Canadian Living
COOKS

Canadian Living
COOKS

**185 Showstopping Recipes from
Canada's Favourite Cooks**

Elizabeth Baird

Daphna Rabinovitch

Emily Richards

and The Canadian Living Test Kitchen

Random House Canada

www.randomhouse.ca

National Library of Canada Cataloguing in Publication

Baird, Elizabeth
    Canadian living cooks : 185 showstopping recipes from Canada's favourite cooks / Elizabeth Baird, Daphna Rabinovitch, Emily Richards and the Canadian Living test kitchen.

Includes index.
ISBN 0-679-31283-8

    1. Cookery. I. Rabinovitch, Daphna II. Richards, Emily III. Title.

TX715.6.B33 2003   641.5   C2003-903057-1

Interior page design: Sharon Foster Design
Photography: Karen Whylie
Illustrations: Elizabeth Simpson

Printed and bound in Canada

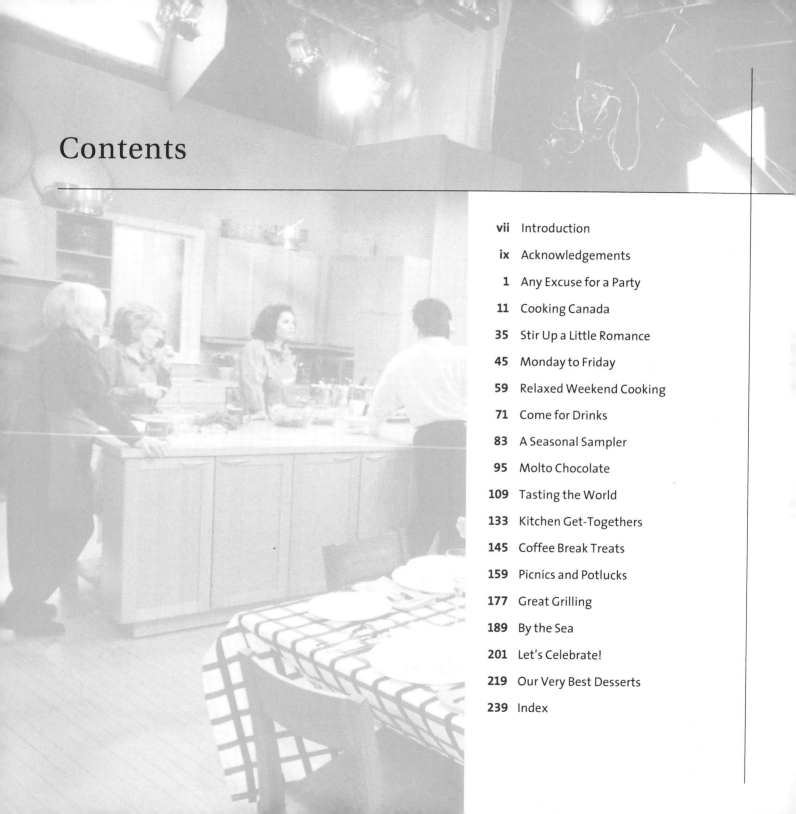

Contents

Introduction

Passion. Without a doubt, that's the main ingredient simmering in the studio of *Canadian Living Cooks*. That's because the three of us take great pride in dishing up smart solutions to everyday cooking challenges for our Food Network Canada viewers. We emphasize superb ingredients, fresh flavours and streamlined techniques, funnelling our collective experiences as cooking teachers through the camera to make each episode inspirational for novice and experienced cooks alike. And as our viewers know, we share a lot of laughs while stirring, sautéing and sampling together. After all, we firmly believe that both preparing and sharing great food should be a most pleasurable experience.

This compendium features our favourite recipes from *Canadian Living Cooks*, with a behind-the-scenes peek at the action in the studio. We work closely with the talented team of producers to plan episodes based on frequently asked questions, on trends and on new dishes we just can't wait to share. We're also proud that many of the recipes draw on our enthusiasm for our families' heritage and rich culinary roots. Themes range from retro desserts to root vegetables, from birthday parties to braising, from easy eggs to exotic fish, from Mexico to the Middle East, from trendy Thai to traditional pie. Good-quality ingredients are a focus, and we are always eager to share our tips on how to shop for them and make the most of them.

We have grouped the recipes into 16 themed chapters that we're sure will inspire you year-round as you cook for and with family and friends. All are Tested Till Perfect in The Canadian Living Test Kitchen, the largest media test kitchen in the country, so you can count on the fact that they'll turn out as beautifully for you as they do for us. Now we invite you to grab your whisk and join us for a smorgasbord of culinary adventures, featuring 185 tantalizing recipes for everyday and entertaining occasions. Happy cooking!

Elizabeth, Daphna and Emily

Cohosts
Elizabeth Baird,
Daphna Rabinovitch
and Emily Richards

Born in Stratford, Ontario, **Elizabeth Baird** graduated from the University of Toronto with a degree in Modern Languages and Literature and pursued a career in teaching for almost 20 years. Cooking and food, however, were overriding passions. And no wonder – she came from a family of outstanding cooks and bakers for whom food was central to every gathering. Encouraged to combine her love of teaching and food, in 1974 she published her first book, *Classic Canadian Cooking* (Lorimer), a best-seller that is still in print. Since her appointment as food editor of *Canadian Living* magazine in 1987, she has edited 25 cookbooks and been honoured with several media and food writing awards. Her reputation for showcasing Canadian products, new Canadian talent and our multicultural food heritage is renowned. So, too, is her belief that food plays an important role in our social fabric. "Sure, we have to eat to live," Elizabeth says, "but food lovingly prepared and lovingly shared encourages us to connect with each other and to nurture and sustain our rituals, traditions and heritages."

What started as quality time spent with her mom baking cookies and concocting stews grew into an all-consuming passion that fuelled a career and a life-long love affair for **Daphna Rabinovitch**. Raised in Ottawa and Montreal, Daphna earned an undergraduate degree in Political Science and Economics at the University of Toronto and a graduate degree in Journalism at Carleton University in Ottawa, but what seemed bred in the bone compelled her to move to San Francisco to train as a chef and pastry chef at the famed Tante Marie's Cooking School. After that came a stint teaching classical Italian cooking alongside Lorenza de' Medici in Tuscany, Italy. She worked as a senior pastry chef in Toronto for several years before joining *Canadian Living* Magazine, first as Test Kitchen manager and later associate food editor. She is the editor of *Canadian Living Cooks Step by Step*, which won the Cuisine Canada Cookbook Award in 2000. Says Daphna, "The simple truth is I adore food – the historical, sociological and cultural aspects of it, the preparation and the enjoyment of it. I get excited about showing viewers how to transform Canada's bounty into delicious everyday and special-occasion meals."

A native of Sault Ste. Marie, Ontario, home economist **Emily Richards** started making bread and pasta at her grandmother's knee when she was only three. Food has always been the touchstone in Emily's family, who trace their roots to southern Italy, so no one was surprised when she decided to pursue a degree in Home Economics at the University of Western Ontario in London, specializing in food and nutrition. Upon graduating, Emily joined the Canadian Living Test Kitchen in 1996. After sharing her fresh approach to memorable meals on *Canadian Living Television*, she went on to contribute her expertise as cohost of *Canadian Living Cooks*. Her enjoyment of teaching grew out of working alongside Bonnie Stern at her cooking school, where she assisted many renowned chefs and authors. Emily nourishes her life with food and family, whether it's preparing dishes at home or at the many cooking classes she presents. "I live by a very simple philosophy: live, love, cook!" says Emily. "The love of food is the core of my life, and I want to invite everyone to enjoy the experience."

Acknowledgements

It's gratifying to have our names on the cover of *Canadian Living Cooks*. But this cookbook is the result of the vision and commitment of a talented group of people, each of whom deserves credit. First, we acknowledge the support of those at the magazine, starting with publisher Debbie Gibson, whose enthusiasm for the book has been contagious, and editor-in-chief Charlotte Empey, whose keen eye and sure judgement have contributed enormously to the style and content. Art director Michael Erb, Canadian Living Test Kitchen staff past and present, associate food editor Andrew Chase, senior editor Beverley Renahan, managing editor Susan Antonacci, business manager Nancy Baker, Canadian Living Online producer Catherine Gray, and support staff Olga Goncalves, Teresa Sousa and Jacqueline Holder all deserve a heartfelt thank-you.

But this book wouldn't be a book if it weren't for our Food Network Canada show, *Canadian Living Cooks* – and the overwhelming number of requests for recipes it has generated. Thanks to Karen Gelbart, vice-president of programming for Food Network Canada, and Michael Quast, who directed studio programming for several seasons. To our supervising producers, Helayna Shekter and Tanya Linton, we offer our thanks for their vision, encouragement and insistence that we try harder, watch the tapes and, yes, smile. The crew organizing the shows, getting ready for the cameras to roll and prodding the cohosts over the past five seasons includes Toni Micelli, Marlowe Ain, Holly Gillanders, Dee-Dee Peel, Sheri Kowall and Anna Michener. Thank you to all. We have nothing but appreciation for the directing staff – on the floor, Todd O'Flaherty, David Berube and the master of all shots, Michael Hooey – and for all the sound technicians, control room staff and camera operators. Dressing the set was a challenge that stylist Robert James met with humour and artistry. In the kitchen, Lucie Richard, Claudia Bianchi, Nilay Usakli, Sandra Watson, Wendy Trusler, Suzanne Kim and Patti Hetherington kept those beautifully prepped dishes coming. As for primping the hosts, Jodi Luke did hair, and Val Chubey and Sue Timewell-Jeffs did makeup. We all look the better for their creativity and concealer. Essential to the show are sponsors, including Longo's for food, Linens 'N Things for props, and Fairweather and Talbots for wardrobe.

As for the people who put the book together, project editor Julia Armstrong heads the list and gets an enormous thank-you from the cohosts. Assisting her on the editorial side were senior editors Beverley Renahan and Christina Anson Mine, copy editors Karen Campbell-Sheviak and Corinna Reeves, and proofreader Jennifer Lloyd. The indexer, your friend indeed when you're looking up a recipe, was Laurie Coulter. Nutrient analysis was prepared by Info Access (1988) Inc. Contributing to the cover were stylist Rachel Mathews, OK Props, and hair and makeup artists Alice Kilpatrick, Elena Pacienza and Jodi Urichuk of The Plutino Group. Daphna's sweater is from The Gap, and Emily's blouse is from The Bay.

A resounding thanks to Random House Canada, especially publisher Anne Collins, senior editor Tanya Trafford, creative director Scott Richardson, designer Sharon Foster, director of production Janine Laporte, director of sales Duncan Shields, director of marketing Linda Scott, deputy director of publicity Sheila Kay, diversified sales manager Marlene Fraser, and senior publicist Frances Bedford.

And you thought it was just the three of us! Would that we could, but we needed the help of all these people and want to tell them how much we appreciate everything they have done to make the cookbook, show and magazine a success. Finally, we say a heartfelt thanks to all our viewers. Tune in again to *Canadian Living Cooks* for more great food and fun.

Any Excuse for a Party

I can always think of a reason to share good food with friends in a relaxed atmosphere. *How about enjoying Friday night with the girls, a Sunday afternoon movie fest or* Hockey Night in Canada *while munching on chicken wings or sandwiches piled high with tender beef or pork? When I had six friends in recently, the Stuffed Jalapeño Peppers were a huge hit – although the 80 I prepared didn't seem to be enough! Whatever you make, call your guests over early to pitch in. With a promise of great food and good laughs, they won't have any excuse not to show up. – Emily*

- Oven-Baked Sesame Chicken Wings
- Poached Shrimp and Crudités with Basil Aïoli
- Caramelized Onion Quesadillas
- Stuffed Jalapeño Peppers
- Italian Sausage Panzerotti
- Cuban Grilled Pork Sandwich
- Spicy Patties
- Beef and Baguette with "Dip"

‹ Emily and Daphna review notes with members of the "Cooks" team

Oven-Baked Sesame Chicken Wings

Tasty chicken in a crisp sesame seed and bread crumb coating appeals to finger food lovers of all ages. Just forget the calories and enjoy. – Elizabeth

3 lb	chicken wings	1.5 kg
1 cup	dry bread crumbs	250 mL
½ cup	grated Parmesan cheese	125 mL
⅓ cup	sesame seeds	75 mL
1 tsp	dried oregano	5 mL
½ tsp	each salt and pepper	2 mL
¼ tsp	cayenne pepper	1 mL
½ cup	butter, melted	125 mL

1 Remove tips (if desired), excess skin and fat from chicken wings.

2 In shallow dish, combine bread crumbs, Parmesan cheese, sesame seeds, oregano, salt, pepper and cayenne. Dip wings into butter; roll in bread crumb mixture to coat completely.

3 Arrange wings, meaty side down, on well-greased rimmed baking sheet. Bake in 375°F (190°C) oven, turning halfway through cooking time, until golden, crisp and juices run clear, 40 to 45 minutes.

Makes 4 servings. PER SERVING: about 743 cal, 45 g pro, 53 g total fat (21 g sat. fat), 20 g carb, 1 g fibre, 170 mg chol, 983 mg sodium. % RDI: 24% calcium, 31% iron, 25% vit A, 10% folate.

fridge **NOTE**

- **Save on cleanup by lining the rimmed baking sheet with foil; grease foil well.**

Poached Shrimp and Crudités with Basil Aïoli

Everybody loves shrimp cocktail, and here is a new way to serve it: dipped in a basil and garlic mayonnaise sauce. – Elizabeth

1 BASIL AÏOLI: In food processor, pulse together basil, garlic, oil, lemon juice, anchovy paste and hot pepper sauce until smooth; mix in mayonnaise. Transfer to bowl. (MAKE-AHEAD: **Cover and refrigerate for up to 24 hours.**)

2 In saucepan, bring 6 cups (1.5 L) water to boil; add onion, lemon, bay leaves, parsley, coriander seeds, peppercorns and salt. Reduce heat, cover and simmer for 15 minutes. Strain into clean saucepan and bring to boil over high heat. Add shrimp; cook until shrimp are pink and opaque, about 3 minutes. Drain and let cool.

3 Bring large saucepan of salted water to boil. One at a time, place asparagus, rapini, green beans, yellow beans and radishes in large sieve; plunge into boiling water and cook just until tender-crisp, 2 to 3 minutes each. Plunge into ice water to stop cooking; drain and arrange on paper towel–lined trays. (MAKE-AHEAD: **Cover and refrigerate for up to 2 hours.**)

4 Cut cucumber lengthwise into quarters; cut each into 8 long pieces. Peel and slice jicama. Arrange all vegetables on platter along with tomatoes and shrimp. Serve with Basil Aïoli.

Makes 20 servings. PER SERVING: about 174 cal, 9 g pro, 12 g total fat (1 g sat. fat), 7 g carb, 3 g fibre, 59 mg chol, 271 mg sodium. % RDI: 5% calcium, 11% iron, 8% vit A, 30% vit C, 21% folate.

1	onion, sliced	1
Half	lemon, sliced	Half
3	bay leaves	3
3	stalks parsley	3
1 tbsp	whole coriander seeds	15 mL
1 tsp	black peppercorns	5 mL
½ tsp	salt	2 mL
2 lb	large shrimp, peeled and deveined	1 kg
8 oz	each asparagus, rapini, green beans, yellow beans and radishes	250 g
1	English cucumber	1
1	jicama (8 oz/250 g)	1
8 oz	cherry tomatoes	250 g
BASIL AÏOLI:		
½ cup	lightly packed fresh basil leaves	125 mL
2	cloves garlic, minced	2
¼ cup	extra-virgin olive oil	50 mL
1 tbsp	lemon juice	15 mL
2 tsp	anchovy paste	10 mL
Dash	hot pepper sauce	Dash
1 cup	mayonnaise	250 mL

Caramelized Onion Quesadillas

The sky's the limit with quesadillas. On the show, I made them with potatoes and chorizo; Brie and caramelized onions make another winner. – Emily

1 tbsp	butter	15 mL
1 tbsp	vegetable oil	15 mL
2	large onions, sliced	2
1 tsp	granulated sugar	5 mL
1 tsp	crumbled dried rosemary	5 mL
4 oz	Brie, sliced (or soft goat cheese or cream cheese)	125 g
Pinch	each salt and pepper	Pinch
2	large (10-inch/25 cm) flour tortillas	2

1 In large skillet, heat butter and oil over high heat; sauté onions, sugar and rosemary, stirring occasionally, for 5 minutes. Reduce heat to medium-high; cook, stirring and scraping bottom of pan often, until onions are golden brown and very soft, 10 to 15 minutes. Let cool to room temperature. (MAKE-AHEAD: **Refrigerate in airtight container for up to 24 hours.**)

2 In small bowl, stir together Brie, salt and pepper; arrange evenly over half of each tortilla. Sprinkle onions over cheese. Fold uncovered half over filling; press edges together. (MAKE-AHEAD: **Cover and refrigerate for up to 3 hours.**)

3 Place on rimmed baking sheet; bake in 425°F (220°C) oven, turning halfway through, until browned and crisp, about 10 minutes. To serve, cut into wedges.

Makes 4 appetizer servings. PER SERVING: about 275 cal, 9 g pro, 16 g total fat (8 g sat. fat), 24 g carb, 2 g fibre, 37 mg chol, 345 mg sodium. % RDI: 7% calcium, 9% iron, 8% vit A, 5% vit C, 29% folate.

" Quesadillas are ideal party food because everyone loves the cheesy inside and crunchy outside, and there are endless filling options for both meat eaters and vegetarians. – *Emily* **"**

Stuffed Jalapeño Peppers

These daringly hot appetizers are favourites of Canadian Living *readers and Test Kitchen staff alike.* – Emily

1 Wearing rubber gloves to protect hands, cut jalapeño peppers in half lengthwise. Using small knife, scrape out seeds and membranes, leaving stems intact.

2 In bowl, combine Cheddar cheese, cream cheese and salsa; stir in ¼ cup (50 mL) of the bread crumbs. Spoon evenly into each pepper half.

3 In small bowl, toss together remaining bread crumbs, parsley and butter; spoon over filling. (MAKE-AHEAD: **Cover and refrigerate for up to 24 hours.**)

4 Bake in 375°F (190°C) oven until topping is golden and crisp, about 20 minutes.

Makes 20 pieces. PER PIECE: about 37 cal, 1 g pro, 3 g total fat (2 g sat. fat), 2 g carb, trace fibre, 9 mg chol, 61 mg sodium. % RDI: 3% calcium, 1% iron, 2% folate, 11% vit A, 32% vit C.

10	jalapeño peppers (8 oz/250 g)	10
½ cup	shredded Cheddar cheese	125 mL
¼ cup	light cream cheese, softened	50 mL
¼ cup	salsa	50 mL
¾ cup	fresh bread crumbs	175 mL
2 tbsp	chopped fresh parsley	25 mL
2 tbsp	butter, melted	25 mL

Italian Sausage Panzerotti

Deep-fried turnovers stuffed with roasted red peppers and sausage make fine party fixings. I love them crunchy and hot from the fryer. – Emily

12 oz	pizza dough	375 g
2 tbsp	extra-virgin olive oil	25 mL
1	small clove garlic, minced	1
1 tsp	minced jalapeño pepper (or ¼ tsp/1 mL hot pepper sauce)	5 mL
2	roasted red peppers, thinly sliced	2
1	red onion, thinly sliced	1
½ cup	pizza or pasta sauce	125 mL
2 cups	shredded mozzarella cheese	500 mL
8 oz	dried Italian sausage packed in oil, patted dry and sliced	250 g
1	egg white, lightly beaten	1
	Vegetable oil for deep-frying	

1 Divide dough into 4 equal parts; roll each into 8-inch (20 cm) circle. Cover and set aside.

2 In bowl, whisk together oil, garlic and jalapeño pepper. Add red peppers and onion; toss to coat.

3 Spread sauce over half of each pizza base; sprinkle with pepper mixture and mozzarella cheese. Top with sausage. Brush edge of dough with egg white. Fold dough over filling to form half-moon shape; pinch edges to seal.

4 Pour enough oil into deep-fryer or deep heavy-bottomed saucepan to come at least 2 inches (5 cm) up side. Heat to 375°F (190°C) or until 1-inch (2.5 cm) cube of bread turns golden in 30 seconds. Gently place 1 or 2 panzerotti into oil; deep-fry, turning once, until golden brown and crisp, about 5 minutes. Drain on paper towel. Repeat with remaining panzerotti.

Makes 4 servings. PER SERVING: about 882 cal, 33 g pro, 57 g total fat (20 g sat. fat), 59 g carb, 3 g fibre, 99 mg chol, 2,007 mg sodium. % RDI: 35% calcium, 25% iron, 35% vit A, 115% vit C, 24% folate.

fridge **NOTE**

- If you don't have a deep-fryer, use a large, deep, wide saucepan.

Cuban Grilled Pork Sandwich

This is memories of Miami, where lineups form at lunchtime for these crusty, goodie-packed sandwiches. – Elizabeth

1 In bowl, whisk together oil, chili powder, garlic, pepper and salt; add pork, turning to coat. (MAKE-AHEAD: **Cover and refrigerate for up to 24 hours.**)

2 Place pork on greased grill over medium-high heat; close lid and grill, turning once, until just a hint of pink remains inside and juices run clear when pork is pierced, 16 to 20 minutes. Transfer to cutting board; let cool. Slice thinly on diagonal.

3 Using serrated knife, cut bread in half horizontally. In small bowl, stir mayonnaise with mustard; spread on cut sides of loaf. Layer ham, pork, pickle slices then cheese on bottom. Sandwich with top half of loaf. (MAKE-AHEAD: **Wrap in foil and refrigerate for up to 6 hours. Unwrap and serve cold. Or heat in large sandwich press, or on baking sheet in 375°F/190°C oven, or on grill over medium heat, pressing lightly, until warmed and toasted on both sides.**) Cut into eighths to serve.

Makes 8 servings. PER SERVING: about 349 cal, 24 g pro, 13 g total fat (4 g sat. fat), 34 g carb, 1 g fibre, 46 mg chol, 822 mg sodium. % RDI: 14% calcium, 16% iron, 19% folate, 7% vit A, 2% vit C.

2 tbsp	vegetable oil	25 mL
1 tbsp	chili powder	15 mL
1	clove garlic, minced	1
¼ tsp	pepper	1 mL
Pinch	salt	Pinch
1	pork tenderloin (12 oz/375 g)	1
1	oblong bread loaf (450 g)	1
¼ cup	light mayonnaise	50 mL
2 tsp	Dijon mustard	10 mL
6 oz	sliced Black Forest ham	175 g
6	slices dill pickle	6
4 oz	sliced Swiss cheese	125 g

Spicy Patties

Shannon Ferrier and the kids at Lord Dufferin School in Toronto put their collective taste buds together to come up with the perfect patty. – Elizabeth

4 cups	all-purpose flour	1 L
4 tsp	baking powder	20 mL
2 tsp	curry powder	10 mL
1 tsp	each salt and turmeric	5 mL
1⅓ cups	shortening	325 mL
½ cup	butter	125 mL
1 cup	cold water	250 mL
CURRIED BEEF FILLING:		
2 tbsp	vegetable oil	25 mL
2	large onions, finely chopped	2
2	cloves garlic, minced	2
2 lb	ground beef	1 kg
1 tbsp	curry powder	15 mL
1½ tsp	each salt and dried thyme	7 mL
1 tsp	pepper	5 mL
Pinch	cayenne pepper	Pinch
1 cup	fresh bread crumbs	250 mL

1 In large bowl, whisk together flour, baking powder, curry powder, salt and turmeric. Using pastry blender or 2 knives, cut in shortening and butter until mixture resembles fine crumbs with a few larger pieces. Pour in water, stirring with fork to make soft dough. Gather into ball; wrap in plastic wrap and refrigerate for 1 hour.

2 CURRIED BEEF FILLING: In large skillet, heat oil over medium heat; cook onions and garlic until softened, about 5 minutes. Transfer onion mixture to bowl; set aside. Increase heat to high; cook beef, stirring to break up pieces, until no longer pink, about 5 minutes. Drain off fat. Stir in onion mixture, curry powder, salt, thyme, pepper and cayenne; reduce heat to medium and cook, stirring, for 3 minutes. Pour in 2 cups (500 mL) water and bring to boil; reduce heat and simmer until most of the water is absorbed, 5 to 10 minutes. Add bread crumbs, stirring just until moist but not runny. Taste and adjust seasoning. Let cool.

3 Divide pastry in half and roll into 2 long sausage shapes. Slice each crosswise into 12 equal pieces. Roll out into 6-inch (15 cm) circles. Divide filling into 24 equal mounds; spoon onto centre of pastry rounds. Wet edges of pastry with water and fold in half, making edges meet. Using fork, press edges together; prick twice. Trim into neat half-moon shape. Place patties on ungreased rimmed baking sheets; bake in 375°F (190°C) oven until crisp and lightly browned, 25 to 30 minutes. (MAKE-AHEAD: **Let cool. Layer between waxed paper in airtight container and freeze for up to 2 weeks. Reheat in 350°F/180°C oven for about 15 minutes.**)

Makes 24 patties. PER PATTY: about 312 cal, 10 g pro, 21 g total fat (7 g sat. fat), 21 g carb, 1 g fibre, 33 mg chol, 385 mg sodium. % RDI: 4% calcium, 16% iron, 4% vit A, 2% vit C, 13% folate.

Beef and Baguette with "Dip"

I first made this sandwich at Don Cherry's restaurant. So in honour of the big coach, serve it to the gang watching Hockey Night in Canada. – Emily

1 Pat roast dry. Using tip of sharp knife, make 24 evenly spaced slits in beef, about ½ inch (1 cm) deep. Quarter garlic cloves lengthwise; insert 1 into each slit. Set aside on greased rack in small roasting pan.

2 In bowl, stir together vinegar, mustard, oil, soy sauce and hot pepper sauce; brush about three-quarters over beef, reserving any remaining mustard mixture. (MAKE-AHEAD: **Cover and refrigerate beef and mustard mixture separately for up to 24 hours.**)

3 Pour enough water into roasting pan to come ½ inch (1 cm) up side. Roast in 500°F (260°C) oven for 30 minutes. Remove from oven. Brush with reserved mustard mixture. Reduce heat to 275°F (140°C); roast until meat thermometer registers 140°F (60°C) for rare, about 40 minutes, or 150°F (65°C) for medium-rare. Transfer to cutting board and tent with foil; let stand for 20 minutes before slicing thinly across the grain. (MAKE-AHEAD: **Let cool completely in refrigerator; cover and refrigerate for up to 2 days. Reheat, moistened with a few spoonfuls of beef stock or dip.**)

4 Meanwhile, skim fat from pan juices. Pour in wine; bring to boil over high heat, scraping up any brown bits from bottom of pan. Boil until reduced by half, about 5 minutes. Pour in stock and return to boil; boil hard until reduced to about 2½ cups (625 mL), about 15 minutes.

5 Slice baguettes crosswise into quarters; halve lengthwise. Drizzle cut sides with 1 tbsp (15 mL) dip, or spread with mustard (if using). Pile beef on bottom slices; sandwich with tops. Serve each sandwich with ¼ cup (50 mL) juices in small bowl for dipping.

Makes 8 servings. PER SERVING: about 391 cal, 33 g pro, 9 g total fat (3 g sat. fat), 41 g carb, 2 g fibre, 50 mg chol, 833 mg sodium. % RDI: 7% calcium, 28% iron, 2% vit C, 36% folate.

Amount	Ingredient	Metric
2 lb	eye of round oven roast	1 kg
6	cloves garlic	6
1 tbsp	balsamic vinegar	15 mL
1 tbsp	grainy mustard	15 mL
2 tsp	vegetable oil	10 mL
1 tsp	soy sauce	5 mL
Dash	hot pepper sauce	Dash
½ cup	dry red wine	125 mL
2½ cups	beef stock	625 mL
2	sourdough baguettes (each 14 inches/35 cm)	2
	Dijon mustard or light mayonnaise or horseradish (optional)	

fridge NOTE

- **The beef slices best when it's cold (the next day).**

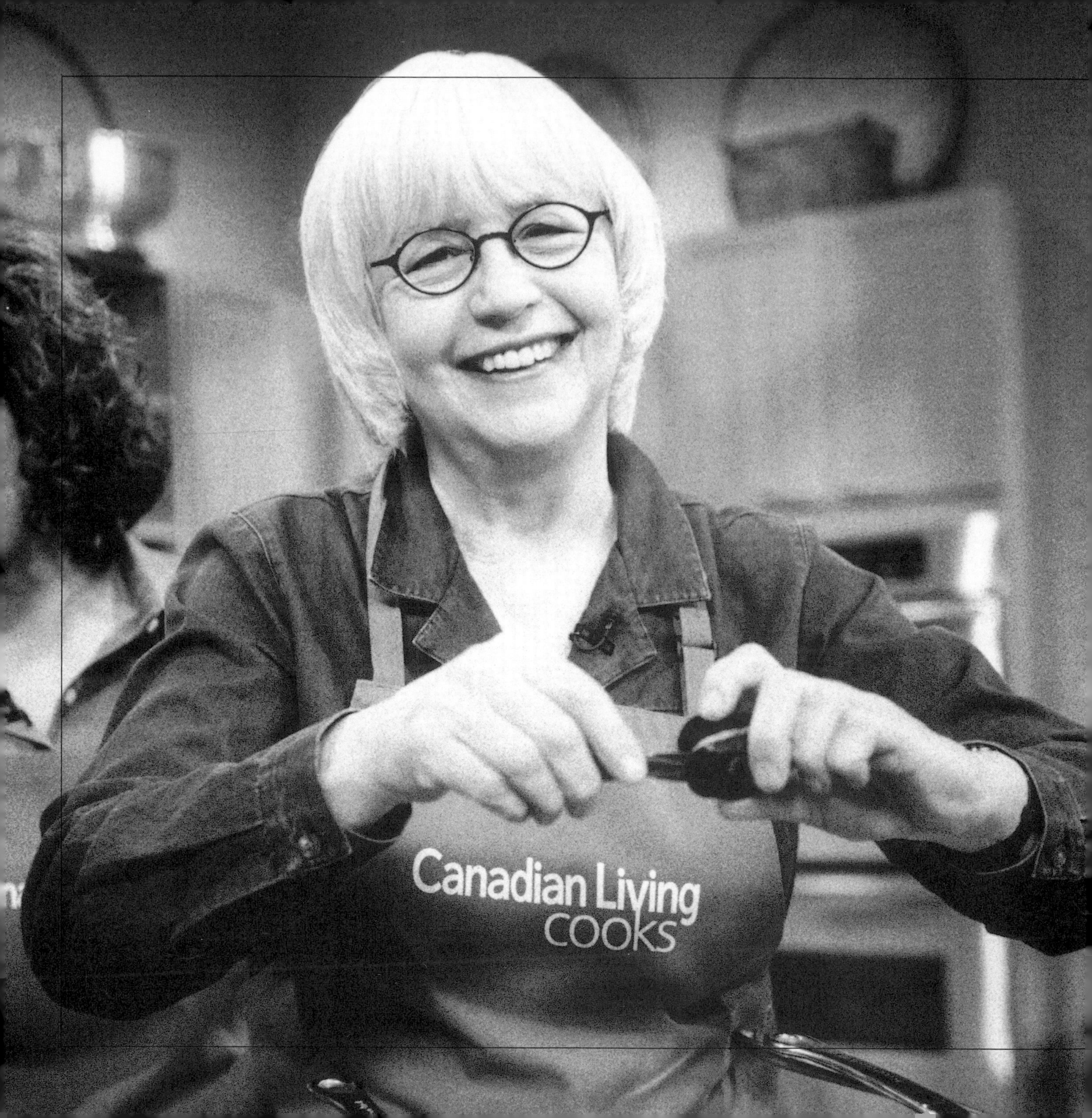
Canadian Living
COOKS

Cooking Canada

*I*n Canada, we are blessed. When it comes to cooking, the ingredients are boundless, the ways of flavouring and preparing them seemingly infinite. In deciding how to represent Canada on the show, Daphna, Emily and I first find inspiration in our backgrounds and our heritages. Then we draw from our travels, dipping our spoons into soup pots in la belle province, forking up Alberta lamb or sampling fresh Atlantic scallops. There's not a corner of the country where we haven't found a delicious dish to share, whether it's a farmhouse classic like butter tarts or a fine dining dish such as Arctic char from stylish Quebec City. We offer you Canada, a tempting place to nibble. Happy cooking and bon appétit. – Elizabeth

- Two-Mushroom Barley Soup
- Baby Greens in Frico Cups
- Wild Rice Salad with Mustard Honey Dressing
- Pan-Fried Cornmeal-Crusted Pickerel
- Lime-Buttered Scallops in Phyllo Baskets
- Arctic Char with Barley Risotto and Curry Sauce
- Salmon Wellington in Shallot Cream Sauce
- Maple Orange Cornish Hens
- Rebel House Buffalo Burger
- Oven-Barbecued Short Ribs with Creamy Chili Biscuits
- Roasted Loin of Pork with Cranberry Stuffing
- Roasted Rack of Lamb with Cumin Garlic Crust
- Beer and Oat Bread
- Buttermilk Pie
- Bumbleberry Pie
- Chocolate Butter Tarts
- Shmoo Torte
- Cookies-and-Cream Torte

Two-Mushroom Barley Soup

Hearty soups like this are a perfect meal, and in my mind hearty and barley are synonymous. Use pearl and pot barley interchangeably. – Daphna

1 oz	dried mushrooms (porcini or shiitake)	30 g
4	carrots	4
8 cups	button mushrooms (1 lb/500 g)	2 L
2 tbsp	vegetable oil	25 mL
2	onions, finely chopped	2
3	cloves garlic, minced	3
1¼ tsp	dried thyme	6 mL
¾ tsp	crumbled dried sage	4 mL
½ tsp	pepper	2 mL
¼ tsp	salt	1 mL
2 tbsp	tomato paste	25 mL
2 tbsp	soy sauce	25 mL
1 tbsp	balsamic or red wine vinegar	15 mL
1 cup	barley	250 mL
6 cups	chicken or vegetable stock	1.5 L
4 cups	packed fresh spinach	1 L

1 In small bowl, pour 1 cup (250 mL) boiling water over dried mushrooms; let stand until softened, about 20 minutes. Strain through cheesecloth-lined sieve, reserving liquid. If using shiitakes, cut off tough stem. Slice mushrooms into thin strips; set aside.

2 Meanwhile, peel carrots; slice diagonally and set aside. Cut off tough stems from button mushrooms; slice caps thickly.

3 In large saucepan, heat oil over medium heat; cook onions and garlic, stirring often, until softened, about 5 minutes. Add carrots and dried and button mushrooms; cook, stirring often, until mushrooms are lightly browned and liquid is evaporated, 15 to 20 minutes.

4 Stir in thyme, sage, pepper and salt. Stir in tomato paste, soy sauce, vinegar and reserved soaking liquid. Add barley; simmer, stirring, until liquid is absorbed and barley is well coated, 1 to 2 minutes.

5 Add stock and 3 cups (750 mL) water; bring to boil. Reduce heat, cover and simmer, stirring occasionally, for 50 minutes. Uncover and cook until slightly thickened, about 20 minutes. (MAKE-AHEAD: **Let cool. Refrigerate in airtight container for up to 2 days. Reheat gently, adding up to ½ cup/125 mL more water to thin if desired.**)

6 Trim spinach; flatten and stack leaves with all stems at 1 end. Starting at long side, roll up tightly; using sharp chef's knife, slice crosswise into ½-inch (1 cm) wide strips. Stir into soup; cook until wilted, about 3 minutes.

Makes 6 servings. PER SERVING: about 280 cal, 11 g pro, 7 g total fat (1 g sat. fat), 46 g carb, 10 g fibre, 0 mg chol, 1,219 mg sodium. % RDI: 10% calcium, 36% iron, 152% vit A, 18% vit C, 45% folate.

Baby Greens in Frico Cups

This cheese cup recipe is from chef Tarrah Laidman-Lodboa, formerly of the Good Earth Cooking School in Ontario's Niagara region. – Daphna

1 Line rimmed baking sheet with parchment paper; set aside.

2 In bowl, mix cheese with flour. Using ¼ cup (50 mL) for each frico cup and baking only 2 at a time, mound cheese mixture, about 6 inches (15 cm) apart, on prepared pan; pat to flatten slightly.

3 Bake in centre of 350°F (180°C) oven just until lightly golden around edge, 11 to 12 minutes, watching carefully to prevent browning. Let stand on pan on rack for 1 minute. Using metal spatula, immediately transfer each round to inverted 2¼- to 2½-inch (5.5 to 6 cm) drinking glass and gently shape round to glass; let cool. (MAKE-AHEAD: **Store in paper towel–lined container at room temperature for up to 2 days.**)

4 DRESSING: In small bowl, whisk together oil, vinegar, salt and pepper; set aside.

5 Cut tomatoes in half and place in bowl. Add basil, chives and 3 tbsp (50 mL) of the dressing; toss to combine. In separate bowl, toss mixed greens with remaining dressing. Arrange ¾ cup (175 mL) greens in each frico cup; top or surround with ½ cup (125 mL) of the tomato mixture.

Makes 8 servings. PER SERVING: about 224 cal, 9 g pro, 19 g total fat (7 g sat. fat), 7 g carb, 2 g fibre, 30 mg chol, 410 mg sodium. % RDI: 22% calcium, 6% iron, 25% vit A, 33% vit C, 28% folate.

2 cups	shredded extra-old white Cheddar cheese	500 mL
1 tbsp	all-purpose flour	15 mL
4 cups	cherry tomatoes	1 L
¼ cup	shredded fresh basil	50 mL
2 tbsp	coarsely chopped fresh chives	25 mL
8 cups	mixed baby greens (about 6 oz/175 g)	2 L
DRESSING:		
⅓ cup	grape-seed oil or extra-virgin olive oil	75 mL
2 tbsp	balsamic vinegar	25 mL
¾ tsp	salt	4 mL
½ tsp	pepper	2 mL

fridge NOTE

- **If frico cups soften when made ahead of time, place on baking sheet and bake in 350°F (180°C) oven for 1 minute, then reshape over inverted glass.**

Wild Rice Salad with Mustard Honey Dressing

This all-season salad features Prairie wild rice, which is actually a marsh grass. I enjoy its chewy texture and nutty flavour. – Daphna

2 cups	wild rice	500 mL
½ cup	diced dried apricots	125 mL
½ cup	diced dried apple	125 mL
⅓ cup	raisins or currants	75 mL
¼ cup	golden raisins	50 mL
MUSTARD HONEY DRESSING:		
2 tbsp	canola oil	25 mL
2 tbsp	orange juice	25 mL
2 tbsp	white wine vinegar	25 mL
4 tsp	Dijon mustard	20 mL
1 tbsp	liquid honey	15 mL
¼ tsp	each salt and pepper	1 mL
¼ cup	chopped fresh mint	50 mL

1 In large pot of boiling salted water, cover and cook wild rice until tender, about 35 minutes. Drain well and transfer to large bowl; add apricots, apple, raisins and golden raisins. Set aside.

2 MUSTARD HONEY DRESSING: In small bowl, whisk together oil, orange juice, vinegar, mustard, honey, salt and pepper. Pour over rice mixture and toss gently.

3 Let salad cool completely; cover and refrigerate until chilled, about 4 hours. (MAKE-AHEAD: **Refrigerate for up to 24 hours.**) To serve, add mint and toss to combine.

Makes 6 to 8 servings. PER EACH OF 8 SERVINGS: about 252 cal, 7 g pro, 4 g total fat (trace sat. fat), 51 g carb, 5 g fibre, 0 mg chol, 118 mg sodium. % RDI: 2% calcium, 13% iron, 6% vit A, 5% vit C, 18% folate.

fridge NOTE

- **Manitoba is renowned for its grains. Try replacing the wild rice in this salad with another Prairie crop, such as pearl barley or wheat berries.**

In the prep kitchen with food assistant Patti Hetherington

Pan-Fried Cornmeal-Crusted Pickerel

Manitoba pickerel is so flavourful when pan-fried in a dilly cornmeal crust.
You'll need 2 lb (1 kg) pickerel, probably two or three fillets. – Emily

1 LEMON SAUCE: In small saucepan, bring cream, lemon rind and juice, and Worcestershire sauce to simmer over medium heat; simmer, stirring occasionally, until reduced by half and thick enough to coat back of spoon, about 7 minutes.

2 Place flour in shallow bowl. In separate shallow bowl, whisk milk with eggs. Place cornmeal, dill, salt and pepper in another shallow bowl. Dip fish, 1 piece at a time, into flour, shaking off excess; dip into milk mixture, then into cornmeal mixture.

3 In skillet, heat butter over medium-high heat; fry fillets, turning once, until fish flakes easily when tested, about 5 minutes. Serve with Lemon Sauce.

Makes 6 servings. PER SERVING: about 395 cal, 34 g pro, 18 g total fat (10 g sat. fat), 22 g carb, 1 g fibre, 231 mg chol, 332 mg sodium. % RDI: 18% calcium, 20% iron, 20% vit A, 5% vit C, 15% folate.

½ cup	all-purpose flour	125 mL
¼ cup	milk	50 mL
2	eggs	2
1 cup	cornmeal	250 mL
2 tbsp	chopped fresh dill	25 mL
½ tsp	salt	2 mL
¼ tsp	pepper	1 mL
2 lb	pickerel fillets, skinned	1 kg
¼ cup	butter or canola oil	50 mL
LEMON SAUCE:		
½ cup	whipping cream	125 mL
½ tsp	grated lemon rind	2 mL
2 tbsp	lemon juice	25 mL
½ tsp	Worcestershire sauce	2 mL

Lime-Buttered Scallops in Phyllo Baskets

Restaurateur and caterer Unni Simenson is famous in Halifax for her fine touch with seafood. – Emily

1 lb	fresh scallops	500 g
¼ tsp	each salt and pepper	1 mL
2 tbsp	butter	25 mL
3	kaffir lime leaves (optional)	3
2 tbsp	gin	25 mL
½ tsp	grated lime rind	2 mL
1 tbsp	lime juice	15 mL
PHYLLO BASKETS:		
3	sheets phyllo pastry	3
2 tbsp	butter, melted	25 mL

1 PHYLLO BASKETS: Lightly brush each phyllo sheet with butter. Stack and cut into 4 rectangles. Press gently into 4 large muffin cups, leaving empty cup between each to allow for overhang. Bake in centre of 400°F (200°C) oven until golden, about 5 minutes. Transfer to rack and let cool.

2 Cut scallops in half crosswise if large. Sprinkle with salt and pepper. In large nonstick skillet, melt butter over medium-high heat; cook scallops and lime leaves (if using), stirring gently, until scallops are firm but still slightly opaque, about 5 minutes. Using slotted spoon, transfer to plate.

3 Add gin and lime rind and juice to pan; bring to simmer. Return scallops to pan, turning gently to coat; heat through. Remove lime leaves (if using). Spoon scallops and liquid into phyllo baskets.

Makes 4 servings. PER SERVING: about 271 cal, 20 g pro, 13 g total fat (8 g sat. fat), 13 g carb, trace fibre, 74 mg chol, 532 mg sodium. % RDI: 3% calcium, 7% iron, 12% vit A, 2% vit C, 10% folate.

fridge NOTE

- For a maritime version of crostini, spread a mixture of avocado, salt, pepper and lime juice over grilled baguette slices. Top with sliced plum tomatoes and grilled scallops; garnish with chopped fresh coriander.

Arctic Char with Barley Risotto and Curry Sauce

At Restaurant Initiale in Quebec City, chef Yvan Lebrun serves this crispy-bottomed fillet of char with sautéed mushrooms. – Elizabeth

1 CURRY SAUCE: In large deep skillet, melt butter over medium heat; cook shallot, stirring occasionally, until softened, about 2 minutes. Add wine and vinegar; bring to boil over high heat. Boil until syrupy, about 5 minutes. Add chicken stock and return to boil; boil vigorously until reduced to 1 cup (250 mL), about 30 minutes. Add cream; boil until thick enough to coat back of spoon, about 5 minutes. (MAKE-AHEAD: **Set aside for up to 30 minutes; reheat.**) Whisk in curry paste and tarragon.

2 BARLEY RISOTTO: In saucepan, bring vegetable stock and wine to simmer; maintain at simmer. Meanwhile, in separate saucepan, heat half of the olive oil over medium heat; cook onion and garlic, stirring occasionally, until softened. Stir in barley. Add hot stock mixture, ½ cup (125 mL) at a time, stirring until liquid evaporates and adding more until all liquid is absorbed and barley is tender, about 45 minutes. Add pepper and salt. (MAKE-AHEAD: **Cover and set aside for up to 20 minutes; reheat if necessary.**) Using fork, stir in remaining olive oil.

3 Meanwhile, in large ovenproof skillet, heat vegetable oil over medium-high heat. Sprinkle fish with salt and pepper. Place, skin side down, in pan; fry until skin is crispy, about 5 minutes. Transfer to 450°F (230°C) oven; roast until fish flakes easily when tested, about 5 minutes.

4 Divide risotto among 4 warmed plates. Arrange fish over top; drizzle sauce around risotto.

Makes 4 servings. PER SERVING: about 786 cal, 58 g pro, 42 g total fat (13 g sat. fat), 39 g carb, 3 g fibre, 202 mg chol, 669 mg sodium. % RDI: 7% calcium, 28% iron, 24% vit A, 3% vit C, 14% folate.

2 tsp	vegetable oil	10 mL
2 lb	arctic char fillets	1 kg
Pinch	each salt and pepper	Pinch
BARLEY RISOTTO:		
3 cups	vegetable stock	750 mL
½ cup	white wine	125 mL
4 tsp	extra-virgin olive oil	20 mL
1	onion, finely chopped	1
1	clove garlic, minced	1
¾ cup	pearl barley, rinsed	175 mL
¼ tsp	pepper	1 mL
Pinch	salt	Pinch
CURRY SAUCE:		
1 tbsp	butter	15 mL
1	shallot, finely chopped	1
½ cup	white wine	125 mL
⅓ cup	white wine vinegar	75 mL
4 cups	unsalted chicken stock	1 L
½ cup	whipping cream	125 mL
1 tbsp	curry paste or powder	15 mL
1½ tsp	minced fresh tarragon	7 mL

Salmon Wellington in Shallot Cream Sauce

Asked to feature top Canadian restaurant entrées, we chose this celebration dish from chef Jean Soulard at Quebec City's Château Frontenac. – Emily

1 lb	salmon fillet (in 1 piece)	500 g
8 cups	packed fresh spinach	2 L
Half	pkg (397 g pkg) frozen puff pastry, thawed	Half
1	egg yolk	1
STUFFING:		
12 oz	boneless halibut, cubed	375 g
1	egg white	1
½ cup	whipping cream	125 mL
2 tbsp	lemon juice	25 mL
1 tbsp	chopped fresh chervil or basil	15 mL
¼ tsp	each salt and pepper	1 mL
SHALLOT CREAM SAUCE:		
½ cup	finely chopped shallots (about 4)	125 mL
⅓ cup	wine vinegar	75 mL
⅓ cup	whipping cream	75 mL
½ cup	cold butter, cubed	125 mL
Pinch	pepper	Pinch

1 STUFFING: In food processor, pulse together halibut and egg white until smooth; blend in cream, lemon juice, chervil, salt and pepper. Transfer to airtight container; refrigerate for 1 hour. (MAKE-AHEAD: **Refrigerate for up to 4 hours.**)

2 Cut salmon crosswise into ½-inch (1 cm) thick slices; cover and refrigerate. Trim spinach, removing stems; rinse and shake off excess water. In large saucepan, cover and cook spinach, with just the water clinging to leaves, just until wilted. Arrange in single layer on paper towels; pat dry.

3 On lightly floured surface, roll out pastry to form 14-inch (35 cm) square. Place on sheet of parchment paper large enough to cover large rimless baking sheet. Cover pastry with spinach, leaving about 1½-inch (4 cm) border at edges. Spread half of the stuffing over spinach; layer with salmon slices, then remaining stuffing.

4 Mix egg yolk with 1 tbsp (15 mL) water; lightly brush some of the egg wash on uncovered top and side borders of pastry. Starting at bottom edge and using paper as support, roll up, pressing egg-washed top edge onto pastry; fold in sides, pressing together lightly. Place roll and paper on rimmed baking sheet. (MAKE-AHEAD: **Cover and refrigerate for up to 4 hours; add 10 minutes to baking time.**) Brush lightly with egg wash. Bake in centre of 400°F (200°C) oven until golden and crisp, about 30 minutes.

> **"** I admire the way Canadian chefs seamlessly weave
> traditional recipes with nouveau philosophies to create
> evocative dishes like this one. – *Daphna* **"**

5 SHALLOT CREAM SAUCE: Meanwhile, in small saucepan, simmer shallots with vinegar over medium-low heat until vinegar is evaporated. Add cream; simmer until reduced by half, about 4 minutes. Whisking constantly, add butter, a few cubes at a time, until creamy. Add pepper.

6 To serve, trim off ends and cut pastry package crosswise into 8 slices. Pool one-quarter of the sauce onto each warmed plate; arrange 2 slices per serving over and to side of sauce.

Makes 4 servings. PER SERVING: about 969 cal, 46 g pro, 74 g total fat (31 g sat. fat), 32 g carb, 3 g fibre, 264 mg chol, 687 mg sodium. % RDI: 19% calcium, 39% iron, 101% vit A, 20% vit C, 79% folate.

fridge NOTE

- The "Wellington" part of our entertaining salmon dish indicates that the fish is encased in puff pastry. We've simplified that component by using frozen puff pastry.

Maple Orange Cornish Hens

Maple syrup conjures memories of sugaring-off parties in Quebec. Here, we feature the homegrown specialty in a lovely entertaining dish. – Daphna

⅓ cup	maple syrup or packed brown sugar	75 mL
⅓ cup	orange juice	75 mL
2 tbsp	white wine (optional)	25 mL
2 tsp	chopped dried rosemary	10 mL
3	Cornish hens (each about 1¼ lb/625 g)	3
1 tbsp	finely grated orange rind	15 mL
Pinch	each salt and pepper	Pinch
	Fresh rosemary sprigs and orange slices	

1 In small saucepan, whisk together maple syrup, orange juice, wine (if using) and rosemary; bring to boil. Boil until slightly thickened, 3 to 5 minutes. Let cool slightly.

2 Meanwhile, cut wing tips from each hen. Using kitchen scissors or sharp knife, cut along each side of backbone; discard backbone. Cut through breastbone to separate into halves. Trim off excess fat and skin. Gently loosen skin from each half of hens, leaving skin attached at back side. Starting at breast, ease in orange rind over flesh under skin.

3 Place hens, skin side up, on foil-lined rimmed baking sheet. Sprinkle with salt and pepper; brush with one-third of the maple glaze. Roast in 375°F (190°C) oven, brushing twice with glaze, until browned and juices run clear when hens are pierced, about 45 minutes. Arrange on serving platter; garnish with rosemary sprigs and orange slices.

Makes 6 servings. PER SERVING: about 350 cal, 26 g pro, 21 g total fat (6 g sat. fat), 13 g carb, trace fibre, 150 mg chol, 75 mg sodium. % RDI: 3% calcium, 10% iron, 4% vit A, 10% vit C, 3% folate.

fridge NOTE

- **After cutting out the backbone, save it to use with other Cornish hen or chicken bones to make stock.**

Rebel House Buffalo Burger

The Rebel House restaurant in Toronto is known for its excellent buffalo burger. Buffalo tastes rich but is very lean. – Emily

1 In skillet, heat oil over medium heat; cook diced onion, stirring occasionally, until softened, about 5 minutes. Let cool.

2 In large bowl, beat egg. Stir in thyme, mustard, horseradish, salt and pepper; mix in cooked onion, beef and buffalo. Shape into four ½-inch (1 cm) thick patties. (MAKE-AHEAD: **Cover and refrigerate for up to 6 hours. Or layer between waxed paper in airtight container and freeze for up to 1 month; thaw in refrigerator.**)

3 Place patties on greased grill over medium-high heat; close lid and grill, turning once, until no longer pink inside, about 10 minutes.

4 Cut rolls in half; place, cut side down, on grill and toast until golden, 1 to 2 minutes. Layer burgers, lettuce, tomato, then red onion on bottoms; sandwich with tops.

Makes 4 servings. PER SERVING: about 425 cal, 32 g pro, 15 g total fat (4 g sat. fat), 41 g carb, 5 g fibre, 112 mg chol, 734 mg sodium. % RDI: 9% calcium, 37% iron, 6% vit A, 20% vit C, 40% folate.

1 tbsp	vegetable oil	15 mL
1	onion, diced	1
1	egg	1
2 tsp	chopped fresh thyme, rosemary or oregano (or ½ tsp/2 mL dried)	10 mL
2 tsp	Dijon mustard	10 mL
2 tsp	horseradish	10 mL
½ tsp	each salt and pepper	2 mL
8 oz	medium ground beef	250 g
8 oz	ground buffalo (or beef)	250 g
4	kaiser rolls or hamburger buns	4
4	leaves lettuce	4
1	tomato, sliced	1
Half	small red onion, thinly sliced	Half

Oven-Barbecued Short Ribs with Creamy Chili Biscuits

For her stew recipe, M. Lee Leuschner of Calgary was grand-prize winner in a recent Canadian Living *Heritage Recipe Contest.* – Emily

3 lb	beef simmering short ribs	1.5 kg
3 tbsp	vegetable oil	50 mL
2	large onions, coarsely chopped	2
3	large cloves garlic, minced	3
2	cans (each 19 oz/540 mL) stewed tomatoes	2
2 cups	beef stock	500 mL
⅓ cup	cider vinegar	75 mL
¼ cup	packed brown sugar	50 mL
3 tbsp	Worcestershire sauce	50 mL
2 tbsp	Dijon mustard	25 mL
1½ tsp	salt	7 mL
1½ tsp	hot pepper sauce	7 mL
½ tsp	each pepper, paprika and turmeric	2 mL
8	sprigs fresh parsley	8
2	thin slices lemon	2
1 lb	potatoes (about 2), peeled and cubed	500 g
1 lb	carrots, peeled and cut diagonally in 2-inch (5 cm) thick slices	500 g

1 One Day Ahead: Arrange ribs in single layer in large shallow roasting pan. Broil 4 inches (10 cm) from heat, turning often, until browned, about 10 minutes.

2 In Dutch oven, heat oil over medium heat; cook onions and garlic, stirring occasionally, until translucent, about 10 minutes.

3 Add tomatoes, stock, vinegar, sugar, Worcestershire sauce, mustard, salt, hot pepper sauce, pepper, paprika, turmeric, parsley and lemon slices. Add ribs and pan drippings; bring to boil. Cover and transfer to 350°F (180°C) oven; bake just until ribs are tender, about 2 hours.

4 Add potatoes and carrots. Bake, covered, until vegetables are tender, about 1 hour. Discard parsley and lemon. Let cool for about 30 minutes. Refrigerate for 24 hours. Remove fat from top.

5 One Hour Before Serving: Bring rib mixture to simmer over medium-high heat, stirring occasionally.

6 CREAMY CHILI BISCUITS: Meanwhile, in small skillet, melt butter over medium heat; cook onion and garlic, stirring occasionally, until softened, about 5 minutes. Let cool.

7 In large bowl, whisk together flour, baking powder, chili powder and salt; stir in cheese and parsley. Blend in onion mixture. Drizzle cream over top, mixing with fork just until dough comes together and adding more cream if necessary. Turn out dough onto lightly floured surface; knead about 10 times. Roll out to ½-inch (1 cm) thickness. Using 2¼-inch (5.5 cm) round cookie cutter, cut out circles; arrange over ribs.

8 Bake, uncovered, in 450°F (230°C) oven until biscuits are puffed and no longer doughy underneath, about 15 minutes.

Makes 6 to 8 servings. PER EACH OF 8 SERVINGS: about 689 cal, 28 g pro, 38 g total fat (17 g sat. fat), 62 g carb, 5 g fibre, 97 mg chol, 1,660 mg sodium. % RDI: 20% calcium, 38% iron, 138% vit A, 43% vit C, 29% folate.

CREAMY CHILI BISCUITS:		
1 tbsp	butter	15 mL
1	onion, finely chopped	1
1	large clove garlic, finely chopped	1
2 cups	all-purpose flour	500 mL
1 tbsp	baking powder	15 mL
2 tsp	chili powder	10 mL
1 tsp	salt	5 mL
¼ cup	grated Parmesan cheese	50 mL
2 tbsp	minced fresh parsley or coriander	25 mL
1 cup	whipping cream (approx)	250 mL

Roasted Loin of Pork with Cranberry Stuffing

A stuffed loin of pork is a dazzling choice for a dinner party. Here's the best of the West: Alberta pork complemented by Prairie sage. – Elizabeth

1 cup	dried cranberries	250 mL
⅓ cup	apple cider	75 mL
½ cup	hazelnuts	125 mL
¼ cup	butter	50 mL
2	large shallots, minced	2
1 tbsp	chopped fresh sage	15 mL
½ tsp	each salt and pepper	2 mL
3 cups	fresh bread crumbs	750 mL
2 tbsp	chopped fresh parsley	25 mL
3 lb	centre-cut boneless single pork loin roast	1.5 kg
1 tbsp	vegetable oil	15 mL
SAUCE:		
1½ tsp	all-purpose flour	7 mL
1½ tsp	butter, softened	7 mL
4	shallots, minced	4
2	cloves garlic, minced	2
1 cup	white wine	250 mL
1 cup	chicken stock	250 mL
¼ tsp	pepper	1 mL

1 In small microwaveable bowl, combine cranberries and cider; cover and microwave at High for 1 minute. Let cool. Spread hazelnuts on rimmed baking sheet; toast in 350°F (180°C) oven or toaster oven until fragrant, about 8 minutes. Transfer to tea towel and rub off most of the skins. Let cool; chop and set aside.

2 In skillet, melt butter over medium-low heat; cook large shallots, sage and half each of the salt and pepper until shallots are softened, about 5 minutes. Transfer to large bowl. Add cranberry mixture, toasted hazelnuts, bread crumbs and parsley; toss to combine.

3 Place pork, fat side up, on cutting board. Starting at right side with knife parallel to board, cut loin in half almost but not all the way through; open flat like book. Starting in centre of opened loin, with knife parallel to board, cut in half on left side almost but not all the way through. Repeat on right side. Open flat. Cover with waxed paper. Using mallet, pound to even thickness.

4 Sprinkle with half each of the remaining salt and pepper. Leaving 1-inch (2.5 cm) border on 1 short side, spread cranberry stuffing over meat. Starting at other short side, roll up tightly. Place seven 12-inch (30 cm) lengths of kitchen string under loin. Tie at top of loin; cut off excess string. Place on rack in roasting pan. Brush with oil; sprinkle with remaining salt and pepper.

“ Canada produces the finest pork in the world.
We can be proud of the contribution our farmers
make to the economy and to our tables. – *Elizabeth* ”

5 Roast in 375°F (190°C) oven until meat thermometer registers 160°F (70°C), about 1 hour and 20 minutes. Transfer to cutting board and tent with foil; let stand for 15 minutes before carving.

6 SAUCE: Meanwhile, in small bowl, stir flour with butter; set aside. Skim fat from roasting pan. Place pan over medium heat. Add shallots and garlic; cook, stirring, for 3 minutes. Add wine; bring to boil over high heat, scraping up any brown bits from bottom of pan. Boil until reduced by half, about 3 minutes. Stir in stock and pepper; return to boil. Stir in flour mixture and boil, stirring, until thickened, about 5 minutes. Strain into gravy boat. Serve with pork.

Makes 8 to 10 servings. PER EACH OF 10 SERVINGS: about 389 cal, 31 g pro, 20 g total fat (7 g sat. fat), 19 g carb, 2 g fibre, 93 mg chol, 363 mg sodium. % RDI: 6% calcium, 14% iron, 6% vit A, 7% vit C, 10% folate.

fridge **NOTE**
- **You can substitute raisins or chopped apples for the cranberries in the stuffing.**

Roasted Rack of Lamb with Cumin Garlic Crust

Edmonton caterer extraordinaire Gail Hall showcases Alberta rack of lamb
with a distinctive southwestern flavour. – Daphna

2	racks of lamb, each about 1½ lb (750 g)	2
¼ cup	cumin seeds	50 mL
¼ cup	extra-virgin olive oil	50 mL
2 tbsp	minced garlic	25 mL
½ tsp	salt	2 mL
¼ tsp	pepper	1 mL

fridge NOTES

- Ask your butcher to cut between the bones so you can easily carve the roasted rack into attractive single chops. Or look for an already chined (backbone removed) rack.

- Roasted plum tomato halves and Middle Eastern couscous are wonderful accompaniments to the lamb.

1 If necessary, trim all but ⅛ inch (3 mm) fat from meaty portion of racks. Place each rack, meaty side up, on cutting board. Using sharp knife, cut line across rack where meaty portion begins, about 3 inches (8 cm) from rib ends. Cut off meat and fat between bared ribs to expose bones. Holding each rack firmly, scrape exposed bones clean.

2 In small dry skillet, toast cumin seeds over medium heat, shaking pan often, until fragrant and slightly darkened, about 5 minutes. Let cool. Transfer to spice grinder; grind coarsely. Transfer to bowl; mix in oil, garlic, salt and pepper. (Or, using mortar and pestle, pound seeds coarsely. Add garlic and pound to make thick, smooth paste. Gradually blend in oil, then salt and pepper.)

3 Evenly spread paste over meaty side of each rack, pushing some between bones. Spread remaining paste on bone side. Place on greased rack in small roasting pan. (MAKE-AHEAD: **Cover and refrigerate for up to 24 hours. Let come to room temperature before roasting.**)

4 Roast in 400°F (200°C) oven until lamb is crusty and browned and meat thermometer registers 140°F (60°C) for rare, about 30 minutes, or to desired doneness. Transfer to cutting board and tent with foil; let stand for 5 minutes. Cut between bones to serve.

Makes 4 to 6 servings. PER EACH OF 6 SERVINGS: about 249 cal, 20 g pro, 18 g total fat (5 g sat. fat), 3 g carb, 1 g fibre, 71 mg chol, 235 mg sodium. % RDI: 5% calcium, 31% iron, 1% vit A, 2% vit C.

Beer and Oat Bread

I like the way large-flake oats provide phenomenal texture in this bread baked at The Kingston Brewing Company in Kingston, Ontario. – Emily

1 Set aside ¼ cup (50 mL) of the oats for topping. In food processor, grind 2 cups (500 mL) of the remaining oats until fine; set aside.

2 Sprinkle remaining oats evenly over rimmed baking sheet; toast in 350°F (180°C) oven for 20 minutes, stirring once. Let cool slightly.

3 Meanwhile, in small bowl, whisk together 1 cup (250 mL) of the flour, the warm water and yeast; let stand until frothy, about 15 minutes.

4 In large bowl, whisk together ale, skim milk powder, sugar and salt; whisk in yeast mixture. Stir in 3 cups (750 mL) of the remaining flour and ground and toasted oats. Stir in enough of the remaining flour to make slightly sticky dough. Turn out onto lightly floured surface; knead until smooth and elastic, about 5 minutes, adding enough of the remaining flour as necessary to prevent sticking. Place in greased bowl, turning to grease all over. Cover with plastic wrap; let rise in warm draft-free place until doubled in bulk, 1 to 1½ hours.

5 Punch down dough; cut in half. Pat each half into 11- x 8-inch (28 x 20 cm) rectangle. Starting at narrow end, roll up into cylinder; pinch along bottom to smooth and seal. Fit into 2 greased 8- x 4-inch (1.5 L) loaf pans. Cover and let rise until doubled in bulk, about 1 hour. Brush loaves lightly with water; sprinkle with reserved oats.

6 Bake in centre of 375°F (190°C) oven until golden and loaves sound hollow when tapped on bottom, about 40 minutes.

Makes 2 loaves, each 12 slices. PER SLICE: about 183 cal, 6 g pro, 1 g total fat (trace sat. fat), 36 g carb, 2 g fibre, 0 mg chol, 302 mg sodium. % RDI: 3% calcium, 16% iron, 1% vit A, 27% folate.

4 cups	large-flake rolled oats (not instant)	1 L
5 cups	all-purpose flour (approx)	1.25 L
1½ cups	warm water	375 mL
2 tbsp	active dry yeast	25 mL
1	bottle (341 mL) pale ale or brown ale	1
½ cup	skim milk powder	125 mL
½ cup	packed brown sugar	125 mL
1 tbsp	salt	15 mL

fridge NOTE

- **This loaf is terrific for sandwiches, for morning toast, with cheese and even for dips and spreads.**

Buttermilk Pie

The genius of Karen Barnaby, executive chef of The Fish House in Stanley Park, Vancouver, shows in this nutty, fennel-seed crust. – Elizabeth

½ cup	whole almonds	125 mL
½ cup	whole hazelnuts	125 mL
1 tsp	coriander seeds	5 mL
½ tsp	fennel seeds	2 mL
½ cup	butter	125 mL
1 cup	graham cracker crumbs	250 mL
FILLING:		
2	pkg (each 8 oz/250 g) cream cheese, softened	2
⅔ cup	granulated sugar	150 mL
3	eggs	3
1 tsp	vanilla	5 mL
¾ cup	buttermilk	175 mL
1⅓ cups	fresh raspberries	325 mL

1 Spread almonds and hazelnuts on rimmed baking sheet, keeping types separate; toast in 350°F (180°C) oven until fragrant, 5 to 10 minutes. Transfer hazelnuts to tea towel and rub off as much of the skins as possible; let cool. Finely chop nuts; place in bowl.

2 In skillet, toast coriander and fennel seeds over medium heat until fragrant, about 2 minutes; add to bowl. In small saucepan, melt butter over medium heat until slightly browned; add to bowl. Add crumbs and mix well. Press over bottom and up side of 10-inch (25 cm) pie plate; set aside.

3 FILLING: In bowl, beat cream cheese with sugar until smooth. In separate bowl, whisk eggs with vanilla; slowly beat into cheese mixture until smooth, scraping down side of bowl occasionally. Gradually beat in buttermilk.

4 Scatter raspberries over pie crust; pour filling over top. Place pie plate in roasting pan; pour enough boiling water into pan to come halfway up side of pie plate. Bake in centre of 350°F (180°C) oven until edge is puffed and centre is set but still jiggly, about 30 minutes. Let cool to room temperature in pan of water on rack. Remove from water bath; refrigerate until chilled, about 2 hours. (MAKE-AHEAD: **Cover and refrigerate for up to 2 days.**)

Makes 8 servings. PER SERVING: about 595 cal, 12 g pro, 47 g total fat (23 g sat. fat), 36 g carb, 3 g fibre, 170 mg chol, 433 mg sodium. % RDI: 13% calcium, 16% iron, 42% vit A, 7% vit C, 16% folate.

Bumbleberry Pie

Serve this fruit-filled pie with a dollop of crème Chantilly – lightly whipped cream sweetened with brown sugar. – Emily

1 On lightly floured surface, roll out a little more than half of the pastry. Fit into 10-inch (25 cm) pie plate. Trim and flute edge. Roll out remaining dough. Using maple leaf cutter, cut out shapes. Refrigerate on rimmed baking sheet until chilled, about 30 minutes.

2 In large saucepan, combine apples, blueberries, raspberries, blackberries, cranberries and plums. In bowl, whisk together sugar, flour, cornstarch and cinnamon; gently stir into fruit mixture along with lemon juice. Cook over medium heat, stirring occasionally, until berries release juices, about 5 minutes. Spoon into prepared pie shell. Arrange pastry leaves over filling. Brush crust and leaves with egg.

3 Bake on rimmed baking sheet in bottom third of 400°F (200°C) oven for 15 minutes. Reduce heat to 350°F (180°C); bake until pastry is golden and filling is bubbling and thickened, about 50 minutes. Let cool on rack.

Makes 8 servings. PER SERVING: about 518 cal, 6 g pro, 19 g total fat (5 g sat. fat), 85 g carb, 7 g fibre, 23 mg chol, 281 mg sodium. % RDI: 3% calcium, 16% iron, 3% vit A, 30% vit C, 24% folate.

Pastry for 10-inch (25 cm) double-crust pie		
2½ cups	apples, peeled and diced	625 mL
2 cups	blueberries	500 mL
2 cups	raspberries	500 mL
1½ cups	blackberries	375 mL
1½ cups	cranberries	375 mL
1½ cups	diced plums	375 mL
1¼ cups	granulated sugar	300 mL
⅓ cup	all-purpose flour	75 mL
3 tbsp	cornstarch	50 mL
½ tsp	cinnamon	2 mL
1 tbsp	lemon juice	15 mL
1	egg, lightly beaten	1

fridge **NOTE**

- Use fresh or frozen berries; increase baking time by 15 minutes if using frozen. If blackberries are unavailable, substitute more raspberries or blueberries.

Chocolate Butter Tarts

Butter tarts were my father's favourite. He always found an excuse to be in the kitchen when my mother was taking them out of the oven. – Elizabeth

1¼ cups	all-purpose flour	300 mL
½ cup	cocoa powder	125 mL
¼ tsp	salt	1 mL
¼ cup	cold butter, cubed	50 mL
¼ cup	shortening, cubed	50 mL
1	egg yolk	1
1 tsp	vinegar	5 mL
FILLING:		
½ cup	packed brown sugar	125 mL
½ cup	corn syrup	125 mL
1	egg	1
2 tbsp	butter, softened	25 mL
1 tsp	each vanilla and vinegar	5 mL
Pinch	salt	Pinch
¼ cup	currants, raisins, chopped pecans or shredded coconut	50 mL
¼ cup	coarsely chopped chocolate chunks	50 mL

1 In large bowl, whisk together flour, cocoa and salt. Using pastry blender or 2 knives, cut in butter and shortening until mixture resembles coarse crumbs with a few larger pieces. In liquid measure, whisk egg yolk with vinegar; add enough ice water to make ⅓ cup (75 mL).

2 Gradually sprinkle egg mixture over flour mixture, stirring briskly with fork until pastry holds together. Press into ball; flatten into disc. Wrap in plastic wrap and refrigerate for 1 hour. (MAKE-AHEAD: **Refrigerate for up to 3 days; let stand at room temperature for 15 minutes before rolling out.**)

3 FILLING: In bowl, vigorously whisk together brown sugar, corn syrup, egg, butter, vanilla, vinegar and salt; set aside.

4 On lightly floured surface, roll out pastry to ⅛-inch (3 mm) thickness. Using 4-inch (10 cm) round cookie cutter (or empty 28-oz/796 mL can), cut out 12 circles, rerolling scraps once if necessary.

5 Fit circles into 2¾- x 1¼-inch (7 x 3 cm) muffin cups. Divide currants and chocolate among pastry shells. Spoon in filling until three-quarters full.

6 Bake in bottom third of 450°F (230°C) oven until filling is puffed and bubbling and pastry is golden, about 12 minutes. Let stand on rack for 1 minute. Run metal spatula around tarts to loosen; carefully slide spatula under tarts and transfer to rack to let cool.

Makes 12 tarts. PER TART: about 253 cal, 3 g pro, 12 g total fat (6 g sat. fat), 36 g carb, 2 g fibre, 51 mg chol, 133 mg sodium. % RDI: 2% calcium, 11% iron, 7% vit A, 10% folate.

Shmoo Torte

This Winnipeg specialty is from Café au Livre, a charming restaurant in McNally Robinson Booksellers. – Elizabeth

1 CAKE: In bowl, sift ¾ cup (175 mL) of the sugar with the flour. In large bowl, beat egg whites until soft peaks form. Beat in almond extract and remaining sugar, 2 tbsp (25 mL) at a time, until stiff glossy peaks form. Sift flour mixture over top, one-quarter at a time, gently folding in after each addition. Fold in chopped pecans. Scrape into ungreased 10-inch (4 L) tube pan. Run spatula through batter to eliminate any large air pockets; smooth top.

2 Bake in centre of 350°F (180°C) oven until top springs back when lightly touched, 45 to 60 minutes. Invert pan; let stand on legs attached to pan, or set on bottle or funnel, until completely cooled.

3 CARAMEL SAUCE: In saucepan, bring butter and half of the cream to boil. Add sugar and remaining cream; return to boil. Reduce heat and simmer for 5 minutes. Remove from heat; set aside to let cool to room temperature.

4 Remove cake from pan. Cut into 3 layers. In large bowl, whip cream, icing sugar and vanilla. Place bottom cake layer, cut side up, on flat cake plate. Using piping bag fitted with star tip, fill hole of cake with whipped cream mixture. Pipe border on top around edge. Pour ¼ cup (50 mL) of the caramel sauce inside border. Repeat layers once. Top with remaining cake layer, cut side down.

5 Spread 3 cups (750 mL) of the cream mixture over top and side. Pipe rosette in centre; pipe border around edge. Spread thin layer of caramel sauce inside border; garnish with pecan halves.

Makes 16 servings. PER SERVING: about 453 cal, 6 g pro, 30 g total fat (15 g sat. fat), 44 g carb, 1 g fibre, 84 mg chol, 101 mg sodium. % RDI: 5% calcium, 6% iron, 22% vit A, 6% folate.

3 cups	whipping cream	750 mL
⅓ cup	icing sugar	75 mL
2 tsp	vanilla	10 mL
16	pecan halves	16
CAKE:		
1½ cups	granulated sugar	375 mL
1 cup	all-purpose flour	250 mL
2 cups	egg whites (about 14 whites)	500 mL
2 tsp	almond extract	10 mL
1 cup	finely chopped pecans	250 mL
CARAMEL SAUCE:		
¼ cup	butter	50 mL
1 cup	whipping cream	250 mL
1 cup	packed brown sugar	250 mL

Cookies-and-Cream Torte

Featuring whipped cream and sweet sliced strawberries, here's the perfect red-and-white cake for a Canada Day party. – Elizabeth

2 tbsp	red currant jelly	25 mL
COOKIE LAYERS:		
1 cup	butter, softened	250 mL
1 cup	granulated sugar	250 mL
2	eggs	2
2 cups	all-purpose flour	500 mL
1 tbsp	grated lemon rind	15 mL
2 tsp	baking powder	10 mL
½ tsp	salt	2 mL
FILLING:		
1 tbsp	unflavoured gelatin	15 mL
3 cups	whipping cream	750 mL
¼ cup	granulated sugar	50 mL
7 cups	sliced strawberries	1.75 L

1 Line 2 rimmed baking sheets with parchment paper; using 9-inch (1.5 L) round metal cake pan as guide, draw 1 circle on each sheet of paper. Set aside.

2 COOKIE LAYERS: In large bowl, beat butter with sugar until combined; beat in eggs, 1 at a time, until fluffy. In small bowl, whisk together flour, lemon rind, baking powder and salt; gradually beat into butter mixture. Spoon one-quarter onto each circle on prepared pan; spread evenly almost to edge.

3 Bake, 1 sheet at a time, in centre of 350°F (180°C) oven until golden around edge and firm to the touch, about 12 minutes. Transfer to rack; let cool. Repeat with remaining batter. (MAKE-AHEAD: **Wrap in plastic wrap and set aside for up to 24 hours or freeze in airtight container for up to 2 weeks.**)

4 FILLING: In small saucepan, sprinkle gelatin over ¼ cup (50 mL) water; let stand for 5 minutes. Heat over medium-low heat until dissolved; let cool slightly. In bowl, whip cream with sugar; beating constantly, pour in gelatin mixture in thin steady stream.

5 Place 1 cookie layer on flat serving platter; spread heaping cupful (250 mL) of the whipped cream mixture over cookie layer. Arrange 2 cups (500 mL) of the strawberries over cookie layer, some with tips pointing out around edge and the rest over cream. Repeat layers twice. Top with remaining cookie layer and whipped cream mixture. Arrange remaining strawberries over top. Cover and refrigerate until cake is softened, about 4 hours. (MAKE-AHEAD: **Refrigerate for up to 24 hours.**)

6 In microwaveable bowl or saucepan, melt jelly; brush over berries.

Makes 12 servings. PER SERVING: about 537 cal, 6 g pro, 38 g total fat (23 g sat. fat), 47 g carb, 3 g fibre, 154 mg chol, 330 mg sodium. % RDI: 8% calcium, 10% iron, 39% vit A, 83% vit C, 20% folate.

Supervising producer Tanya Linton

fridge NOTE

- **Summer's the perfect time for an ice-cream pie. Here's an easy one: In a prepared graham cracker crumb crust, layer softened orange sherbet with vanilla ice cream and refreeze; top with a scattering of shaved orange-flavoured chocolate or crushed orange candies.**

Stir Up a Little Romance

*S*avouring food with your beloved can definitely be a romantic affair, whether you feed each other oysters or gaze at one another over spoonfuls of silky chocolate pudding. I am always seduced by the fresh fig, especially when it's cloaked in a salty slice of prosciutto. Remember, if your date drops a piece of bread in the cheese fondue, custom dictates that he/she has to kiss the cook. (Here's hoping!) What I think is truly romantic is when two people get up close and personal with a skillet and tongs to create a masterpiece together. Love is in the air, and in the kitchen. – Emily

- Oysters on the Half Shell
- Grilled Figs Wrapped in Prosciutto with Balsamic Drizzle
- Artichokes with Two Dipping Sauces
- True Canadian Cheese Fondue
- Seared Peppercorn Sirloin
- Sweetheart Waffles with Cherry Berry Sauce
- Chocolate Hazelnut Pots de Crème

‹ Prop assistant Anna Michener and Emily give a final stir before cameras roll

Oysters on the Half Shell

When I'm buying oysters, I tap the shell: a sharp, cracking sound indicates a live oyster; dead oysters sound dull and hollow. – Elizabeth

36	oysters	36
6	lemon wedges	6
	Large sprigs fresh parsley	
¼ tsp	pepper	1 mL

fridge NOTE

- If you prefer to buy already shucked in-shell oysters, look for those with clean – not milky – liquor and very little odour. Keep refrigerated and serve the same day.

1 Make bed of crushed ice on 6 deep plates; place in freezer.

2 Using stiff brush, scrub oyster shells under cool water. Shuck oysters over sieve set over bowl. Using oyster knife and thick glove or cloth, and holding oyster curved shell down, insert tip of blade into hinge and twist. Once seal is broken, wipe blade clean, reinsert it and slide it along inside of flat upper shell to cut oyster from top shell. Slide blade under oyster to sever it from lower shell. Hold shell level to keep as much liquor as possible with oyster. Discard flat upper shells. Balance oysters in bottom shells on bed of ice.

3 Garnish each plate with lemon wedge and parsley sprigs. Season with pepper.

Makes 6 pieces. PER PIECE: about 59 cal, 6 g pro, 2 g total fat (1 g sat. fat), 4 g carb, trace fibre, 45 mg chol, 177 mg sodium. % RDI: 4% calcium, 41% iron, 3% vit A, 12% vit C, 4% folate.

> " Hail to all lovers who enjoy puckering up to a few fortifying oysters. – *Elizabeth* "

Grilled Figs Wrapped in Prosciutto with Balsamic Drizzle

I encourage you to eat figs with gusto and abandon, seductively scooping out the seeds with your tongue. How voluptuous! – Emily

1 Halve figs; cut prosciutto in half lengthwise. Wrap basil leaf then prosciutto piece around each fig. Place on plate; cover and refrigerate for 1 hour. (MAKE-AHEAD: **Refrigerate for up to 8 hours.**) Brush fig packages with oil.

2 Place fig packages on greased grill over medium-low heat; close lid and grill, turning once, until warmed through and prosciutto is barely browned around edges, about 2 minutes. Divide frisée among 4 plates. Place fig packages on top. Drizzle with balsamic vinegar and top with cheese.

Makes 4 servings. PER SERVING: about 115 cal, 4 g pro, 6 g total fat (2 g sat. fat), 13 g carb, 2 g fibre, 8 mg chol, 195 mg sodium. % RDI: 10% calcium, 4% iron, 7% vit A, 5% vit C, 17% folate.

4	fresh black or green figs	4
4	thin slices prosciutto	4
8	large fresh basil leaves	8
1 tbsp	extra-virgin olive oil	15 mL
2 cups	torn frisée leaves	500 mL
2 tbsp	balsamic vinegar	25 mL
¾ oz	Parmigiano-Reggiano cheese, shaved	25 g

fridge NOTE

- **Substitute peeled slices of fresh peach or mango for the figs.**

Artichokes with Two Dipping Sauces

Tender, succulent artichokes are easy to cook and fun to eat. Dip leaves cold into Aïoli or hot into Ginger Beurre Blanc Sauce. – Elizabeth

4	large artichokes (about 2 lb/1 kg total)	4
Half	lemon	Half
AÏOLI:		
2	small cloves garlic, minced	2
¼ tsp	salt	1 mL
⅔ cup	light mayonnaise	150 mL
1 tsp	lemon juice	5 mL
OR		
GINGER BEURRE BLANC SAUCE:		
⅔ cup	dry white wine	150 mL
2 tsp	minced gingerroot	10 mL
1 tsp	grated lemon rind	5 mL
½ cup	butter, diced	125 mL
Pinch	each salt and pepper	Pinch

1 Trim off each artichoke stem so artichoke stands level. As you work, rub cut surface with lemon to prevent discolouration. Using sharp knife, cut off pointed top of each artichoke parallel to base. Using scissors, cut off remaining prickly tips of leaves.

2 Place steamer basket over 1 inch (2.5 cm) boiling water in large pot; place artichokes upside down in basket. Reduce heat, cover and steam, adding boiling water to maintain level, until leaf from centre can be pulled out easily, about 35 minutes. Let cool slightly.

3 Push back central leaves to expose fuzzy choke. Using small spoon, scoop out and discard choke and attached purplish leaves. (MAKE-AHEAD: **To serve cold, cover and refrigerate for up to 8 hours.**)

4 AÏOLI: Meanwhile, on cutting board, sprinkle garlic with salt. Using side of chef's knife or fork, rub together to form paste. In small bowl, whisk together mayonnaise, lemon juice and garlic paste. (MAKE-AHEAD: **Cover and refrigerate for up to 4 hours.**)

5 OR GINGER BEURRE BLANC SAUCE: Meanwhile, in small saucepan, bring wine, ginger and lemon rind to boil over medium heat; reduce heat and simmer until reduced by half, about 5 minutes. Remove from heat; whisk in butter, a few pieces at a time, until blended. Whisk in salt and pepper.

6 To serve hot, place Ginger Beurre Blanc Sauce in small bowl. To serve cold, fill centre of artichoke with Aïoli. To eat, pull off leaf and dip in sauce; pull between teeth to release flesh. Cut base, or heart, into pieces.

Makes 4 servings. PER SERVING WITH AÏOLI: about 165 cal, 3 g pro, 12 g total fat (1 g sat. fat), 13 g carb, 5 g fibre, 0 mg chol, 486 mg sodium. % RDI: 4% calcium, 8% iron, 2% vit A, 15% vit C, 20% folate. PER SERVING WITH GINGER BEURRE BLANC SAUCE: about 267 cal, 3 g pro, 23 g total fat (14 g sat. fat), 10 g carb, 5 g fibre, 62 mg chol, 318 mg sodium. % RDI: 5% calcium, 9% iron, 23% vit A, 15% vit C, 20% folate.

fridge NOTES

- Artichokes are so much fun to eat! Use your fingers to remove the leaves one by one, dip them into the sauce, then draw them through your teeth to scrape off the delicious flesh.

- When buying artichokes, size doesn't matter. Look for tightly furled leaves that form as compact a ball as possible. They should feel firm; if flabby, they are old. Sometimes the tips will be slightly brown, but that is fine.

True Canadian Cheese Fondue

*Before diving into the fondue, toast the evening with kir – a dash of cassis
topped with white wine.* – Elizabeth

2 cups	dry white wine	500 mL
1	clove garlic, minced	1
5½ cups	Oka cheese, shredded (1⅓ lb/670 g)	1.375 L
3 cups	extra-old Cheddar cheese, shredded (12 oz/375 g)	750 mL
2 tbsp	cornstarch	25 mL
1½ tsp	Dijon mustard	7 mL
1 tsp	Worcestershire sauce	5 mL
¼ tsp	pepper	1 mL
Pinch	each grated nutmeg and cayenne pepper	Pinch
1 tbsp	whisky	15 mL
2	baguettes (French sticks), cut in 1-inch (2.5 cm) cubes	2
1	each apple and pear, cored and cubed	1

1 Pour all but 2 tbsp (25 mL) of the wine into fondue pot; add garlic and bring to simmer over medium heat on stove top.

2 Add Oka and Cheddar cheeses; stir with wooden spoon until melted. Dissolve cornstarch in remaining wine; stir in mustard, Worcestershire sauce, pepper, nutmeg and cayenne. Add to fondue pot and bring to simmer, stirring; simmer for 1 minute. Stir in whisky.

3 Place pot over medium-low heat of fondue burner on table, adjusting heat as necessary to maintain low simmer and stirring often. Serve with baguette, apple and pear cubes to skewer and dip into cheese mixture.

Makes 6 servings. PER SERVING: about 968 cal, 50 g pro, 54 g total fat (32 g sat. fat) 65 g carb, 4 g fibre, 199 mg chol, 1,598 mg sodium. % RDI: 112% calcium, 28% iron, 60% vit A, 5% vit C, 59% folate.

Seared Peppercorn Sirloin

With its sophisticated flavour, this steak is best for an adult dinner party.
Use a cast-iron skillet; it holds heat well and can go in the oven. – Daphna

1 Place peppercorns in plastic bag. Using smooth side of mallet or bottom of heavy saucepan, crush peppercorns to size of sesame seeds. In small bowl, combine peppercorns, garlic, 2 tbsp (25 mL) of the oil and mustard. (MAKE-AHEAD: **Cover and refrigerate for up to 4 hours.**)

2 Trim fat from steak. Spread peppercorn mixture around edge of steak; sprinkle with salt. In ovenproof skillet, heat remaining oil over high heat. Sear steak on both sides until golden brown, about 2 minutes per side. Roast in 425°F (220°C) oven, turning once, until medium-rare, about 15 minutes, or until desired doneness. Transfer to cutting board and tent with foil; let stand for 5 minutes before slicing thinly across the grain.

3 In same pan, bring wine and stock to boil, scraping up any brown bits from bottom of pan; boil for 2 minutes. Strain through fine-mesh sieve; return sauce to pan. Add cream; boil for 1 minute. Add any accumulated juices from steak. Serve with steak.

Makes 4 to 6 servings. PER EACH OF 6 SERVINGS: about 291 cal, 33 g pro, 15 g total fat (4 g sat. fat), 3 g carb, trace fibre, 78 mg chol, 326 mg sodium. % RDI: 5% calcium, 30% iron, 2% vit A, 2% vit C, 5% folate.

2 tbsp	black peppercorns	25 mL
2	cloves garlic, minced	2
3 tbsp	extra-virgin olive oil	50 mL
2 tbsp	Dijon mustard	25 mL
1	top sirloin grilling steak, 1 inch (2.5 cm) thick (about 2 lb/1 kg)	1
¼ tsp	salt	1 mL
½ cup	red wine	125 mL
½ cup	beef stock	125 mL
2 tbsp	whipping cream	25 mL

Sweetheart Waffles with Cherry Berry Sauce

Beaten egg whites create fluffy waffles. As with any waffle recipe, you can make the batter into pancakes if you don't have a waffle iron. – Elizabeth

1½ cups	all-purpose flour	375 mL
2 tbsp	granulated sugar	25 mL
2 tsp	baking powder	10 mL
¼ tsp	salt	1 mL
3	eggs, separated	3
1½ cups	milk	375 mL
1 tsp	vanilla	5 mL
2 tbsp	vegetable oil	25 mL
CHERRY BERRY SAUCE:		
1½ cups	frozen sour cherries, thawed	375 mL
1 cup	each frozen strawberries and raspberries, thawed	250 mL
¼ cup	frozen blueberries, thawed	50 mL
¼ cup	granulated sugar	50 mL
2 tbsp	cornstarch	25 mL
1 tsp	vanilla	5 mL

1 CHERRY BERRY SAUCE: In saucepan, bring cherries, strawberries, raspberries, blueberries, sugar, ¼ cup (50 mL) water and cornstarch to boil over medium-high heat, stirring gently; cook until thickened, about 1 minute. Stir in vanilla. Keep warm.

2 In large bowl, whisk together flour, 1 tbsp (15 mL) of the sugar, baking powder and salt. In separate bowl, whisk together egg yolks, milk and vanilla; pour over flour mixture and whisk until smooth.

3 In clean bowl, beat egg whites until soft peaks form. Sprinkle with remaining sugar; beat until stiff peaks form. Fold one-quarter into batter; fold in remaining egg whites.

4 Heat waffle iron. For each waffle, brush iron lightly with some of the oil; pour in generous ½ cup (125 mL) of the batter. Close lid and cook until steam stops and waffle is crisp and golden, 4 to 5 minutes. Serve warm with sauce.

Makes 8 servings. PER SERVING: about 245 cal, 7 g pro, 7 g total fat (1 g sat. fat), 39 g carb, 2 g fibre, 84 mg chol, 185 mg sodium. % RDI: 10% calcium, 12% iron, 9% vit A, 15% vit C, 9% folate.

VARIATION

Sweetheart Waffles with Apple Cinnamon Sauce: Add ½ tsp (2 mL) cinnamon to dry ingredients for waffles. Replace Cherry Berry Sauce with Apple Cinnamon Sauce: In saucepan, melt 2 tbsp (25 mL) butter with ¼ cup (50 mL) packed brown sugar over medium-high heat. Add 4 cups (1 L) thickly sliced peeled apples and ½ tsp (2 mL) cinnamon. Cover and cook, stirring once, until apples are tender, about 5 minutes.

fridge NOTE

- Sink your teeth into a chocolate chip waffle sandwich. Mix chocolate chips into the batter, then sandwich a scoop of creamy vanilla ice cream between two cooked waffles.

Chocolate Hazelnut Pots de Crème

The perfect seduction to end a romantic dinner. Refrigerate it ahead, then serve with whipped cream. I like to add dazzle with gold flakes. – Emily

1 In saucepan, bring 1½ cups (375 mL) of the cream just to boil; pour over chocolate in bowl and stir until melted.

2 In separate bowl, whisk egg yolks with sugar; whisk in one-third of the chocolate mixture. Stir in remaining chocolate mixture, hazelnut liqueur and vanilla. Pour into six 6-oz (175 mL) custard cups or ramekins; place in 13- x 9-inch (3.5 L) metal cake pan. Pour in enough boiling water to come halfway up sides of cups.

3 Bake in centre of 325°F (160°C) oven until set around edge but still slightly jiggly in centre, about 20 minutes. Remove cups from pan; let cool on rack to room temperature. Cover and refrigerate until chilled. (MAKE-AHEAD: **Refrigerate for up to 24 hours.**)

4 In bowl, whip remaining cream. Using piping bag or spoon, pipe onto centre of each cup. Garnish with chopped hazelnuts.

Makes 6 servings. PER SERVING: about 536 cal, 8 g pro, 50 g total fat (28 g sat. fat), 25 g carb, 4 g fibre, 323 mg chol, 40 mg sodium. % RDI: 9% calcium, 18% iron, 36% vit A, 11% folate.

2 cups	whipping cream	500 mL
6 oz	bittersweet chocolate, chopped	175 g
6	egg yolks	6
⅓ cup	granulated sugar	75 mL
2 tbsp	hazelnut or almond liqueur	25 mL
Dash	vanilla	Dash
1 tbsp	chopped toasted hazelnuts	15 mL

fridge NOTE

- **Cosy up to your loved one with an interactive dessert, such as chocolate fondue. Serve it with a luscious platter of fruit and some crunchy baby biscotti.**

NO ENTRANCE

Monday to Friday

It's one thing to throw a great dinner party every once in a while and garner a reputation as a fine cook. It's quite another to feel inspired putting supper on the table Monday to Friday, when time's short and everyone's hungry. But making the time to be together around the table is a priority, and preparing tasty and healthy food is the significant draw that gets everybody there. Weeknight suppers are a cornerstone of cooking in The Canadian Living Test Kitchen and on our show. We liken the creation of Monday-to-Friday meals to painting a picture around favourite family ingredients. Included in the art is time-saving, affordability, nutrition and, of course, great taste. – Elizabeth

- Pasta with Mushroom Bolognese
- Fusilli with Broccoli, Garlic and Anchovies
- Creamy Walnut Pasta Shells
- Pasta with Spinach and Potatoes
- Tuna, Roasted Pepper and Arugula Fettuccine
- Lemony Chicken Pasta
- Chili Orange Grilled Chicken Breasts
- Chicken Tortilla Bundles
- Moroccan Chicken with Couscous
- Romano Pork Chops
- Black Bean and Sausage Soup
- Lamb Shoulder Chops in Tomato Sauce

Pasta with Mushroom Bolognese

You will never miss the meat in this robust sauce. Bucatini is a tubular pasta that's slightly thicker than spaghetti. – Daphna

2 tbsp	extra-virgin olive oil	25 mL
1	onion, chopped	1
4	cloves garlic, minced	4
1	each carrot and stalk celery, diced	1
8 cups	finely chopped mushrooms (1½ lb/750 g)	2 L
1 cup	vegetable stock	250 mL
½ tsp	each salt and pepper	2 mL
Pinch	nutmeg	Pinch
1	bay leaf	1
1	can (28 oz/796 mL) diced tomatoes	1
¼ cup	tomato paste	50 mL
12 oz	bucatini or spaghetti pasta	375 g
½ cup	grated Parmesan cheese	125 mL

1 In large heavy saucepan, heat oil over medium-high heat; sauté onion, garlic, carrot, celery and mushrooms, stirring occasionally, until no liquid remains, about 15 minutes.

2 Add stock, salt, pepper, nutmeg and bay leaf; cook, stirring occasionally, until reduced by half, about 5 minutes.

3 Add tomatoes and tomato paste; bring to boil. Reduce heat and simmer until sauce is thick enough to mound on spoon, about 20 minutes. Discard bay leaf. (MAKE-AHEAD: **Refrigerate in airtight container for up to 24 hours; reheat before continuing.**)

4 Meanwhile, in large pot of boiling salted water, cook pasta until tender but firm, 8 to 10 minutes. Drain well and return to pot; add sauce and toss to coat. Sprinkle with Parmesan cheese to serve.

Makes 4 servings. PER SERVING: about 545 cal, 22 g pro, 13 g total fat (4 g sat. fat), 88 g carb, 10 g fibre, 10 mg chol, 1,233 mg sodium. % RDI: 26% calcium, 43% iron, 63% vit A, 70% vit C, 74% folate.

Fusilli with Broccoli, Garlic and Anchovies

My friend Jo Carlino introduced me to the heady mixture of garlic and anchovies with broccoli. I pass it on with pleasure. – Elizabeth

1 In large pot, combine 20 cups (5 L) water and 2 tbsp (25 mL) salt; bring to boil. Add pasta; cook for 8 minutes. Add broccoli; cook until tender-crisp and pasta is tender but firm, about 2 minutes. Drain well and return to pot.

2 Meanwhile, in skillet, heat oil over medium-low heat; cook garlic, stirring occasionally, for 3 minutes. Add anchovies and pepper; cook, stirring, until anchovies are dissolved, about 3 minutes. Fill pasta bowls with hot water to warm.

3 Add anchovy mixture, bread crumbs and half of the Parmesan cheese to pasta mixture; toss to coat. Empty water from bowls; spoon in pasta. Sprinkle with remaining cheese to serve.

Makes 4 servings. PER SERVING: about 596 cal, 22 g pro, 25 g total fat (5 g sat. fat), 71 g carb, 5 g fibre, 21 mg chol, 1,081 mg sodium. % RDI: 23% calcium, 24% iron, 9% vit A, 60% vit C, 68% folate.

5 cups	fusilli or orecchiette pasta (12 oz/375 g)	1.25 L
4 cups	broccoli florets	1 L
⅓ cup	extra-virgin olive oil	75 mL
4	cloves garlic, minced	4
1	pkg (50 g) flat anchovy fillets (about 8), chopped	1
¼ tsp	pepper	1 mL
¾ cup	fresh bread crumbs	175 mL
½ cup	grated Parmesan cheese	125 mL

fridge NOTE

- You can use anchovy paste instead of anchovies; about 2 tbsp (25 mL) will replace eight fillets. Look for tubes of the paste in coolers in the deli section of supermarkets.

Creamy Walnut Pasta Shells

Enjoy this crunchy, creamy blue cheese pasta as a first course for a dinner party with friends. – Emily

⅓ cup	chopped walnuts	75 mL
2 tbsp	butter	25 mL
2 tsp	chopped fresh thyme (or ½ tsp/2 mL dried)	10 mL
¾ cup	10% cream	175 mL
4 oz	blue cheese, Stilton or Gorgonzola, crumbled	125 g
Pinch	pepper	Pinch
4 cups	medium-size shell pasta or gnocchi pasta (12 oz/375 g)	1 L
2 tbsp	chopped fresh parsley	25 mL

1 In large skillet, toast walnuts over medium heat, stirring occasionally, until fragrant, 5 to 7 minutes.

2 Add butter and thyme; cook for 30 seconds. Add cream, blue cheese and pepper; simmer over medium-low heat, stirring occasionally, until slightly thickened and cheese is melted, about 5 minutes.

3 Meanwhile, in large pot of boiling salted water, cook pasta until tender but firm, 8 to 10 minutes. Drain well and return to pot; add sauce and toss to coat. Serve sprinkled with parsley.

Makes 4 servings. PER SERVING: about 587 cal, 20 g pro, 26 g total fat (12 g sat. fat), 68 g carb, 4 g fibre, 51 mg chol, 698 mg sodium. % RDI: 21% calcium, 18% iron, 17% vit A, 3% vit C, 63% folate.

> **"** I always keep some cream in the fridge for stirring up a velvety sauce for quick pasta suppers. You don't need much for rich flavour. – *Emily* **"**

A serious moment: the cohosts
review their recipes

Pasta with Spinach and Potatoes

*Comfort foods warm the soul and satisfy the tummy. When I'm in need of
cosy carbs, I think of this classic combo from Italy.* – Daphna

1 In large pot of boiling salted water, cook potato and pasta for
6 minutes. Stir in spinach; cook until pasta is tender but firm, 2 to
4 minutes. Reserving ⅓ cup (75 mL) cooking liquid, drain pasta mixture; return to pot.

2 Meanwhile, in skillet, heat oil over low heat; cook garlic, stirring
often, until softened, about 5 minutes. Stir in anchovy paste, pepper
and hot pepper flakes.

3 Add garlic mixture and reserved cooking liquid to pasta mixture;
toss to coat. Serve sprinkled with Parmesan cheese.

Makes 4 servings. PER SERVING: about 631 cal, 21 g pro, 18 g total fat (3 g sat. fat),
97 g carb, 7 g fibre, 7 mg chol, 575 mg sodium. % RDI: 20% calcium, 39% iron, 57% vit A,
18% vit C, 119% folate.

1	large baking potato, peeled and diced	1
5½ cups	orecchiette or fusilli pasta (1 lb/500 g)	1.375 L
1	pkg (10 oz/284 g) fresh spinach, coarsely chopped	1
¼ cup	extra-virgin olive oil	50 mL
4	cloves garlic, minced	4
1 tbsp	anchovy paste (or 5 anchovies, minced)	15 mL
¼ tsp	pepper	1 mL
Pinch	hot pepper flakes	Pinch
¼ cup	grated Parmesan cheese	50 mL

Tuna, Roasted Pepper and Arugula Fettuccine

Fresh pasta cooks in about three minutes. For extra flavour, add chopped black olives to the dish and serve with grated Parmesan cheese. – Elizabeth

12 oz	fresh fettuccine	375 g
2	cans (each 170 g) solid white tuna, drained	2
2	roasted red peppers, chopped	2
1	clove garlic, minced	1
½ tsp	pepper	2 mL
¼ tsp	salt	1 mL
¼ cup	extra-virgin olive oil	50 mL
2 tbsp	lemon juice	25 mL
1	bunch arugula, shredded	1

1 In large pot of boiling salted water, cook pasta until tender but firm, about 3 minutes.

2 Meanwhile, in large serving bowl, break tuna into chunks; add red peppers, garlic, pepper and salt. In small bowl, gradually whisk oil into lemon juice; pour half over tuna mixture and mix well.

3 Reserving ½ cup (125 mL) of the cooking liquid, drain pasta; place on tuna mixture. Pour remaining oil mixture over top; add arugula and toss, moistening with reserved cooking liquid as desired.

Makes 4 servings. PER SERVING: about 484 cal, 29 g pro, 18 g total fat (3 g sat. fat), 53 g carb, 3 g fibre, 90 mg chol, 615 mg sodium. % RDI: 7% calcium, 16% iron, 33% vit A, 175 % vit C, 76 % folate.

fridge NOTE

- **For a meal in minutes, sauté rapini in oil, roasted garlic and pinch hot pepper flakes; toss with your favourite short pasta and sprinkle with grated Parmesan or Romano cheese.**

Lemony Chicken Pasta

To keep the pasta warm, I fill my pasta bowls with hot water just before toss-ing the pasta with sauce. Then I drain the bowls, fill and serve. – Daphna

1 In large pot of boiling salted water, cook pasta until tender but firm, 8 to 10 minutes. Reserving ½ cup (125 mL) of the cooking liquid, drain and return to pot.

2 Meanwhile, cut chicken breasts crosswise into slices. In nonstick skillet, melt butter over medium-high heat; cook chicken, stirring occasionally, until no longer pink inside, about 5 minutes. Add garlic; cook, stirring, for 1 minute.

3 Add reserved cooking liquid, ricotta cheese, half of the Parmesan cheese, lemon rind and juice, salt, pepper and nutmeg; bring to simmer. Add spinach; cook, stirring, just until wilted. Pour over pasta and toss to coat. Serve sprinkled with remaining Parmesan cheese.

Makes 4 servings. PER SERVING: about 568 cal, 41 g pro, 13 g total fat (7 g sat. fat), 70 g carb, 5 g fibre, 81 mg chol, 819 mg sodium. % RDI: 32% calcium, 32% iron, 54% vit A, 17% vit C, 94% folate.

4 cups	penne pasta (12 oz/375 g)	1 L
12 oz	boneless skinless chicken breasts	375 g
1 tbsp	butter	15 mL
3	cloves garlic, minced	3
1 cup	light ricotta cheese	250 mL
¼ cup	grated Parmesan cheese	50 mL
1 tsp	grated lemon rind	5 mL
2 tbsp	lemon juice	25 mL
½ tsp	salt	2 mL
¼ tsp	pepper	1 mL
Pinch	nutmeg	Pinch
4 cups	packed trimmed spinach, shredded	1 L

fridge **NOTE**

- While supper is cooking, your family will enjoy nibbling on this simple appetizer: Fill Belgian endive spears with a mixture of chopped tomatoes, basil, garlic, green onion and a splash of extra-virgin olive oil.

Chili Orange Grilled Chicken Breasts

Save time with this two-dinner dish. Make enough chicken breasts for one night, saving two for Chicken Tortilla Bundles (opposite) the next. – Elizabeth

¾ cup	pasta or tomato sauce	175 mL
¼ cup	thawed orange juice concentrate	50 mL
2 tbsp	chili powder	25 mL
1 tbsp	cider vinegar	15 mL
1 tsp	grated orange rind	5 mL
4	cloves garlic, minced	4
½ tsp	each salt and pepper	2 mL
6	chicken breasts (3 lb/1.5 kg total)	6

1 In large glass dish, combine pasta sauce, orange juice concentrate, chili powder, vinegar, orange rind, garlic, salt and pepper; add chicken, turning to coat. Cover and refrigerate for 4 hours, turning occasionally. (MAKE-AHEAD: **Refrigerate for up to 12 hours.**)

2 Reserving marinade, place chicken, skin side down, on greased grill over medium heat; close lid and grill for 20 minutes. Turn and brush with reserved marinade; grill until no longer pink inside, about 25 minutes. (Refrigerate 2 of the breasts until cold; wrap and refrigerate for up to 2 days for making Chicken Tortilla Bundles, page 53.)

Makes 4 servings (plus enough for Chicken Tortilla Bundles, page 53). PER EACH OF 4 SERVINGS (WITHOUT SKIN): about 255 cal, 34 g pro, 8 g total fat (2 g sat. fat), 12 g carb, 1 g fibre, 103 mg chol, 443 mg sodium. % RDI: 3% calcium, 9% iron, 15% vit A, 32% vit C, 6% folate.

fridge NOTES

- Serve the hot grilled chicken breasts with skewers of mini potatoes and baby vegetables grilled alongside.

- To complement the Chicken Tortilla Bundles, toss a Bibb lettuce salad with sliced avocado and a lemon juice and olive oil dressing.

Chicken Tortilla Bundles

There's no such thing as dreary leftovers when this chicken is added to cheese and hearty beans in a crispy grilled wrap. – Daphna

1 Remove chicken meat from bone; shred into large bowl. Stir in cheese, beans, salsa, corn and green pepper. Divide evenly among tortillas; fold sides over filling and roll up. Brush bundles with oil.

2 Place bundles, seam side down, on greased grill over medium heat. Close lid and grill, turning once, until golden and crisp, 12 to 15 minutes.

Makes 4 servings. PER SERVING: about 569 cal, 37 g pro, 23 g total fat (10 g sat. fat), 54 g carb, 8 g fibre, 89 mg chol, 984 mg sodium. % RDI: 35% calcium, 26% iron, 23% vit A, 48% vit C, 24% folate.

2	Chili Orange Grilled Chicken Breasts (recipe, page 52)	2
1½ cups	shredded Monterey Jack or old Cheddar cheese	375 mL
1 cup	canned red kidney beans, drained and rinsed	250 mL
¾ cup	salsa	175 mL
½ cup	corn kernels	125 mL
½ cup	chopped sweet green pepper	125 mL
4	large (10-inch/25 cm) flour tortillas	4
2 tsp	vegetable oil	10 mL

Blocking the moves: Elizabeth, Daphna, Sheri Kowall, Dee-Dee Peel, Robert James, Holly Gillanders, Tanya Linton and director Michael Hooey

Moroccan Chicken with Couscous

I'm lucky to have visited Morocco, especially the souks *(markets), where great pyramids of spices invite you to cook.* – Elizabeth

½ cup	orange juice	125 mL
3 tbsp	extra-virgin olive oil	50 mL
1 tbsp	liquid honey	15 mL
¾ tsp	each ground cumin, coriander and salt	4 mL
½ tsp	each cinnamon, paprika, dried mint and pepper	2 mL
4	boneless skinless chicken breasts (1 lb/500 g total)	4
2	cloves garlic, minced	2
1	small onion, chopped	1
¼ cup	diced dried apricots	50 mL
1 cup	couscous	250 mL
1	zucchini, shredded	1

1 In small bowl, whisk together 1 tsp (5 mL) of the orange juice, 2 tbsp (25 mL) of the oil, honey, cumin, coriander, ¼ tsp (1 mL) of the salt, the cinnamon, paprika, mint and half of the pepper. Place chicken on broiler pan or foil-lined rimmed baking sheet; brush 1 side with half of the spice mixture. Broil chicken, turning halfway through and brushing with remaining spice mixture, until glazed and no longer pink inside, about 15 minutes.

2 Meanwhile, in saucepan, heat remaining oil over medium heat; cook garlic, onion and remaining salt and pepper, stirring occasionally, until softened, about 5 minutes.

3 Add 1 cup (250 mL) water, remaining orange juice and apricots; bring to boil. Stir in couscous and zucchini; cover and remove from heat. Let stand for 5 minutes; fluff with fork. Serve with chicken.

Makes 4 servings. PER SERVING: about 455 cal, 33 g pro, 12 g total fat (2 g sat. fat), 53 g carb, 3 g fibre, 67 mg chol, 502 mg sodium. % RDI: 4% calcium, 16% iron, 9% vit A, 22% vit C, 20% folate.

Romano Pork Chops

This piquant breading is golden crisp, and the pork cooks evenly and quickly because it's pounded until thin. – Emily

1 Trim fat from chops. One at a time, place chops between waxed paper and pound with mallet to about ¼-inch (5 mm) thickness. On plate, mix together cheese, bread crumbs, Cajun seasoning and lemon rind. Spread flour on separate plate. In shallow bowl, lightly beat eggs. Coat each chop in flour, shaking off excess. Dip into egg then into bread crumb mixture to coat both sides.

2 In large skillet, heat oil over medium-high heat; fry chops, in 2 batches and turning once, until golden brown, about 6 minutes. Garnish with lemon wedges.

Makes 4 servings. PER SERVING: about 456 cal, 41 g pro, 24 g total fat (9 g sat. fat), 18 g carb, 1 g fibre, 194 mg chol, 596 mg sodium. % RDI: 34% calcium, 20% iron, 12% vit A, 3% vit C, 14% folate.

4	boneless pork loin chops	4
1 cup	grated Romano or pecorino cheese	250 mL
½ cup	dry bread crumbs	125 mL
2 tsp	Cajun seasoning	10 mL
1 tsp	grated lemon rind	5 mL
¼ cup	all-purpose flour	50 mL
2	eggs	2
2 tbsp	vegetable oil	25 mL
	Lemon wedges	

fridge **NOTE**

- **In Canada, Romano is a pecorino-style cheese made from cow's milk and bearing the name Romano because of its origins in the Rome area. These cheeses can also be made from ewe's milk and are always salty and piquant – ideal for pastas and a nice foil for pork chops.**

Black Bean and Sausage Soup

Such a satisfying soup – requiring only five ingredients and taking less than 20 minutes to cook. That's what you want for weeknights. – Emily

2	smoked sausages (4 oz/125 g), diced	2
1	onion, finely chopped	1
2 tsp	ground cumin	10 mL
2 tbsp	tomato paste	25 mL
1	can (19 oz/540 mL) black beans, drained and rinsed	1

1 In large saucepan, brown sausages over medium heat. Add onion and cumin; cook, stirring occasionally, until softened, about 2 minutes.

2 Add tomato paste; cook, stirring, for 1 minute. Add beans and 4 cups (1 L) water; bring to boil. Reduce heat, cover and simmer for 15 minutes.

Makes 4 servings. PER SERVING: about 221 cal, 13 g pro, 7 g total fat (2 g sat. fat) 27 g carb, 7 g fibre, 15 mg chol, 424 mg sodium. % RDI: 5% calcium, 24% iron, 2% vit A, 8% vit C, 65% folate.

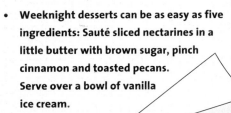

fridge NOTE

- **Weeknight desserts can be as easy as five ingredients:** Sauté sliced nectarines in a little butter with brown sugar, pinch cinnamon and toasted pecans. Serve over a bowl of vanilla ice cream.

" Many viewers have told me they were surprised to discover how full of flavour this soup is with only five ingredients. – *Emily* **"**

Lamb Shoulder Chops in Tomato Sauce

This Greek-inspired skillet supper is delicious served with rice pilaf or couscous. Accompany it with a mixed green salad. – Elizabeth

1 In shallow dish, whisk together flour, oregano, salt and pepper; press lamb chops into mixture, turning to coat. Reserve remaining flour mixture.

2 In large nonstick skillet, heat oil over medium-high heat; brown chops all over. Transfer to plate.

3 Add reserved flour mixture to pan; cook, stirring, over medium heat for 1 minute. Stir in tomatoes, stock, olives, green pepper, lemon rind and juice, and cinnamon; bring to boil.

4 Return chops and any accumulated juices to pan; cover and simmer over medium-low heat, turning once, until chops are fork-tender, about 15 minutes.

Makes 4 servings. PER SERVING: about 377 cal, 29 g pro, 21 g total fat (8 g sat. fat), 17 g carb, 2 g fibre, 690 mg sodium. % RDI: 8% calcium, 29% iron, 9% vit A, 52% vit C, 15% folate.

¼ cup	all-purpose flour	50 mL
2 tsp	dried oregano	10 mL
¼ tsp	each salt and pepper	1 mL
4	lamb shoulder chops (1½ lb/750 g total)	4
1 tbsp	extra-virgin olive oil	15 mL
1	can (19 oz/540 mL) stewed tomatoes	1
¼ cup	beef stock	50 mL
¼ cup	chopped pitted black olives	50 mL
Half	sweet green pepper, chopped	Half
1 tsp	grated lemon rind	5 mL
1 tbsp	lemon juice	15 mL
Pinch	cinnamon	Pinch

fridge NOTE

- If the lamb chops have a round bone, score the meat around the bone so that the chops cook evenly and don't curl.

Relaxed Weekend Cooking

*W*e look forward to weekends for a reprieve from the week's routines – a chance to putter. So weekend cooking should be leisurely whenever possible. That's where we come in, sharing stylish recipes that require almost no babysitting but deliver great rewards. Take the Miami Glazed Ribs, for example. The Saturday after I made them on the show, Mike, one of our cameramen, cooked them to rave reviews. He's been making them ever since. Many of these dishes simmer away in the oven or on the stove top for hours, allowing you time to indulge in the other joys of the weekend. – Daphna

- Chicken in a Clay Pot
- Classic Roast Chicken and Gravy
- Rabbit with White Wine Sauce
- Miami Glazed Ribs
- Veal Cutlets with Homemade Tomato Sauce
- Pork and Mushroom Stew
- Honey-Roasted Ribs
- Lemon Ricotta Pancakes
- Chocolate Cranberry Twist

◀ Daphna and floor director David Berube between segments

Chicken in a Clay Pot

This is one of my mother's signature dishes. The clay baker steams the chicken beautifully, browning it at the same time. – Daphna

1	large red onion, thickly sliced	1
2	potatoes, peeled and cut in chunks	2
3	carrots, cut in chunks	3
3	cloves garlic	3
1 tsp	salt	5 mL
½ tsp	pepper	2 mL
1	chicken (about 4 lb/2 kg)	1
Half	lemon	Half
2 tbsp	balsamic vinegar	25 mL
1 tbsp	soy sauce	15 mL
1 tsp	liquid honey	5 mL
1 tsp	dried thyme	5 mL

1 Soak both halves of clay baker in water for 20 minutes; drain and pat dry. In bottom of baker, arrange onion slices in single layer along centre. Arrange potatoes, carrots and garlic around sides, leaving centre of onion layer uncovered. Sprinkle with half each of the salt and pepper.

2 Remove giblets and neck, if present, from chicken. Rinse chicken inside and out; pat dry with paper towels. Stuff cavity with lemon. Tie legs together with kitchen string; tuck wings under back. Place, breast side up, over onions in baker.

3 In small bowl, combine vinegar, soy sauce and honey; pour over chicken. Sprinkle with thyme and remaining salt and pepper.

4 Place in centre of oven; turn on oven to 400°F (200°C). Roast until juices run clear when thigh is pierced and meat thermometer inserted in thigh registers 185°F (85°C), about 2 hours.

Makes 4 servings. PER SERVING: about 499 cal, 41 g pro, 23 g total fat (6 g sat. fat), 33 g carb, 4 g fibre, 143 mg chol, 992 mg sodium. % RDI: 6% calcium, 19% iron, 141% vit A, 18% vit C, 17% folate.

fridge NOTE

- **When cooking food in an unglazed clay pot or baker, presoaking in water and the cold-oven start are essential to avoid breakage and maintain succulence. The clay absorbs the water and releases it as the chicken cooks, creating a moist environment.**

Classic Roast Chicken and Gravy

Cooks know how easy it is to roast a good-size chicken to golden crisp perfection – and the happy reaction it gets around the table. – Elizabeth

1 Remove giblets and neck, if present, from chicken. Rinse chicken inside and out; pat dry with paper towels.

2 Place onion and garlic in cavity. Squeeze juice from lemon and set aside; add lemon half to cavity.

3 Tie legs together with kitchen string; tuck wings under back. Brush all over with oil; sprinkle with thyme, rosemary, salt and pepper. Place, breast side up, on rack in roasting pan. Roast, uncovered, in 325°F (160°C) oven for 1½ hours.

4 Roast, basting occasionally with pan juices, until juices run clear when thigh is pierced and meat thermometer inserted in thigh registers 185°F (85°C), about 1½ hours. Transfer chicken to platter and tent with foil; let stand for 10 minutes before carving.

5 Skim fat from pan juices. Sprinkle flour over juices; cook over medium-high heat, whisking, for 1 minute. Gradually pour in chicken stock and reserved lemon juice, whisking until smooth and thickened, about 3 minutes. Pour into warmed gravy boat.

6 Cut string holding legs together; discard onion, lemon and garlic. Using kitchen scissors, cut chicken into 2 breast and 2 leg portions. Cut each breast in half diagonally. Cut through each leg at joint to separate into drumsticks and thighs. Serve with gravy.

Makes 6 servings. PER SERVING: about 300 cal, 32 g pro, 17 g total fat (4 g sat. fat), 3 g carb, trace fibre, 116 mg chol, 291 mg sodium. % RDI: 1% calcium, 11% iron, 4% vit A, 3% vit C, 5% folate.

1	chicken (about 5 lb/2.2 kg)	1
Half	onion	Half
4	cloves garlic	4
Half	lemon	Half
1 tbsp	extra-virgin olive oil or butter	15 mL
¾ tsp	dried thyme	4 mL
¼ tsp	crumbled dried rosemary	1 mL
¼ tsp	each salt and pepper	1 mL
2 tbsp	all-purpose flour	25 mL
¾ cup	chicken stock	175 mL

Rabbit with White Wine Sauce

This heritage recipe comes from the Pusateri family, owners of Pusateri's, Toronto's finest specialty grocery store. – Daphna

⅓ cup	all-purpose flour	75 mL
¼ tsp	each salt and pepper	1 mL
2	rabbits (each about 2 lb/1 kg), each cut in 6 pieces	2
3 tbsp	extra-virgin olive oil	50 mL
1 tbsp	butter	15 mL
3	cloves garlic, smashed	3
2	each onions, stalks celery and small carrots, diced	2
1 cup	white wine	250 mL
2 cups	chicken stock	500 mL
2 tbsp	chopped fresh Italian parsley	25 mL

1 In plastic bag, combine flour, salt and pepper. In batches, add rabbit pieces and shake to coat, reserving any remaining flour mixture.

2 In large shallow Dutch oven, heat 2 tbsp (25 mL) of the oil over medium-high heat; brown rabbit, in batches and adding remaining oil as necessary, about 10 minutes. Transfer to plate.

3 Reduce heat to medium. Melt butter in pan; cook garlic, stirring, until golden, about 1 minute. Discard garlic. Add onions, celery and carrots; cook, stirring occasionally, until softened, about 10 minutes. Sprinkle with any reserved flour mixture; cook, stirring, for 1 minute.

4 Stir in wine; bring to boil, scraping up any brown bits from bottom of pan. Boil until reduced by half, about 2 minutes. Add stock; bring to boil. Return rabbit to pan; reduce heat, cover and simmer until tender and juices run clear when rabbit is pierced, about 40 minutes. Transfer rabbit to serving platter.

5 Increase heat and bring sauce to boil; boil until reduced to about 3 cups (750 mL), about 5 minutes. Sprinkle parsley over rabbit; serve with sauce.

Makes 6 servings. PER SERVING: about 464 cal, 49 g pro, 22 g total fat (6 g sat. fat), 12 g carb, 2 g fibre, 136 mg chol, 461 mg sodium. % RDI: 5% calcium, 33% iron, 63% vit A, 7% vit C, 16% folate.

fridge NOTE

- You can replace the rabbit with 4 lb (2 kg) skinless chicken pieces.

Kitchen assistant Elanora Reyes

Miami Glazed Ribs

Turn an everyday cut of meat into a not-so-everyday dish. Slow cooking brings out the fall-off-the-bone succulence of short ribs. – Daphna

1 In large pot, cover ribs with cold water; bring to boil. Reduce heat, cover and simmer until fork-tender, about 45 minutes. Drain and transfer to 13- x 9-inch (3 L) glass baking dish.

2 In saucepan, combine coffee, molasses, vinegar, tomato paste, Worcestershire sauce, ginger, salt, allspice and hot pepper sauce; bring to boil. Reduce heat and simmer until reduced to 2⅔ cups (650 mL), about 15 minutes. Pour over ribs, turning to coat; let cool. Cover tightly with foil and refrigerate for 4 hours. (MAKE-AHEAD: **Refrigerate for up to 24 hours.**)

3 Bake in 325°F (160°C) oven for 30 minutes. Uncover, turn ribs and bake, basting occasionally, until meat almost falls off bone and sauce is thickened, about 45 minutes.

Makes 6 servings. PER SERVING: about 520 cal, 32 g pro, 25 g total fat (11 g sat. fat), 43 g carb, 1 g fibre, 84 mg chol, 525 mg sodium. % RDI: 12% calcium, 44% iron, 5% vit A, 17% vit C, 5% folate.

4 lb	beef simmering short ribs	2 kg
1⅔ cups	brewed coffee	400 mL
1 cup	fancy molasses	250 mL
⅔ cup	cider vinegar	150 mL
½ cup	tomato paste	125 mL
2 tbsp	Worcestershire sauce	25 mL
1 tbsp	ground ginger	15 mL
1 tsp	salt	5 mL
¼ tsp	ground allspice	1 mL
¼ tsp	hot pepper sauce	1 mL

Veal Cutlets with Homemade Tomato Sauce

When it comes to weekend comfort dishes, this is one of my family's favourites. We usually serve it up with pasta or gnocchi. – Emily

¼ cup	all-purpose flour	50 mL
½ tsp	salt	2 mL
½ tsp	pepper	2 mL
1	egg	1
¾ cup	dry Italian bread crumbs	175 mL
¼ cup	grated Parmesan or Romano cheese	50 mL
1 tsp	dried oregano	5 mL
1 lb	veal cutlets	500 g
¼ cup	extra-virgin olive oil (approx)	50 mL
TOMATO SAUCE:		
2	cans (each 28 oz/796 mL) plum tomatoes	2
¼ cup	extra-virgin olive oil	50 mL
8	sprigs fresh Italian parsley	8
4	leaves fresh basil	4
2	cloves garlic	2
1	onion, halved	1
1 tbsp	dried oregano	15 mL
1 tsp	salt	5 mL
½ tsp	hot pepper flakes	2 mL

1 TOMATO SAUCE: In blender, purée tomatoes until smooth; pour into saucepan. Add oil, parsley, basil, garlic, onion, oregano, salt and hot pepper flakes; bring to boil. Reduce heat, partially cover and simmer until thickened, about 2 hours.

2 Meanwhile, in shallow bowl, combine flour and half each of the salt and pepper. In another shallow bowl, whisk egg with 3 tbsp (50 mL) water. In third shallow bowl, combine bread crumbs, 2 tbsp (25 mL) of the Parmesan cheese and oregano. Sprinkle remaining salt and pepper over veal. Dredge each cutlet in flour mixture, then dip into egg, letting excess drip off. Coat evenly in bread crumb mixture. Place on waxed paper–lined rimmed baking sheet. (MAKE-AHEAD: **Cover and refrigerate for up to 4 hours.**)

3 In large nonstick skillet, heat oil over medium-high heat; fry cutlets, in batches and adding more oil if necessary, turning once, until light golden, about 3 minutes.

4 Ladle 2 cups (500 mL) of the tomato sauce into 13- x 9-inch (3 L) glass baking dish. Top with cutlets, overlapping slightly; ladle remaining sauce over top. Sprinkle with remaining cheese. Cover with foil and bake in 350°F (180°C) oven until sauce is bubbling and veal is very tender and no longer pink inside, about 30 minutes.

Makes 4 servings. PER SERVING: about 609 cal, 37 g pro, 33 g total fat (6 g sat. fat), 43 g carb, 5 g fibre, 140 mg chol, 2,258 mg sodium. % RDI: 24% calcium, 41% iron, 29% vit A, 98% vit C, 38% folate.

Pork and Mushroom Stew

Serve this stew with creamy mashed potatoes. The beef stock gives a rich, meaty flavour to both the oyster mushrooms and the sauce. – Elizabeth

1 Trim roast and cut into 1-inch (2.5 cm) cubes. In large bowl, whisk together flour and half each of the Italian herb seasoning, salt and pepper; add pork, in batches, and toss to coat. Reserve any remaining flour mixture. In large Dutch oven, heat oil over medium-high heat; brown pork in batches. Transfer to plate.

2 Drain any fat from pan. Reduce heat to medium; cook chopped onions, garlic and remaining Italian herb seasoning, salt and pepper, stirring occasionally, until onions are softened, about 5 minutes.

3 Stir in pearl onions and reserved flour mixture; cook, stirring occasionally, for 5 minutes. Add stock and bay leaf; bring to boil, scraping up any brown bits from bottom of pan. Return pork and any accumulated juices to pan.

4 Cover and simmer over medium-low heat (or in 350°F/180°C oven) until pork is tender, about 1 hour. Stir in mushrooms and peas; simmer, uncovered, until mushrooms are tender and sauce is slightly thickened, about 15 minutes. Discard bay leaf. (MAKE-AHEAD: **Let cool for 30 minutes; refrigerate, uncovered, in shallow airtight container until cold. Cover and refrigerate for up to 24 hours or freeze for up to 2 weeks; thaw in refrigerator for 48 hours before reheating.**)

Makes 6 to 8 servings. PER EACH OF 8 SERVINGS: about 280 cal, 27 g pro, 13 g total fat (3 g sat. fat), 13 g carb, 2 g fibre, 71 mg chol, 427 mg sodium. % RDI: 5% calcium, 20% iron, 1% vit A, 10% vit C, 14% folate.

3 lb	boneless pork shoulder butt roast	1.5 kg
⅓ cup	all-purpose flour	75 mL
2 tsp	Italian herb seasoning	10 mL
½ tsp	each salt and pepper	2 mL
3 tbsp	vegetable oil	50 mL
2	onions, chopped	2
4	cloves garlic, minced	4
2 cups	pearl onions, peeled	500 mL
2 cups	beef or chicken stock	500 mL
1	bay leaf	1
4 cups	oyster or button mushrooms (about 12 oz/375 g), trimmed	1 L
½ cup	frozen peas	125 mL

fridge NOTE

- You can make this stew in a slow-cooker: Follow steps 1 to 3; transfer to slow-cooker. Cover and cook on Low until pork is tender, 6 to 7 hours. Stir in mushrooms and peas; cover and cook until mushrooms are tender, about 1 hour. Discard bay leaf.

Honey-Roasted Ribs

Sweet and sticky barbecued ribs are one of the highlights of summer. Serve with corn on the cob and lots of serviettes. – Elizabeth

3 lb	pork back or side ribs	1.5 kg
1	head garlic	1
¾ cup	ketchup	175 mL
½ cup	liquid honey	125 mL
3 tbsp	cider vinegar	50 mL
1 tbsp	Worcestershire sauce	15 mL
1 tsp	dry mustard	5 mL

fridge NOTE

- **To add a smoky flavour to your grill, place some hardwood chips, such as soaked and drained hickory, mesquite or cherrywood, in a foil pan with holes punched in the bottom; place the pan over the burner of your gas barbecue. The aroma will intensify whatever you're grilling. Replenish the chips as needed.**

1 Trim excess fat from ribs; cut into single ribs. Place in large pot and cover with cold water; bring just to boil. Skim off foam. Reduce heat, cover and simmer until ribs are fork-tender, about 40 minutes. Drain well and refrigerate until ribs are cool.

2 Meanwhile, trim ¼ inch (5 mm) off top of garlic head; wrap head loosely in foil. Roast in 400°F (200°C) oven or toaster oven until very soft when squeezed, about 45 minutes.

3 Meanwhile, in large bowl, stir together ketchup, honey, vinegar, Worcestershire sauce and mustard.

4 Squeeze roasted garlic pulp out of skin; mash into ketchup mixture until blended. Add ribs, turning to coat. Cover and refrigerate for 4 hours. (MAKE-AHEAD: **Refrigerate for up to 24 hours or flatten bag and freeze for up to 2 weeks. Let thaw in refrigerator overnight.**)

5 Reserving sauce, place ribs on greased grill over medium-high heat; close lid and grill, brushing often with reserved sauce and turning once, until browned, 10 to 15 minutes.

Makes 4 servings. PER SERVING: about 669 cal, 36 g pro, 36 g total fat (13 g sat. fat), 54 g carb, 1 g fibre, 84 mg chol, 716 mg sodium. % RDI: 5% calcium, 16% iron, 5% vit A, 18% vit C, 8% folate.

Lemon Ricotta Pancakes

Serve the pancakes English-style, with lemon wedges to squeeze over the top and icing sugar for a sweet touch. Garnish with fresh berries. – Daphna

1 In large bowl, whisk together flour, granulated sugar, baking powder and salt.

2 Press ricotta through fine sieve into separate large bowl. Whisk in egg, milk, butter and lemon rind; pour over dry ingredients and stir just until moistened (batter may be slightly lumpy).

3 Heat large skillet or griddle over medium heat; brush lightly with vegetable oil (optional for nonstick pans). Pour ¼ cup (50 mL) batter per pancake into pan, spreading with spatula to form 5-inch (12 cm) circle; cook until bottom is golden and bubbles break on top but do not fill in, 1½ to 2 minutes. Turn and cook until golden on bottom, 1 to 2 minutes. Repeat with remaining batter, brushing skillet with more oil as necessary.

4 Transfer to warmed plates. Using small sieve, sift icing sugar over pancakes. Garnish with lemon wedges and blueberries.

Makes 4 servings. PER SERVING: about 443 cal, 13 g pro, 19 g total fat (11 g sat. fat), 55 g carb, 2 g fibre, 105 mg chol, 688 mg sodium. % RDI: 26% calcium, 19% iron, 22% vit A, 12% vit C, 33% folate.

1½ cups	all-purpose flour	375 mL
1 tbsp	granulated sugar	15 ml
1 tbsp	baking powder	15 mL
½ tsp	salt	2 mL
½ cup	extra-smooth ricotta cheese	125 mL
1	egg	1
1½ cups	milk	375 mL
¼ cup	butter, melted, or vegetable oil	50 mL
2 tsp	finely grated lemon rind	10 mL
¼ cup	icing sugar	50 mL
4	lemon wedges	4
½ cup	fresh blueberries or sliced strawberries	125 mL

fridge NOTE

- **Have fun with pancake batter. Use a squirt bottle to form whimsical shapes, such as shamrocks, pumpkins or hearts, or the pancake lovers' initials.**

Chocolate Cranberry Twist

*This fabulous-looking, cranberry-studded loaf makes an innovative
centrepiece for a festive brunch table.* – Daphna

¼ cup	granulated sugar	50 mL
½ cup	warm water	125 mL
1	pkg active dry yeast (or 2¼ tsp/11 mL)	1
½ cup	milk	125 mL
¼ cup	butter	50 mL
1 tsp	salt	5 mL
3	eggs	3
4 cups	all-purpose flour (approx)	1 L
FILLING:		
¼ cup	packed brown sugar	50 mL
⅓ cup	corn syrup	75 mL
¾ cup	dried cranberries or raisins	175 mL
⅔ cup	chocolate chips	150 mL
⅓ cup	chopped pecans	75 mL
1 tsp	cinnamon	5 mL
ICING:		
¼ cup	icing sugar, sifted	50 mL
2 tsp	milk	10 mL
2 tsp	butter, melted	10 mL

1 Grease 10-inch (3 L) springform pan; set aside.

2 In large bowl, dissolve 1 tsp (5 mL) of the sugar in warm water. Sprinkle in yeast; let stand until frothy, about 10 minutes. Meanwhile, in small saucepan over medium heat, heat together milk, remaining sugar, butter and salt until butter is melted; let cool to lukewarm. Beat 2 of the eggs; whisk into yeast mixture. Whisk in milk mixture. Stir in 3½ cups (875 mL) of the flour to make soft, slightly sticky dough.

3 Turn out onto lightly floured surface; knead until smooth and elastic, about 10 minutes, adding enough of the remaining flour as necessary to prevent sticking. Place in greased bowl, turning to grease all over. Cover with plastic wrap; let rise in warm draft-free place until doubled in bulk, about 1 hour.

4 FILLING: In bowl, mix sugar with corn syrup; stir in cranberries, chocolate chips and pecans. Punch down dough; turn out onto lightly floured surface. Roll out into 18- x 11-inch (45 x 28 cm) rectangle. Spread filling over dough, pressing into surface; sprinkle with cinnamon. Starting at 1 long edge, roll up tightly; pinch seam to seal.

5 Place, seam side down, on work surface; cut in half lengthwise. Keeping cut sides up, twist halves together; place in prepared pan, shaping into ring. Pinch ends together to seal. Cover with plastic wrap; let rise until doubled in bulk, about 1 hour.

6 Beat remaining egg; brush over loaf. Bake in centre of 350°F (180°C) oven until golden, about 35 minutes. Run knife around edge of pan; transfer loaf to rack and let cool.

> **"** While a little heightened effort is required
> to make this braid, I guarantee you will be
> rewarded by the glorious results. – *Daphna* **"**

7 ICING: Stir together icing sugar, milk and butter; drizzle over loaf. (MAKE-AHEAD: **Wrap in plastic wrap and store at room temperature for up to 24 hours.**)

Makes 1 loaf, 16 slices. PER SLICE: about 282 calories, 5 g pro, 9 g total fat (4 g sat. fat), 46 g carb, 2 g fibre, 50 mg chol, 202 mg sodium. % RDI: 3% calcium, 16% iron, 5% vit A, 2% vit C, 12% folate.

VARIATION

Bread Machine Chocolate Cranberry Twist (for dough only): Use 4 cups (1 L) flour. Into pan of 1½- to 2-lb (750 g to 1 kg) machine, add (in order) warm water, milk, eggs, melted butter, sugar, salt, flour and yeast. Choose dough setting. Shape and bake as directed.

fridge NOTES

- For a variation, use ½ cup (125 mL) raspberry jam or marmalade instead of the filling.

- Careful measuring of ingredients is important for best results when baking. Lightly spoon dry ingredients into a measuring cup, filling until heaping. Level off by running the straight edge of a knife across the top. Do not pack or tap the measure when filling. (Brown sugar, however, should be packed lightly until it holds the shape of the measure when turned out.)

Come for Drinks

*N*ow, that's music to my ears. Not that *drinking is the point. It's the warmth – the casual but careful style of entertaining that means a sit-down visit, a pleasant glass and good food to sustain the conversation. For these occasions, we three all agree on one thing: lots of flavour. And, while you're at it, how about finding it in countries where taste is king? Case in point: the robust, rusty red smoked spice from Spain that lends its savour to the pink plumpness of our paprika shrimp. We think it helps if the appetizers we serve are easy to pass around and pick up, by hand or with a toothpick. Please join us as we pause for a delicious little nibble and raise a glass. – Elizabeth*

- Smoked Salmon and Radish Dip
- Warm Mushroom Salad on Garlic Toasts
- Chickpeas with Chorizo Sausage
- Warm Garlic Bean Crostini
- Potato Pancakes with Smoked Salmon and Dill Crème Fraîche
- Mushroom Tenderloin Cubes
- Wilted Greens with Raisins, Pine Nuts and Garlic Croûtes
- Garlic Paprika Shrimp
- Gravlax
- Buckwheat Blini

Smoked Salmon and Radish Dip

This tasty, crunchy dip is from associate food editor Andrew Chase, whose mother serves it often. It's perfect for a wedding or baby shower. – Elizabeth

¾ cup	sour cream	175 mL
½ cup	low-fat pressed cottage cheese	125 mL
½ cup	cream cheese, softened	125 mL
Pinch	each salt and pepper	Pinch
4 oz	smoked salmon, finely chopped	125 g
½ cup	finely chopped red radishes (about half bunch)	125 mL
⅓ cup	finely chopped red onion	75 mL
2 tbsp	chopped fresh chives (optional)	25 mL

1 In large bowl, beat together sour cream, cottage cheese, cream cheese, salt and pepper. Stir in salmon, radishes, onion, and chives (if using). Transfer to serving bowl. (MAKE-AHEAD: **Refrigerate in airtight container for up to 2 days; let stand at room temperature for 30 minutes before serving.**)

Makes 2 cups (500 mL). PER 1 TBSP (15 mL): about 30 cal, 2 g pro, 2 g total fat (1 g sat. fat), 1 g carb, trace fibre, 7 mg chol, 42 mg sodium. % RDI: 1% calcium, 1% iron, 2% vit A, 2% vit C, 1% folate.

fridge NOTES

- **Smoked salmon varies in the degree of saltiness; you can omit the salt and taste for seasoning just before serving, if desired.**

- **If you want to lighten the dip a little, use light sour cream and light cream cheese.**

" Deliver eye appeal as well as delicious flavour: scoop the dip into a vaselike glass dish surrounded by vegetables arranged in a variety of glassware. – *Elizabeth* "

Warm Mushroom Salad on Garlic Toasts

Even restaurant-style dishes can be affordable but still have flair. We created
this appetizer for our $10-a-person dinner party. – Daphna

1 Slice baguette diagonally into 12 slices, each ½ inch (1 cm) thick and 4 inches (10 cm) long. Brush both sides with all but 1 tsp (5 mL) of the oil. Toast on rimmed baking sheet in 375°F (190°C) oven, turning once, until firm and crusty, about 8 minutes. Immediately rub both sides with cut side of garlic halves; set aside. (MAKE-AHEAD: **Store in airtight container for up to 2 days.**)

2 DRESSING: Meanwhile, in small bowl, whisk together vinegar, mustard, soy sauce, sugar and salt; whisk in oil. (MAKE-AHEAD: **Set aside for up to 4 hours; whisk before continuing.**)

3 In large nonstick skillet, heat remaining oil over medium-high heat; cook mushrooms, thyme and pepper, in batches if necessary, until browned and moisture is evaporated, about 10 minutes. Remove from heat. (MAKE-AHEAD: **Set aside for up to 2 hours; reheat before continuing.**) Pour dressing over top and toss to coat.

4 Place spinach leaf on each plate. Divide ½ cup (125 mL) of the mushroom mixture among 3 toasts and stack on 1 of the plates in spiral fashion, overlapping tips slightly. Repeat with remaining toasts and mushroom mixture. Sprinkle toasts and plate rims with parsley.

Makes 4 servings. PER SERVING: about 281 cal, 6 g pro, 15 g total fat (2 g sat. fat), 31 g carb, 4 g fibre, 0 mg chol, 519 mg sodium. % RDI: 5% calcium, 24% iron, 4% vit A, 13% vit C, 32% folate.

1	piece (10 inches/25 cm) baguette (French stick)	1
2 tbsp	extra-virgin olive oil	25 mL
1	large clove garlic, halved	1
8 cups	sliced mushrooms	2 L
½ tsp	dried thyme	2 mL
¼ tsp	pepper	1 mL
4	spinach or lettuce leaves	4
2 tbsp	chopped fresh parsley	25 mL
DRESSING:		
2 tbsp	balsamic vinegar	25 mL
1 tsp	Dijon mustard	5 mL
1 tsp	soy sauce	5 mL
½ tsp	granulated sugar	2 mL
¼ tsp	salt	1 mL
2 tbsp	extra-virgin olive oil	25 mL

Chickpeas with Chorizo Sausage

Tapas are both fun to serve and fun to eat. The bite-size portions make them perfect party mingle food. – Emily

2 tbsp	extra-virgin olive oil	25 mL
1	onion, finely chopped	1
4	cloves garlic, minced	4
¼ tsp	dried thyme	1 mL
Pinch	each ground cloves and cinnamon	Pinch
1	bay leaf	1
4	cured air-dried chorizo sausages (about 6 oz/175 g total)	4
5 cups	chicken or vegetable stock	1.25 L
2	cans (each 19 oz/540 mL) chickpeas, drained and rinsed	2
¼ tsp	pepper	1 mL

1 In large skillet or shallow Dutch oven, heat oil over medium heat; cook onion, garlic, thyme, cloves, cinnamon and bay leaf, stirring occasionally, until onion is softened, about 5 minutes.

2 Cut chorizo into ½-inch (1 cm) thick slices and add to pan; fry, stirring often, until mixture is golden, about 8 minutes.

3 Stir in stock and chickpeas; bring to boil. Reduce heat and simmer, stirring often, until liquid thickens and coats chickpeas, about 15 minutes. Discard bay leaf. Stir in pepper.

Makes 6 servings. PER SERVING: about 382 cal, 18 g pro, 18 g total fat (5 g sat. fat), 36 g carb, 7 g fibre, 25 mg chol, 1,368 mg sodium. % RDI: 5% calcium, 19% iron, 10% vit C, 41% folate.

fridge NOTE

- **Because sausage and canned chickpeas are already salted, choose unsalted homemade chicken stock or sodium-reduced stock.**

Warm Garlic Bean Crostini

Partially crushing the beans gives the mixture a chunkier texture than the usual bean or chickpea dips, such as hummus. – Emily

1 Cut baguette diagonally into 24 slices; broil on rimmed baking sheet until golden, about 30 seconds per side. Set aside.

2 In nonstick skillet, heat oil over medium heat; cook garlic, sage and pepper, stirring, until garlic is golden, about 1 minute.

3 In bowl, mash one-third of the kidney beans. Add mashed and whole beans, and lemon rind and juice to pan; cook until hot, about 3 minutes. Spoon heaping tablespoonful (15 mL) onto each baguette slice. Garnish with sage (if using).

Makes 24 pieces. PER PIECE: about 66 cal, 2 g pro, 2 g total fat (trace sat. fat), 10 g carb, 2 g fibre, 0 mg chol, 124 mg sodium. % RDI: 1% calcium, 4% iron, 2% vit C, 7% folate.

1	baguette (French stick)	1
2 tbsp	extra-virgin olive oil	25 mL
3	cloves garlic, minced	3
½ tsp	crumbled dried sage	2 mL
¼ tsp	pepper	1 mL
1	can (19 oz/540 mL) white kidney beans, drained and rinsed	1
1 tsp	grated lemon rind	5 mL
1 tbsp	lemon juice	15 mL
	Fresh sage or parsley leaves (optional)	

Potato Pancakes with Smoked Salmon and Dill Crème Fraîche

I adore making potato pancakes. How can anybody eat just three? Use a stainless steel skillet; a nonstick one won't make them as crispy. – Daphna

5	baking potatoes (2½ lb/1.25 kg total)	5
2	small onions, quartered	2
3	eggs	3
3 tbsp	all-purpose flour	50 mL
¾ tsp	salt	4 mL
¼ tsp	pepper	1 mL
	Vegetable oil for frying	
8 oz	smoked salmon slices	250 g
DILL CRÈME FRAÎCHE:		
1 cup	whipping cream	250 mL
3 tbsp	plain yogurt	50 mL
2 tbsp	lemon juice	25 mL
2 tbsp	chopped fresh dill	25 mL

1 DILL CRÈME FRAÎCHE: In bowl, whisk together cream, yogurt and lemon juice. Cover and refrigerate until thickened and set, about 12 hours. Stir in dill. (MAKE-AHEAD: **Refrigerate for up to 24 hours; let stand at room temperature for 30 minutes.**)

2 Peel potatoes. By hand, or in food processor using shredder blade, alternately shred onions and potatoes. Transfer to colander. Using hands, squeeze out as much moisture as possible. Discard liquid. Transfer to large bowl. Mix in eggs, flour, salt and pepper; let stand for 5 minutes. Pour off any liquid.

3 In large skillet, heat ¼ inch (5 mm) oil over high heat until hot but not smoking. Add scant ¼ cup (50 mL) of the potato mixture per pancake, leaving about 1 inch (2.5 cm) between each; flatten slightly with back of spoon. Fry, turning once, until crisp around edges and golden brown, about 6 minutes. Transfer to paper towel–lined racks to drain. Remove any overcooked bits from pan, adding oil as necessary.

4 Cut salmon into pieces if large; arrange over hot pancakes and top with Dill Crème Fraîche.

Makes 6 to 8 servings. PER EACH OF 8 SERVINGS: about 431 cal, 11 g pro, 32 g total fat (9 g sat. fat), 26 g carb, 2 g fibre, 115 mg chol, 481 mg sodium. % RDI: 5% calcium, 7% iron, 15% vit A, 17% vit C, 12% folate.

Mushroom Tenderloin Cubes

Porcini mushrooms are a high-end ingredient, but a little goes a long way to intensify the flavour of these sophisticated appetizers. – Daphna

1 Cut beef into 1-inch (2.5 cm) cubes; place in bowl. Mix in half of the brandy; let stand for 10 minutes. Trim stems off white mushrooms; set caps aside.

2 In spice grinder or using mortar and pestle, grind porcini mushrooms to fine powder. In shallow dish, stir together ground porcini mushrooms, salt and pepper. Drain beef; coat, a few pieces at a time, in porcini mushroom mixture.

3 In large skillet over medium-high heat, melt 1 tbsp (15 mL) of the butter; in 2 batches, sear beef cubes on all sides, about 1 minute per batch. Transfer to plate. Wipe out pan.

4 In same pan over medium heat, melt remaining butter; fry mushroom caps and thyme, stirring, for 3 minutes. Add soy sauce, sugar and remaining brandy; cook, stirring, until mushrooms are glazed and no liquid remains, about 30 seconds. Let cool.

5 For each piece, thread 1 mushroom cap and 1 beef cube onto toothpick. Place on rimmed baking sheet. (MAKE-AHEAD: **Wrap in plastic wrap and refrigerate for up to 8 hours.**)

6 Bake in 450°F (230°C) oven until heated through, about 5 minutes. Transfer to warmed serving platter; garnish with chives.

Makes 38 pieces. PER PIECE: about 32 cal, 3 g pro, 2 g total fat (1 g sat. fat), 1 g carb, trace fibre, 9 mg chol, 63 mg sodium. % RDI: 4% iron, 1% vit A, 1% folate.

1¼ lb	beef tenderloin or strip loin grilling steak	625 g
2 tbsp	brandy	25 mL
2 cups	small white mushrooms (about 8 oz/250 g)	500 mL
1	pkg (14 g) dried porcini mushrooms	1
½ tsp	each salt and pepper	2 mL
2 tbsp	butter	25 mL
1 tsp	chopped fresh thyme (or ¼ tsp/1 mL dried)	5 mL
2 tsp	soy sauce	10 mL
¼ tsp	granulated sugar	1 mL
1 tbsp	chopped fresh chives	15 mL

Wilted Greens with Raisins, Pine Nuts and Garlic Croûtes

What's interesting about this attractive dish is that you find it served every-where from Genoa to Sicily and Catalonia to Provence. – Daphna

½ cup	golden raisins	125 mL
5	anchovy fillets	5
4 cups	packed baby spinach	1 L
1	thin baguette (French stick) or Calabrese loaf (300 to 340 g)	1
5	large cloves garlic, minced	5
⅓ cup	extra-virgin olive oil	75 mL
½ tsp	each salt and pepper	2 mL
½ cup	pine nuts or slivered almonds	125 mL

fridge NOTES

- Serve with lemon wedges or drizzle lemon juice over top.

- For a casual get-together, accompany this dish with a selection of olives and a bowl of red and yellow teardrop tomatoes.

1 In small bowl, cover raisins with boiling water; let stand for 15 minutes. Drain and set aside. Meanwhile, soak anchovies in cold water for 10 minutes; drain and set aside.

2 Wash spinach, trimming if necessary; shake off excess water. Chop coarsely. Transfer, in batches if necessary, to large skillet or saucepan; cover and cook over medium-high heat until wilted, about 5 minutes. Drain in sieve and let cool; press out excess liquid. Set aside.

3 Cut baguette into ¼-inch (5 mm) thick slices. Arrange in single layer on rimmed baking sheets. In small saucepan, warm just over half of the garlic in ¼ cup (50 mL) of the oil over low heat until fragrant, about 2 minutes; stir in half each of the salt and pepper. Brush over bread, leaving garlic bits in pan. Toast bread in 350°F (180°C) oven, turning once, until crisp and golden, 10 to 15 minutes; set aside.

4 Meanwhile, spread pine nuts on small rimmed baking sheet; toast in 350°F (180°C) oven until golden, about 8 minutes. Set aside.

5 In large skillet, heat remaining oil over medium heat; cook remaining garlic, salt and pepper for 2 minutes. Add anchovies; mash until smooth. Add spinach and raisins; toss together and heat through until spinach is coated. Arrange in centre of warmed serving dish; sprinkle with toasted pine nuts and surround with croûtes.

Makes 6 servings. PER SERVING: about 377 cal, 10 g pro, 21 g total fat (3 g sat. fat), 41 g carb, 5 g fibre, 3 mg chol, 646 mg sodium. % RDI: 10% calcium, 31% iron, 30% vit A, 8% vit C, 49% folate.

Garlic Paprika Shrimp

Smoked paprika adds a magnificent dimension to shrimp. Buy it at specialty food shops or substitute sweet paprika. – Daphna

1 In skillet, heat oil over medium heat; cook garlic, stirring occasionally, until softened but not browned, about 2 minutes. Add shrimp and paprika; cook, stirring, until shrimp are well coated and beginning to turn pink, about 2 minutes.

2 Stir in wine, tomato paste and salt; increase heat to high and boil until liquid coats shrimp, about 2 minutes. Stir in parsley.

Makes 14 to 16 pieces. PER EACH OF 16 PIECES: about 44 cal, 5 g pro, 2 g total fat (trace sat. fat), 1 g carb, trace fibre, 32 mg chol, 69 mg sodium. % RDI: 1% calcium, 5% iron, 4% vit A, 3% vit C, 1% folate.

2 tbsp	extra-virgin olive oil	25 mL
6	cloves garlic, minced	6
1 lb	large raw shrimp, peeled and deveined	500 g
1 tbsp	smoked paprika	15 mL
⅓ cup	white wine	75 mL
2 tsp	tomato paste	10 mL
¼ tsp	salt	1 mL
2 tbsp	chopped fresh parsley or coriander	25 mL

Gravlax

Gravlax, or cured salmon, is a Scandinavian specialty available in fancy food stores and restaurants. Find out how easy it is to cure your own. – Elizabeth

1 tbsp	peppercorns	15 mL
⅓ cup	granulated sugar	75 mL
¼ cup	pickling or kosher salt	50 mL
2 lb	centre-cut salmon fillet (skin on)	1 kg
⅓ cup	chopped fresh dill	75 mL
2 tbsp	brandy or aquavit	25 mL
	Small fresh dill sprigs	
	Buckwheat Blini (recipe, page 81)	
MUSTARD SAUCE:		
3 tbsp	Dijon mustard	50 mL
2 tbsp	liquid honey	25 mL
1 tbsp	chopped fresh dill	15 mL

1 Five days before serving, coarsely crush peppercorns with bottom of heavy saucepan. Mix together peppercorns, sugar and salt; spread over both sides of salmon. Spread one-third of the chopped dill in centre of large piece of plastic wrap; top with fish, skin side down.

2 Drizzle with brandy; spread remaining chopped dill over top. Wrap tightly in plastic wrap; place on small rimmed baking sheet. Place small cutting board on fish; weigh down with 2 full 28-oz (796 mL) cans. Refrigerate for 5 days, turning fish daily.

3 MUSTARD SAUCE: In small bowl, mix together mustard, honey and chopped dill. (MAKE-AHEAD: **Cover and refrigerate for up to 3 days.**)

4 Unwrap fish; using paper towel, brush off most of the dill. (MAKE-AHEAD: **Wrap in plastic wrap and refrigerate for up to 5 days.**) Slice thinly at 45-degree angle; cut each slice in half and place on Buckwheat Blini. Drizzle with Mustard Sauce; garnish with dill sprig.

Makes about 50 pieces. PER PIECE: about 71 cal, 5 g pro, 3 g total fat (1 g sat. fat), 6 g carb, trace fibre, 18 mg chol, 594 mg sodium. % RDI: 1% calcium, 2% iron, 2% vit A, 2% vit C, 5% folate.

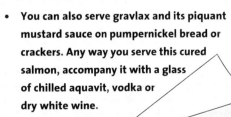

fridge NOTE

- You can also serve gravlax and its piquant mustard sauce on pumpernickel bread or crackers. Any way you serve this cured salmon, accompany it with a glass of chilled aquavit, vodka or dry white wine.

Buckwheat Blini

Serve with gravlax, or with sour cream and your choice of toppings: white-fish caviar, or smoked salmon, mackerel or oysters. – Elizabeth

1 In bowl, dissolve ½ tsp (2 mL) of the sugar in warm water. Sprinkle in yeast; let stand until frothy, about 10 minutes. In separate bowl, beat egg, milk and remaining sugar. Add all-purpose and buckwheat flours and salt; beat for 1 minute. Beat in yeast mixture and half of the butter. Cover with plastic wrap; let rise in warm place until doubled in bulk, about 1 hour.

2 Heat nonstick skillet over medium heat; brush lightly with some of the remaining butter. Without stirring, spoon batter into pan by scant 2 tablespoonfuls (25 mL) to make 2¼-inch (5.5 cm) blini. Cook until bubbles form on top that do not fill in, about 1 minute. Turn and cook until bottoms are golden, about 30 seconds.

Makes 50 blini. PER PIECE: about 29 cal, 1 g pro, 1 g total fat (1 g sat. fat), 4 g carb, trace fibre, 7 mg chol, 38 mg sodium. % RDI: 1% calcium, 1% iron, 1% vit A, 3% folate.

1½ tsp	granulated sugar	7 mL
¼ cup	warm water	50 mL
1½ tsp	active dry yeast	7 mL
1	egg	1
1½ cups	lukewarm milk	375 mL
1 cup	all-purpose flour	250 mL
¾ cup	buckwheat flour	175 mL
½ tsp	salt	2 mL
¼ cup	butter, melted	50 mL

" People love helping themselves to blini and toppings to create their own masterpieces. – *Elizabeth* **"**

A Seasonal Sampler

How lucky we are to live in Canada, with its distinct seasons and such glorious produce to reflect each one. We three share an excitement about picking fresh strawberries in spring, slicing into the first plump tomato of the summer and reacquainting our appetites with hearty soups as autumn arrives. Truly, our cup (or vegetable crisper!) runneth over when we consider the number of markets all across Canada, their stalls overflowing with fruits and vegetables just begging to be the muse for a dinner party. It's that bounty that inspires most of my menu planning. And the same is true on Canadian Living Cooks *and at the magazine, where seasonality of food is one of the cornerstones of recipe development. Here are a few of our favourites.* – Daphna

- Fresh Fava Bean Soup
- Five Lilies Soup
- Fried Green Tomato Sandwiches
- Onion, Apple and Gruyère Tart
- Stuffed Squash for Two
- Cold Sesame Swiss Chard Leaves
- Spaghetti Squash with Mushroom and Pearl Onion Ragout
- Scalloped Brussels Sprouts
- Plum Frangipane Tart
- Tarte Tatin

Fresh Fava Bean Soup

You'll be happy to know that if fresh fava beans are not available for this fabulous soup, you can use frozen baby lima beans instead. – Elizabeth

5 lb	fresh fava beans	2.2 kg
3 tbsp	extra-virgin olive oil	50 mL
1	onion, finely chopped	1
4	cloves garlic, minced	4
¼ tsp	hot pepper flakes	1 mL
4 cups	vegetable stock	1 L
2 cups	diced plum tomatoes	500 mL
2 tbsp	chopped fresh Italian parsley	25 mL
¼ tsp	salt	1 mL
¼ cup	shaved Pecorino Romano or Grana Padano cheese	50 mL

1 Shell beans, discarding pods. In large pot of boiling salted water, cook beans for 2 minutes. Drain and chill under cold water; drain again. Pinch skin of each bean to break at 1 end; squeeze out bean, discarding skin. Set aside.

2 In large saucepan, heat oil over medium heat; cook onion, garlic and hot pepper flakes, stirring occasionally, until softened, about 5 minutes. Add stock, tomatoes and fava beans; bring to boil. Reduce heat to medium-low, cover and simmer for 10 minutes. Stir in parsley and salt. Ladle into bowls. Sprinkle with cheese.

Makes 4 servings. PER SERVING: about 265 cal, 12 g pro, 14 g total fat (3 g sat. fat), 26 g carb, 7 g fibre, 6 mg chol, 1,258 mg sodium. % RDI: 11% calcium, 24% iron, 16% vit A, 90% vit C, 49% folate.

"" I wait all year for fresh fava beans. There's nothing like locally grown vegetables and fruit in season. – *Elizabeth* ""

Five Lilies Soup

The lily family offers everything from bouquets of blooms to aromatic onions, garlic, leeks, shallots and chives. – Emily

1 In saucepan, heat oil over medium-high heat; sauté onions, celery, shallots, garlic, thyme, marjoram, salt and pepper, stirring occasionally, until onions are completely softened and just beginning to turn golden, about 10 minutes.

2 Transfer half of the mixture to blender or food processor; purée until smooth. Return to pan.

3 Add stock, leeks, wine and bay leaf; bring to boil. Reduce heat and simmer until leeks are tender-crisp, about 10 minutes. Discard bay leaf. (MAKE-AHEAD: **Let cool for 30 minutes; refrigerate, uncovered, until cold. Cover and refrigerate in airtight container for up to 3 days. Rewarm over low heat.**) Stir in vinegar. Ladle into warmed soup bowls.

4 TOPPING: Mix together chives, garlic and lemon rind. Place mound in centre of each bowl.

Makes 8 servings. PER SERVING: about 106 cal, 5 g pro, 4 g total fat (1 g sat. fat), 11 g carb, 2 g fibre, 0 mg chol, 647 mg sodium. % RDI: 4% calcium, 7% iron, 1% vit A, 12% vit C, 10% folate.

2 tbsp	extra-virgin olive oil	25 mL
4 cups	chopped onions	1 L
1 cup	finely chopped celery	250 mL
⅓ cup	sliced shallots	75 mL
2	cloves garlic, minced	2
1 tbsp	chopped fresh thyme	15 mL
2 tsp	chopped fresh marjoram	10 mL
½ tsp	each salt and pepper	2 mL
5 cups	chicken or vegetable stock	1.25 L
1 cup	sliced leeks (white and light green parts)	250 mL
¾ cup	dry white wine	175 mL
1	bay leaf	1
1 tbsp	sherry vinegar	15 mL
TOPPING:		
2 tbsp	chopped fresh chives	25 mL
1	clove garlic, minced	1
1 tbsp	finely grated lemon rind	15 mL

Fried Green Tomato Sandwiches

This is no ordinary sandwich – the bread is actually the tomatoes. Use beef-steak tomatoes with some rosiness; all green will be too tart. – Daphna

4 oz	goat cheese, softened	125 g
2 tbsp	finely chopped green onions or fresh chives	25 mL
1 tbsp	chopped fresh parsley	15 mL
1 tbsp	chopped fresh basil	15 mL
1 tbsp	chopped fresh thyme	15 mL
1 tsp	finely grated lemon rind	5 mL
1 tsp	salt	5 mL
½ tsp	pepper	2 mL
½ cup	all-purpose flour	125 mL
2	eggs	2
¾ cup	coarse cornmeal	175 mL
4	green tomatoes (about 1¾ lb/875 g total)	4
¼ cup	extra-virgin olive oil (approx)	50 mL

1 In bowl and using wooden spoon, beat together goat cheese, onions, parsley, basil, thyme, lemon rind and ¼ tsp (1 mL) each of the salt and pepper. Place flour in shallow dish; mix in ½ tsp (2 mL) of the salt and remaining pepper. Beat eggs in separate shallow dish; place cornmeal in third dish. Set aside.

2 Cut each tomato into four ¼-inch (5 mm) thick slices. Pat dry with paper towels. Sprinkle with remaining salt.

3 Spread heaping tablespoonful (15 mL) of the goat cheese mixture evenly over half of the tomato slices; sandwich with remaining slices.

4 Keeping sandwiches intact, carefully dredge in flour mixture to coat, tapping off excess. Dip in egg, then in cornmeal to coat.

5 In large skillet, heat 2 tbsp (25 mL) of the oil over medium heat; fry 4 of the sandwiches, turning once and adding more oil if necessary, until golden and tomatoes are fork-tender, 10 to 12 minutes. Repeat with remaining oil and sandwiches, keeping cooked sandwiches warm in 350°F (180°C) oven.

Makes 8 sandwiches, or 4 side-dish servings. PER EACH OF 8 SANDWICHES: about 196 cal, 7 g pro, 11 g total fat (3 g sat. fat), 18 g carb, 2 g fibre, 39 mg chol, 256 mg sodium. % RDI: 4% calcium, 10% iron, 12% vit A, 40% vit C, 11% folate.

fridge **NOTE**

- In summer, opt for fresh herbs. The rest of the year, you can substitute dried by calculating one-third of the amount of fresh. If you have fresh parsley, add a little chopped to enhance the dried herbs.

Onion, Apple and Gruyère Tart

Use cooking apples, such as Northern Spy, Crispin or Golden Delicious.
They keep their shape and are full of flavour. – Elizabeth

1 PASTRY: In large bowl, whisk together flour, salt and dry mustard. Using pastry blender or 2 knives, cut in butter until in coarse crumbs. In liquid measure and using fork, beat egg yolk with vinegar until frothy; pour in enough ice water to make ⅓ cup (75 mL). Drizzle over flour mixture, stirring briskly with fork until dough holds together. Press into ball; flatten into disc. Wrap in plastic wrap and refrigerate for 30 minutes. (MAKE-AHEAD: **Refrigerate for up to 3 days; let stand at room temperature for 15 minutes before rolling out.**)

2 On lightly floured surface, roll out pastry into 12-inch (30 cm) circle; fit over bottom and all the way up side of 8-inch (2 L) springform pan. Refrigerate until firm, about 30 minutes. Line pastry with foil; fill evenly with pie weights or dried beans. Bake in bottom third of 400°F (200°C) oven for 20 minutes. Remove weights and foil; bake until light golden, about 10 minutes. Let cool on rack.

3 Meanwhile, in skillet, melt butter over medium heat; cook onion, stirring often, until softened, about 5 minutes. Increase heat to medium-high; add apples and cook for 2 minutes. Set aside.

4 In bowl, whisk together eggs, cream, parsley, chives, rosemary, Dijon mustard, salt and pepper. Sprinkle half of the cheese evenly over prepared crust. Spread apple mixture over top. Slowly pour egg mixture over top; sprinkle with remaining cheese.

5 Bake in bottom third of 375°F (190°C) oven until golden and knife inserted in centre comes out clean, about 30 minutes.

Makes 4 main-course, or 6 appetizer, servings. PER EACH OF 4 MAIN-COURSE SERVINGS: about 769 cal, 23 g pro, 53 g total fat (30 g sat. fat), 52 g carb, 4 g fibre, 386 mg chol, 895 mg sodium. % RDI: 37% calcium, 24% iron, 53% vit A, 12% vit C, 46% folate.

1 tbsp	butter	15 mL
1	onion, chopped	1
2	apples (unpeeled), grated	2
4	eggs	4
1 cup	18% cream	250 mL
2 tbsp	chopped fresh parsley	25 mL
1 tbsp	chopped fresh chives	15 mL
2 tsp	chopped fresh rosemary	10 mL
1 tsp	Dijon mustard	5 mL
¼ tsp	each salt and pepper	1 mL
1 cup	shredded Gruyère cheese	250 mL
PASTRY:		
1½ cups	all-purpose flour	375 mL
½ tsp	salt	2 mL
½ tsp	dry mustard	2 mL
½ cup	cold butter, cubed	125 mL
1	egg yolk	1
1 tsp	vinegar	5 mL
	Ice water	

Stuffed Squash for Two

Acorn squash is gorgeous when heaped with a savoury stuffing. Just double or triple the amounts for more servings. – Elizabeth

2	acorn squash	2
1 tbsp	butter	15 mL
1	onion, minced	1
½ cup	finely chopped celery	125 mL
½ cup	chopped mushrooms	125 mL
2	cloves garlic, minced	2
2 tbsp	tomato paste	25 mL
1 cup	fresh bread crumbs	250 mL
1 cup	shredded Cheddar or Jarlsberg cheese	250 mL
¼ cup	sunflower seeds	50 mL
½ tsp	salt	2 mL
¼ tsp	pepper	1 mL
2 tbsp	grated Parmesan cheese	25 mL

1 Lay each squash on side. Cut out about one-third of each lengthwise into wedge; peel wedge, dice and reserve. Scoop out seeds from remaining squash; cut thin slice off bottom of each to level. Place in microwaveable dish; microwave at High until tender, 12 to 15 minutes.

2 Meanwhile, in nonstick skillet, melt butter over medium heat; cook reserved diced squash, onion and celery, stirring occasionally, until softened, about 5 minutes. Add mushrooms and garlic; cook, stirring often, for 2 minutes. Stir in tomato paste; cook for 1 minute.

3 In bowl, combine onion mixture, bread crumbs, Cheddar cheese, sunflower seeds, salt and pepper. Divide between squash, mounding if necessary; sprinkle with Parmesan cheese. Bake in 450°F (230°C) oven until golden and heated through, 7 to 10 minutes.

Makes 2 servings. PER SERVING: about 632 cal, 27 g pro, 37 g total fat (18 g sat. fat), 56 g carb, 12 g fibre, 80 mg chol, 1,260 mg sodium. % RDI: 61% calcium, 38% iron, 37% vit A, 60% vit C, 57% folate.

Prop assistant Anna Michener clears the
set between segments

Cold Sesame Swiss Chard Leaves

*While this Asian dressing is perfect with robust Swiss chard, you can
substitute spinach instead, if you like.* – Elizabeth

1 Remove stems from Swiss chard and reserve for another use. In large pot of boiling salted water, cook leaves for 1 minute. Drain in colander and rinse under cold water; press to extract as much liquid as possible. Transfer to bowl.

2 In small bowl, whisk together soy sauce, sesame seeds, sesame oil and sugar; pour over leaves and toss to coat.

Makes 4 servings. PER SERVING: about 88 cal, 5 g pro, 4 g total fat (1 g sat. fat), 12 g carb, 5 g fibre, 0 mg chol, 1,328 mg sodium. % RDI: 13% calcium, 41% iron, 75% vit A, 72% vit C, 11% folate.

2	bunches Swiss chard (about 2½ lb/1.25 kg total)	2
4 tsp	soy sauce	20 mL
1 tbsp	sesame seeds, toasted	15 mL
2 tsp	sesame oil	10 mL
1 tsp	granulated sugar	5 mL

Spaghetti Squash with Mushroom and Pearl Onion Ragout

A stylish vegetarian dish is a welcome component of any meal, and this one especially will find favour with both vegetarians and non. – Emily

1	spaghetti squash (about 3 lb/1.5 kg)	1
1 lb	pearl onions	500 g
⅓ cup	extra-virgin olive oil	75 mL
2 tsp	granulated sugar	10 mL
2	stalks celery, diced	2
1	carrot, diced	1
1	sweet red pepper, diced	1
1 tsp	each salt and pepper	5 mL
¼ tsp	each dried thyme and sage	1 mL
1 lb	mixed exotic mushrooms (such as oyster, shiitake and cremini), trimmed and thinly sliced	500 g
2	cloves garlic, minced	2
1 cup	vegetable stock	250 mL
3 tbsp	soy sauce	50 mL
2 tbsp	balsamic vinegar	25 mL
2 tbsp	tomato paste	25 mL
1 tbsp	butter, softened	15 mL
1 tbsp	all-purpose flour	15 mL
2 tbsp	chopped fresh Italian parsley	25 mL

1 Using fork, pierce squash all over. Roast in roasting pan in 375°F (190°C) oven, turning twice, until tender when pressed, 1¼ hours.

2 In saucepan of boiling water, blanch onions for 1 minute. Transfer to bowl of ice water. Peel; cut any large onions in half.

3 In large skillet, heat 2 tbsp (25 mL) of the oil over medium heat; cook onions and sugar, stirring often, until onions start to turn golden, about 15 minutes. Stir in celery, carrot, red pepper, half each of the salt and pepper, the thyme and sage; cook, stirring often, until onions are deep caramel colour, about 10 minutes. Transfer to bowl.

4 Add 2 tbsp (25 mL) of the remaining oil to pan; cook mushrooms and garlic, stirring, until no liquid remains and mushrooms are starting to turn golden brown, about 10 minutes.

5 Return onion mixture to pan along with stock, soy sauce, vinegar and tomato paste; cook, stirring, for 5 minutes. Meanwhile, stir butter with flour. Add to pan; cook, stirring gently, until sauce is thickened, about 2 minutes.

6 Cut squash in half lengthwise and scoop out seeds. Using fork, pull apart strands and place in bowl; discard skin. Add remaining oil, salt and pepper; toss to coat. Mound on plates; spoon ragout over top. Garnish with parsley.

Makes 4 servings. PER SERVING: about 378 cal, 8 g pro, 22 g total fat (4 g sat. fat), 43 g carb, 8 g fibre, 9 mg chol, 1,630 mg sodium. % RDI: 10% calcium, 23% iron, 65% vit A, 117% vit C, 31% folate.

Scalloped Brussels Sprouts

Béchamel, a traditional French "mother" sauce, makes a creamy sauce for brussels sprouts. Try it over broccoli and cauliflower, too. – Emily

1 Trim brussels sprouts; cut X in base of each. In saucepan of boiling salted water, cover and cook brussels sprouts until tender-crisp, 7 to 9 minutes. Drain and chill under cold water; press out excess water with towel. Cut in half if large; place in greased shallow 8-cup (2 L) casserole dish.

2 In saucepan, melt butter over medium heat; cook onion and thyme, stirring occasionally, until onion is softened, about 5 minutes. Sprinkle with flour; cook, stirring, for 1 minute. Add milk; cook, stirring, until thickened, 6 to 8 minutes. Remove from heat; stir in cheese, salt and pepper. Pour over brussels sprouts.

3 TOPPING: In bowl, stir together bread crumbs, cheese and melted butter. (MAKE-AHEAD: **Cover and refrigerate brussels sprouts mixture and topping separately for up to 24 hours.**)

4 Cover and bake brussels sprouts mixture in 375°F (190°C) oven for 30 minutes. Uncover and sprinkle with topping; bake until golden and bubbling, about 20 minutes.

Makes 8 servings. PER SERVING: about 284 cal, 15 g pro, 17 g total fat (10 g sat. fat), 21 g carb, 5 g fibre, 51 mg chol, 729 mg sodium. % RDI: 37% calcium, 14% iron, 25% vit A, 117% vit C, 38% folate.

2 lb	brussels sprouts	1 kg
2 tbsp	butter	25 mL
1	onion, chopped	1
¼ tsp	dried thyme	1 mL
¼ cup	all-purpose flour	50 mL
2 cups	milk, warmed	500 mL
1½ cups	shredded Gruyère cheese	375 mL
¾ tsp	salt	4 mL
¼ tsp	pepper	1 mL
TOPPING:		
1½ cups	fresh bread crumbs	375 mL
½ cup	shredded Gruyère, Cheddar or Gouda cheese	125 mL
2 tbsp	butter, melted	25 mL

VARIATION

Scalloped Brussels Sprouts and Chestnuts: Add 1½ cups (375 mL) cooked chestnuts to the brussels sprouts mixture.

Plum Frangipane Tart

Have you been asked to bring a dessert to a dinner party but don't know what?
This classic custard and fruit tart is ideal and easy to transport. – Daphna

⅔ cup	ground almonds	150 mL
¼ cup	granulated sugar	50 mL
2 tbsp	butter, softened	25 mL
1	egg	1
¼ tsp	almond extract	1 mL
2 tbsp	all-purpose flour	25 mL
5	plums or peaches (about 1 lb/500 g), pitted	5
3 tbsp	apricot jam, melted and strained	50 mL
PASTRY:		
1½ cups	all-purpose flour	375 mL
2 tbsp	granulated sugar	25 mL
4 tsp	cornstarch	20 mL
¾ cup	cold butter, cubed	175 mL

1 PASTRY: In large bowl, whisk together flour, sugar and cornstarch. Using pastry blender or 2 knives, cut in butter until mixture clumps together. With floured hands, press evenly into bottom and up side of 9-inch (23 cm) round tart pan with removable bottom. Cover and refrigerate until chilled, about 1 hour. (MAKE-AHEAD: **Refrigerate for up to 3 days.**)

2 Using fork, prick bottom of tart shell all over; bake in bottom third of 350°F (180°C) oven until starting to turn golden, about 15 minutes. Let cool completely on rack.

3 Meanwhile, in bowl, beat together almonds, sugar and butter; beat in egg and almond extract. Stir in flour. Spread over prepared crust. Cut plums into thin wedges; nestle in filling, cut side down, in single layer of concentric circles.

4 Bake in bottom third of 375°F (190°C) oven until firm to the touch and tester inserted in centre comes out clean, about 30 minutes. Let cool on rack for 15 minutes. Remove side of pan. Brush jam over filling and crust. Let cool completely. Serve at room temperature. (MAKE-AHEAD: **Set aside at room temperature for up to 3 hours.**)

Makes 8 servings. PER SERVING: about 412 cal, 6 g pro, 25 g total fat (13 g sat. fat), 43 g carb, 2 g fibre, 87 mg chol, 217 mg sodium. % RDI: 3% calcium, 11% iron, 21% vit A, 7% vit C, 19% folate.

Tarte Tatin

This French apple dessert is made in a skillet, then baked in the oven. Serve it warm with whipped cream or crème fraîche. – Daphna

1 In large bowl, whisk together flour, sugar and salt. Using pastry blender or 2 knives, cut in butter until crumbly. In liquid measure, stir vinegar with enough ice water to make ¼ cup (50 mL). Drizzle over flour mixture, stirring briskly with fork until dough holds together when pressed, adding a few more drops of ice water if necessary. Press into ball; flatten into disc. Wrap in plastic wrap and refrigerate for 30 minutes. (MAKE-AHEAD: **Refrigerate for up to 3 days; let stand at room temperature for 15 minutes before rolling out.**)

2 FILLING: Meanwhile, peel, quarter and core apples; cut each quarter in half lengthwise. In bowl, toss apples with lemon juice. In 8-inch (20 cm) cast-iron skillet, melt butter over medium-high heat. Add sugar; cook, stirring, until starting to bubble, 3 to 5 minutes. Remove from heat. Discarding juice, arrange single layer of apples, cut side down, in concentric circles in pan. Layer remaining apples over top. Cook over medium heat, basting with syrup, until apples begin to soften and syrup starts to thicken, about 15 minutes. Cover and cook until top layer is just tender, about 5 minutes. Remove from heat; let cool for 5 minutes.

3 On lightly floured surface, roll out dough into 10-inch (25 cm) circle; cut 4 small steam vents. Loosely roll pastry around rolling pin; unroll over apples. Trim excess and press edge down between apples and pan. Bake in centre of 425°F (220°C) oven until pastry is golden, about 25 minutes. Let stand until bubbling subsides, about 4 minutes. Invert heatproof serving plate over pastry. Wearing oven mitts, grasp plate and pan; invert tart onto plate. Transfer apples stuck in pan over top.

Makes 8 servings. PER SERVING: about 389 cal, 2 g pro, 18 g total fat (11 g sat. fat), 59 g carb, 5 g fibre, 47 mg chol, 75 mg sodium. % RDI: 1% calcium, 6% iron, 17% vit A, 10% vit C, 10% folate.

1 cup	all-purpose flour	250 mL
1 tbsp	granulated sugar	15 mL
¼ tsp	salt	1 mL
½ cup	unsalted butter, cubed	125 mL
1 tsp	vinegar	5 mL
	Ice water	
FILLING:		
8	Northern Spy or Golden Delicious apples (about 4 lb/2 kg)	8
2 tbsp	lemon juice	25 mL
¼ cup	unsalted butter	50 mL
¾ cup	granulated sugar	175 mL

fridge **NOTE**

- **For safety's sake, wear oven mitts when inverting the tart onto the plate; caramelized sugar is extremely hot.**

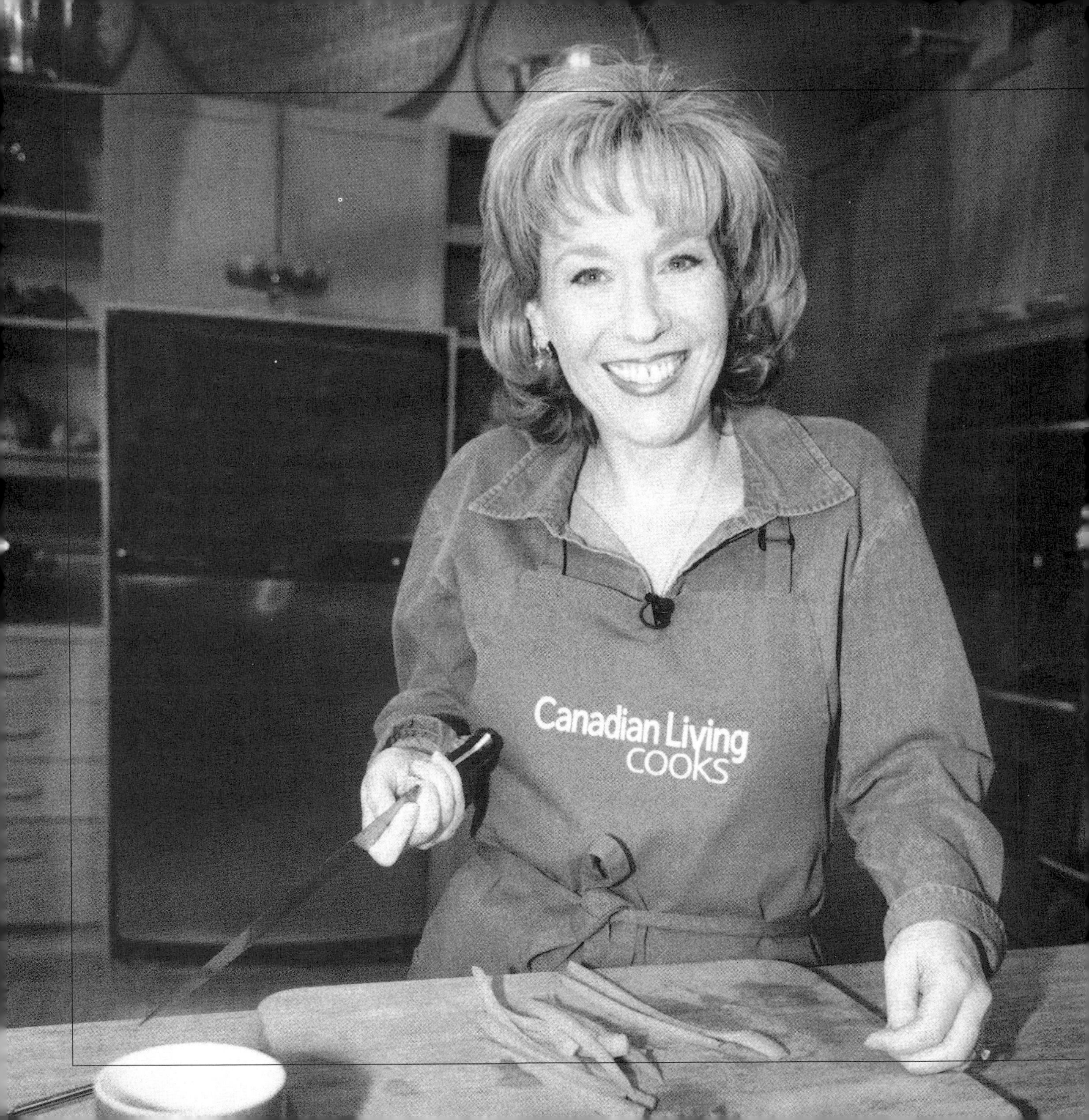
Canadian Living
COOKS

Molto Chocolate

*A*h, *chocolate. The elixir of the gods. I can't remember a time when I didn't love chocolate: as a child awaiting my mother's Black Forest cake, or as a pastry chef concocting chocolate fantasies. I still adore baking with chocolate and discovering all its nuances. And I know I'm not alone. We're so enamoured of chocolate that we have devoted an episode to it each TV season – to top ratings from viewers, who can't seem to get enough either. The thing is that chocolate is so versatile. It pairs magnificently with nuts, caramel, fruits and, of course, other kinds of chocolate. And although it's sublime on its own, it can be sculpted, melted, moussed or baked into any number of divine creations like these, all developed to deliver maximum chocolate voltage!* – Daphna

- Raspberry White Chocolate Tart with Mascarpone
- Double Whammy Chocolate Cream Pie
- Chocolate Silk Macadamia Nut Tart
- Chocolate Caramel Pecan Torte
- Sunken Chocolate Raspberry Cakelets with Raspberry Sauce
- Blueberry Chocolate Squares
- Mud Pie Cookies
- Cranberry White Chocolate Bark
- Truffles

Raspberry White Chocolate Tart with Mascarpone

This decadent dessert is a study in textural contrasts: flaky phyllo, velvety mascarpone and rows of raspberries, like a crown of jewels. – Daphna

3	sheets phyllo pastry	3
3 tbsp	butter, melted	50 mL
3 oz	white chocolate, chopped	90 g
3 cups	raspberries	750 mL
1 cup	mascarpone cheese	250 mL
¼ cup	10% cream	50 mL
4 tsp	granulated sugar	20 mL
½ tsp	vanilla	2 mL

fridge NOTE

- This mascarpone filling is simply divine all on its own. Use dessert spoons or an oval ice-cream scoop to form the filling into oval-shaped quenelles; plate and garnish with a selection of fresh berries tossed lightly with a little sugar.

1 Cut each sheet of phyllo pastry in half lengthwise to make two 17- x 6-inch (43 x 15 cm) sheets. Lay 1 sheet on work surface, keeping remainder covered with damp tea towel to prevent drying out. Brush sheet with butter; top with another sheet so edges are not perfectly aligned and all 8 corners are visible. Repeat with remaining phyllo and butter.

2 Gently fit into 14- x 4-inch (35 x 10 cm) tart pan with removable bottom. Turn edges under and ruffle, allowing some to hang over edge. Line with foil; fill evenly with pie weights or dried beans. Bake in centre of 375°F (190°C) oven for 10 minutes. Remove weights and foil. Prick bottom of shell all over; bake until golden, about 5 minutes longer. Let cool completely on rack. Remove from pan and place on serving plate.

3 In bowl over saucepan of hot (not boiling) water, melt white chocolate, stirring occasionally; pour about two-thirds over crust. (MAKE-AHEAD: **Set aside for up to 2 hours. Remelt reserved white chocolate if necessary.**) Arrange 1 cup (250 mL) of the raspberries over chocolate. In bowl, beat together mascarpone, cream, sugar and vanilla; spread over raspberries. Arrange remaining raspberries over filling. Drizzle with remaining chocolate.

Makes 8 servings. PER SERVING: about 293 cal, 3 g pro, 23 g total fat (14 g sat. fat), 20 g carb, 2 g fibre, 60 mg chol, 108 mg sodium. % RDI: 6% calcium, 4% iron, 5% vit A, 20% vit C, 10% folate.

Double Whammy Chocolate Cream Pie

Chocolate in the crisp crust, chocolate cream filling and chocolate curls on top – a perfect dessert for chocolate lovers. – Daphna

1 CHOCOLATE CRUST: In bowl, whisk together flour, cocoa, sugar and salt. Using pastry blender or 2 knives, cut in butter and shortening until mixture resembles fine crumbs with a few larger pieces. Sprinkle with water, stirring with fork just until dough holds together when pressed. Knead lightly 5 or 6 times to form ball; flatten into disc. Wrap in plastic wrap and refrigerate for 30 minutes.

2 On lightly floured surface, roll out dough to ¼-inch (5 mm) thickness. Fit into 9-inch (23 cm) pie plate; trim and flute edge. Chill until firm, about 30 minutes. Using fork, prick pastry all over. Line with foil; fill with pie weights or dried beans. Bake in centre of 400°F (200°C) oven for 20 minutes. Remove weights and foil; bake until no longer doughy in centre, about 10 minutes. Let cool on rack.

3 FILLING: In saucepan, heat milk over medium-high heat until bubbles form around edge. In bowl, combine sugar, cornstarch and salt; gradually whisk in milk. Return to saucepan. Add chocolate; cook over medium heat, whisking, until boiling and thickened, 4 to 7 minutes.

4 Remove from heat; whisk one-quarter of the hot mixture into egg yolks. Whisk back into saucepan. Reduce heat and simmer for 1 minute; stir in butter and vanilla. Pour into bowl and place plastic wrap directly on surface; refrigerate until cold and firm.

5 Spoon filling into pie shell; smooth top. Whip cream; spread or pipe over filling. Shave semisweet chocolate to form curls; sprinkle over cream. Cover loosely with plastic wrap and refrigerate until filling is set, about 2 hours. (MAKE-AHEAD: **Refrigerate for up to 24 hours.**)

Makes 8 servings. PER SERVING: about 520 cal, 8 g pro, 36 g total fat (19 g sat. fat), 48 g carb, 4 g fibre, 139 mg chol, 363 mg sodium. % RDI: 14% calcium, 18% iron, 24% vit A, 2% vit C, 17% folate.

¾ cup	whipping cream	175 mL
1 oz	semisweet chocolate	30 g
FILLING:		
3 cups	milk	750 mL
½ cup	granulated sugar	125 mL
⅓ cup	cornstarch	75 mL
½ tsp	salt	2 mL
4 oz	bittersweet chocolate, chopped	125 g
3	egg yolks	3
2 tbsp	butter	25 mL
2 tsp	vanilla	10 mL
CHOCOLATE CRUST:		
1 cup	all-purpose flour	250 mL
¼ cup	cocoa powder	50 mL
¼ cup	granulated sugar	50 mL
¼ tsp	salt	1 mL
¼ cup	cold butter, cubed	50 mL
¼ cup	cold shortening, cubed	50 mL
3 tbsp	cold water	50 mL

Chocolate Silk Macadamia Nut Tart

While it may take some time to prepare this caramel and chocolate ganache tart, the end result is pure pleasure. – Daphna

2 cups	chocolate wafer crumbs	500 mL
⅓ cup	butter, melted	75 mL
CARAMEL FILLING:		
¾ cup	granulated sugar	175 mL
2 tbsp	corn syrup	25 mL
⅓ cup	butter, cut in pieces	75 mL
⅔ cup	chopped macadamia nuts	150 mL
¼ cup	whipping cream	50 mL
CHOCOLATE SILK:		
⅔ cup	whipping cream	150 mL
6 oz	bittersweet chocolate, chopped	175 g
2 tbsp	butter	25 mL
TOPPING:		
½ cup	macadamia nuts	125 mL
½ cup	granulated sugar	125 mL
¾ cup	whipping cream	175 mL

1 In bowl, stir wafer crumbs with butter until moistened. Press onto bottom and up side of 9-inch (23 cm) round or square tart pan with removable bottom. Bake in centre of 350°F (180°C) oven until set, about 10 minutes. Let cool completely on rack.

2 CARAMEL FILLING: In heavy saucepan, bring sugar, 3 tbsp (50 mL) water and corn syrup to boil; boil, without stirring but brushing down side with pastry brush dipped in cold water, until mixture turns caramel colour, about 8 minutes. Remove from heat; whisk in butter. Whisk in nuts and cream. Pour into prepared crust. Refrigerate until set, about 1 hour.

3 CHOCOLATE SILK: In clean saucepan, heat cream just until boiling; pour over chocolate and butter in bowl, whisking until smooth. Let cool slightly. Pour over caramel filling. Refrigerate until set, about 8 hours. (MAKE-AHEAD: **Cover and refrigerate for up to 2 days.**)

4 TOPPING: Arrange nuts closely together on foil-lined rimmed baking sheet. In clean saucepan, bring sugar and 2 tbsp (25 mL) water to boil; boil, without stirring but brushing down side with pastry brush dipped in cold water, until mixture turns caramel colour, 5 to 7 minutes. Pour over nuts; let cool completely. (MAKE-AHEAD: **Store topping, uncovered, for up to 24 hours.**) Break into pieces; chop finely in food processor.

5 Remove side of tart pan; slide tart onto serving platter, removing bottom. In bowl, whip cream; spoon into pastry bag fitted with rosette tip. Pipe border of rosettes around edge of tart. Sprinkle with nut topping.

Makes 12 servings. PER SERVING: about 548 cal, 4 g pro, 42 g total fat (20 g sat. fat), 46 g carb, 2 g fibre, 80 mg chol, 165 mg sodium. % RDI: 5% calcium, 12% iron, 24% vit A, 3% folate.

fridge **NOTE**

- **Blanched almonds can replace macadamia nuts; you can even omit the nut topping and use ½ cup (125 mL) chopped toasted macadamia nuts instead.**

Chocolate Caramel Pecan Torte

This decadent, velvety dessert dazzler is one of my favourite chocolate cakes.
See the Fridge Note for how to make chocolate shards like a pro. – Daphna

4 oz	unsweetened chocolate, chopped	125 g
2¼ cups	all-purpose flour	550 mL
2¼ cups	packed brown sugar	550 mL
1 tsp	baking soda	5 mL
½ tsp	baking powder	2 mL
¼ tsp	salt	1 mL
1 cup	sour cream	250 mL
½ cup	butter, softened	125 mL
3	eggs	3
1 tsp	vanilla	5 mL
2 cups	pecan pieces	500 mL
CARAMEL:		
1½ cups	granulated sugar	375 mL
⅔ cup	whipping cream	150 mL
¼ cup	butter	50 mL
TOPPING:		
2½ cups	whipping cream	625 mL
¾ cup	Chocolate Shards (see Fridge Note, page 101)	175 mL
⅓ cup	pecan halves, toasted	75 mL

1 Grease three 9-inch (1.5 L) round metal cake pans; line bottoms with parchment paper. Set aside.

2 In heatproof bowl over saucepan of hot (not boiling) water, melt chocolate; let cool slightly.

3 In large bowl, whisk together flour, brown sugar, baking soda, baking powder and salt; beat in sour cream and butter. Beat in eggs, 1 at a time, beating well after each addition; beat in chocolate and vanilla. Beat for 2 minutes, scraping down side of bowl occasionally. Gradually stir in 1 cup (250 mL) water. Divide evenly among prepared pans; sprinkle pecans over top.

4 Bake in centre of 350°F (180°C) oven until cake tester inserted in centre comes out clean, 30 to 35 minutes. Let cool in pans on racks for 15 minutes. Turn out onto racks and peel off paper; let cool completely. (MAKE-AHEAD: **Wrap in plastic wrap and store for up to 24 hours.**)

5 CARAMEL: In heavy saucepan, stir sugar with ⅓ cup (75 mL) water over medium heat until dissolved, brushing down side of pan with pastry brush dipped in cold water. Bring to boil; boil vigorously, without stirring but brushing down side of pan, until dark amber, about 10 minutes. Holding pan at arm's length and averting face, add cream; whisk until smooth. Whisk in butter until smooth. Let cool. (MAKE-AHEAD: **Refrigerate in airtight container for up to 3 days; reheat slightly before using.**)

6 TOPPING: In bowl, whip cream. Place 1 cake layer, pecan side up, on cake plate. Drizzle with 2 tbsp (25 mL) of the caramel. Spread 1 cup (250 mL) of the whipped cream over top. Drizzle with 2 tbsp (25 mL) of the remaining caramel, being careful not to let any drip down side. Repeat layers once.

7 Top with remaining cake layer. Spread remaining whipped cream over top and side; smooth surface. Drizzle 2 tbsp (25 mL) of the remaining caramel over top. Garnish with Chocolate Shards and pecan halves. Serve with remaining caramel.

Makes 12 to 16 servings. PER EACH OF 16 SERVINGS: about 692 cal, 7 g pro, 45 g total fat (21 g sat. fat), 71 g carb, 4 g fibre, 128 mg chol, 253 mg sodium. % RDI: 10% calcium, 19% iron, 29% vit A, 16% folate.

fridge NOTE

Garnish this torte and your other dessert masterpieces with chocolate shards. Here's how to create them.

- **In heatproof bowl over saucepan of hot (not boiling) water, melt 4 oz (125 g) semisweet chocolate. Spread evenly on rimmed baking sheet; refrigerate until firm, about 15 minutes.**

- **Place baking sheet on damp tea towel; let stand for 3 minutes. Bracing pan against body, slowly scrape metal spatula through chocolate toward body to make shards. Refrigerate pan for 3 to 4 minutes if chocolate gets too soft. (*MAKE-AHEAD: Refrigerate in single layer in airtight container for up to 2 days.*) Makes 1½ cups (375 mL).**

Sunken Chocolate Raspberry Cakelets with Raspberry Sauce

Each soft, rich cake sinks in the middle to become the perfect receptacle for a scoop of sorbet. Garnish the plate with a few berries. – Daphna

6 oz	bittersweet chocolate, chopped	175 g
⅓ cup	butter	75 mL
4	eggs, separated	4
⅔ cup	granulated sugar	150 mL
2 tbsp	cocoa powder, sifted	25 mL
	Raspberry Sauce (see Fridge Note, below)	
1 cup	raspberry sorbet	250 mL

fridge NOTE

- **Raspberry Sauce: In blender or food processor, pulse 1 pkg (300 g) frozen raspberries, thawed, ⅓ cup (75 mL) water, 2 tbsp (25 mL) granulated sugar and 1 tsp (5 mL) lemon juice until smooth; press through fine sieve to remove seeds. *(MAKE-AHEAD: Refrigerate in airtight container for up to 1 week.)* Makes 1½ cups (375 mL).**

1 Grease eight 6-oz (175 mL) ramekins or custard cups; line bottoms with parchment paper. Set aside.

2 In large bowl over saucepan of hot (not boiling) water, melt chocolate with butter until smooth; set aside.

3 In another heatproof bowl over saucepan of gently simmering water, whisk egg yolks with ½ cup (125 mL) of the sugar; cook, whisking constantly, until light and thickened, about 8 minutes. Fold one-quarter into chocolate mixture; fold in remaining yolk mixture. Set aside.

4 In large bowl, beat egg whites until soft peaks form; beat in remaining sugar, 2 tbsp (25 mL) at a time, until stiff peaks form. Fold cocoa and one-third of the egg whites into chocolate mixture; fold in remaining egg whites. Spoon into prepared ramekins. Bake in centre of 350°F (180°C) oven until puffed and edges are set, about 20 minutes. (MAKE-AHEAD: **Cover and refrigerate for up to 24 hours.**)

5 Invert cakes onto dessert plates; remove paper. Garnish each plate with Raspberry Sauce; top cakes with scoop of raspberry sorbet.

Makes 8 servings. PER SERVING: about 330 cal, 6 g pro, 22 g total fat (13 g sat. fat), 35 g carb, 4 g fibre, 117 mg chol, 113 mg sodium. % RDI: 4% calcium, 15% iron, 12% vit A, 15% vit C, 11% folate.

Blueberry Chocolate Squares

These squares hover deliciously between candy and cookie. Serve after dinner with coffee. – Elizabeth

1 Line 8-inch (2 L) square metal cake pan with parchment paper, leaving a few inches of overhang; set aside.

2 In bowl, toss cookie crumbs with butter until moistened; press firmly onto bottom of prepared pan. Sprinkle with blueberries; set aside.

3 In saucepan, bring cream to boil; pour over chocolate in heat-proof bowl and stir until melted. Let cool slightly; spoon evenly over berries. Refrigerate until firm, about 2 hours. (MAKE-AHEAD: **Cover and refrigerate for up to 24 hours.**)

4 To serve, use paper overhang to transfer to cutting board. Cut into squares.

Makes 16 pieces. PER PIECE: about 172 cal, 2 g pro, 11 g total fat (7 g sat. fat), 19 g carb, 1 g fibre, 18 mg chol, 73 mg sodium. % RDI: 3% calcium, 1% iron, 4% vit A, 3% vit C, 2% folate.

2 cups	amaretto cookie crumbs	500 mL
¼ cup	butter, melted	50 mL
1½ cups	fresh wild blueberries	375 mL
⅓ cup	whipping cream	75 mL
8 oz	white chocolate, finely chopped	250 g

fridge NOTE

- **You can make tantalizing candies by folding small wild blueberries into cooled melted white or milk chocolate. Then drop by spoonfuls onto a waxed paper–lined baking sheet. Store in the refrigerator.**

Mud Pie Cookies

If you love the intense chocolate of brownies, then I guarantee you'll find these sweet drops irresistible. – Elizabeth

6 oz	bittersweet chocolate, chopped	175 g
4 oz	unsweetened chocolate, chopped	125 g
⅓ cup	butter	75 mL
1¼ cups	granulated sugar	300 mL
3	eggs	3
2 tsp	vanilla	10 mL
1 cup	all-purpose flour	250 mL
1 tsp	baking powder	5 mL
¼ tsp	salt	1 mL
1¼ cups	chocolate chips	300 mL
¾ cup	miniature marshmallows (optional)	175 mL
¾ cup	chopped walnuts	175 mL

1 Line rimless baking sheets with parchment paper or leave ungreased; set aside.

2 In large heatproof bowl over saucepan of hot (not boiling) water, melt bittersweet and unsweetened chocolates and butter, stirring occasionally, until about three-quarters melted. Remove from heat and let finish melting; stir until smooth. Whisk in sugar; whisk in eggs, 1 at a time, and vanilla.

3 In separate bowl, whisk together flour, baking powder and salt. Pour over chocolate mixture; stir just until combined. Sprinkle chocolate chips, marshmallows (if using) and walnuts over top; stir to combine. Drop by heaping tablespoonfuls (15 mL), about 2 inches (5 cm) apart, onto prepared pans.

4 Bake, 1 sheet at a time, in centre of 350°F (180°C) oven until firm around edge but still soft in centre, 10 to 12 minutes. Let stand on pans on rack until firm, about 5 minutes; transfer to racks and let cool completely. (MAKE-AHEAD: **Layer between waxed paper in airtight container and store at room temperature for up to 5 days or freeze for up to 2 weeks.**)

Makes about 64 cookies. PER COOKIE: about 84 cal, 1 g pro, 5 g total fat (3 g sat. fat), 9 g carb, 1 g fibre, 12 mg chol, 26 mg sodium. % RDI: 1% calcium, 4% iron, 1% vit A, 3% folate.

Cranberry White Chocolate Bark

A bark is melted chocolate studded with various ingredients: raisins, dried fruit, coconut. It's fun to make with kids. – Daphna

1 lb	white chocolate, chopped	500 g
1 cup	dried cranberries	250 mL
1 cup	pistachios, shelled	250 mL

1 In heatproof bowl over saucepan of hot (not boiling) water, melt chocolate, stirring occasionally. Stir in cranberries and pistachios. Pour onto foil-lined rimmed baking sheet; using palette knife or rubber spatula, spread into 12- x 8- inch (30 x 20 cm) rectangle.

2 Refrigerate until hardened, about 1 hour. Break into pieces. (MAKE-AHEAD: **Wrap in plastic wrap and refrigerate in airtight container for up to 1 week.**)

Makes about 32 pieces. PER PIECE: about 109 cal, 2 g pro, 6 g total fat (3 g sat. fat), 12 g carb, 1 g fibre, 3 mg chol, 13 mg sodium. % RDI: 3% calcium, 1% iron, 2% vit C, 2% folate.

VARIATIONS

Fruit and Nut Chocolate Bark: Substitute semisweet or bittersweet chocolate for the white chocolate. Substitute 1 cup (250 mL) each raisins and unsalted roasted peanuts for the dried cranberries and pistachios.

Apricot and Ginger White Chocolate Bark: Substitute 1¼ cups (300 mL) slivered dried apricots and ¼ cup (50 mL) finely chopped candied ginger for the dried cranberries and pistachios.

Milk Chocolate Toffee Pecan Bark: Substitute milk chocolate for the white chocolate. Refrigerate 3 bars (each 56 g) toffee until brittle; chop with large sharp knife and substitute along with 1 cup (250 mL) chopped toasted pecans for the cranberries and pistachios. (If desired, substitute 1 cup/250 mL chopped hard butterscotch candies or 1 pkg/225 g toffee bits for the 3 toffee bars.)

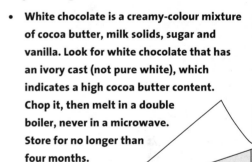

fridge NOTE

- **White chocolate is a creamy-colour mixture of cocoa butter, milk solids, sugar and vanilla. Look for white chocolate that has an ivory cast (not pure white), which indicates a high cocoa butter content. Chop it, then melt in a double boiler, never in a microwave. Store for no longer than four months.**

Truffles

What a good excuse to get together with a friend for an afternoon of truffle making! Surprisingly easy, truffles are a most seductive candy. – Elizabeth

WHITE CHOCOLATE TRUFFLES:

¾ cup	whipping cream	175 mL
¼ cup	butter	50 mL
1 lb	white chocolate, chopped	500 g
1 tbsp	orange liqueur	15 mL

DARK CHOCOLATE TRUFFLES:

1 cup	whipping cream	250 mL
¼ cup	butter	50 mL
1 lb	semisweet or bittersweet chocolate, chopped	500 g
1 tbsp	dark rum	15 mL

MILK CHOCOLATE TRUFFLES:

⅔ cup	whipping cream	150 mL
¼ cup	butter	50 mL
12 oz	milk chocolate, chopped	375 g
1 tbsp	hazelnut liqueur	15 mL

DIPPING CHOCOLATE:

1 lb	white chocolate, chopped	500 g
1 lb	semisweet or bittersweet chocolate, chopped	500 g
1 lb	milk chocolate, chopped	500 g

1 Line rimmed baking sheets with waxed or parchment paper; set aside.

2 WHITE CHOCOLATE TRUFFLES: In small saucepan, bring cream and butter just to boil; stir until butter melts. Pour over white chocolate in bowl; stir until melted and smooth. (If necessary, continue stirring over double boiler to completely melt chocolate.) Stir in liqueur. Cover with plastic wrap and refrigerate until firm, about 12 hours.

3 DARK CHOCOLATE TRUFFLES: Follow method for White Chocolate Truffles.

4 MILK CHOCOLATE TRUFFLES: Follow method for White Chocolate Truffles.

5 Scoop out level tablespoonfuls (15 mL) of each type of truffle mixture; roll each into ball and place on prepared pans. Refrigerate until cold, about 1 hour.

6 DIPPING CHOCOLATE: In metal bowl over saucepan of hot (not boiling) water, melt white chocolate, stirring, until candy thermometer registers 85° to 90°F (30° to 32°C). Remove from over water. One at a time and using long fork, submerge white chocolate truffles in melted chocolate. Tap fork gently against side of pan to remove excess. Slide truffle off fork onto baking sheet. Refrigerate until chocolate is set, about 30 minutes.

> " Truffles can top off a fine meal just as tastily as an elaborate dessert. – *Elizabeth* "

7 Using semisweet chocolate for dark chocolate truffles and milk chocolate for milk chocolate truffles, repeat dipping to make about 130 truffles in total.

8 Use excess dipping chocolate and dipping fork to drizzle decorative designs on truffles, such as dark chocolate drizzles on white chocolate truffles and white chocolate drizzles on dark chocolate truffles.

Makes about 130 truffles. PER WHITE CHOCOLATE TRUFFLE: about 116 cal, 1 g pro, 8 g total fat (5 g sat. fat), 11 g carb, 0 g fibre, 11 mg chol, 27 mg sodium. % RDI: 3% calcium, 2% vit A, 1% folate. PER DARK CHOCOLATE TRUFFLE: about 115 cal, 1 g pro, 7 g total fat (4 g sat. fat), 12 g carb, 1 g fibre, 9 mg chol, 12 mg sodium. % RDI: 1% calcium, 4% iron, 3% vit A, 2% folate. PER MILK CHOCOLATE TRUFFLE: about 168 cal, 2 g pro, 12 g total fat (7 g sat. fat), 16 g carb, 1 g fibre, 17 mg chol, 39 mg sodium. % RDI: 5% calcium, 3% iron, 5% vit A, 1% folate.

fridge NOTE

When storing chocolate, follow these tips.

- **Wrap, then overwrap, to prevent moisture and odour absorption. Store in a cool, dry place for up to six months (no more than four months for white chocolate).**

- **If you've had chocolate on hand for a while and it has developed a grey or white film, don't worry. This slight discolouration, referred to as "bloom," results from exposure to moisture or extreme changes in temperature. When the chocolate is melted, the discolouration will disappear.**

- **Frozen chocolate must always be thawed completely, without unwrapping, in order to prevent moisture from forming on the surface.**

Tasting the World

Whether it's cumin from Mexico or cinnamon from Morocco, I love to fill my kitchen with enticing aromas from around the world. My husband and I have fun travelling the globe through themed dinner parties: we ask everyone to bring a dish from a different country and an accompanying regional wine to discover. Guests have a blast talking about past trips and where they want to go next. We three cooks get lots of requests to showcase different cuisines, so we have made them a significant part of our show, taking our kitchen on a number of exciting food journeys, then bringing classic tastes right to your table – no airfare necessary! – Emily

- Chinese Hot and Sour Soup
- Caldo Verde
- Soupe au Pistou
- Harira
- Gyoza
- Cod and Potato Ovals
- Crab Sui Mai
- Falafels
- Potato Gnocchi
- Hot and Spicy Noodle Salad
- Caldeirada
- Steamed Fish with Shiitake Mushrooms
- Portuguese African Chicken
- Chicken Saltimbocca
- Chicken Braised with Chestnuts and Shiitake Mushrooms
- Lamb Tagine with Artichokes and Mint
- Panforte
- Traditional Mexican Flan
- Spiced Coffee Granita

◀ The boom camera moves around to come in close and get all the overhead shots

Chinese Hot and Sour Soup

Cellophane noodles, a.k.a. bean thread noodles, are made from the starch of mung beans, the legume that gives us bean sprouts. – Daphna

6	dried shiitake mushrooms (or 1 cup/250 mL sliced fresh shiitake mushrooms)	6
1 oz	cellophane noodles	30 g
8 oz	firm tofu	250 g
8 oz	boneless pork loin chops	250 g
4 tsp	cornstarch	20 mL
5 cups	chicken stock	1.25 L
¼ cup	rice vinegar	50 mL
2 tbsp	soy sauce	25 mL
2 tsp	granulated sugar	10 mL
½ tsp	white pepper	2 mL
2	eggs	2
1 tbsp	whole fresh coriander leaves	15 mL
1 tsp	sesame oil	5 mL
2	green onions, sliced	2

1 In small bowl, cover mushrooms with 1 cup (250 mL) warm water; let stand until softened, about 20 minutes. Drain, reserving liquid. Remove stems. Slice caps finely; set aside.

2 In large bowl of warm water, soak noodles for 5 minutes. Drain and place in pile on cutting board; cut pile in half. Set aside.

3 Cut tofu into thin slices. Cut pork into thin strips; toss with 1 tsp (5 mL) of the cornstarch.

4 In large pot, bring stock to simmer. Add mushrooms and reserved soaking liquid, noodles, tofu, pork, vinegar, soy sauce, sugar and pepper; simmer for 3 minutes.

5 In small bowl, whisk remaining cornstarch with 1 tbsp (15 mL) cold water; stir into soup and simmer for 2 minutes. Remove from heat.

6 In small bowl, whisk eggs with 1 tbsp (15 mL) water; drizzle into soup, stirring slowly with spoon to form streamers. Stir in coriander leaves, sesame oil and onions.

Makes 6 servings. PER SERVING: about 230 cal, 20 g pro, 7 g total fat (2 g sat. fat), 24 g carb, 3 g fibre, 85 mg chol, 1,046 mg sodium. % RDI: 9% calcium, 16% iron, 3% vit A, 2% vit C, 22% folate.

Caldo Verde

The greens are the heroes of this Portuguese soup – hence the name "green soup" – while the sausage is considered just a flavouring. – Daphna

1 In large saucepan, bring 6 cups (1.5 L) water, potatoes, onion, parsley and salt to boil. Reduce heat, cover and simmer until potatoes are tender, about 20 minutes.

2 In blender or food processor or using immersion blender, purée soup, in batches, and return to pan.

3 Meanwhile, trim stems and ribs from collard greens; shred leaves finely. Add shredded leaves, sausage and pepper to puréed soup. Cook until greens are tender, about 20 minutes. Gently stir in oil.

Makes 4 to 6 servings. PER EACH OF 6 SERVINGS: about 258 cal, 10 g pro, 17 g total fat (5 g sat. fat), 16 g carb, 2 g fibre, 29 mg chol, 1,001 mg sodium. % RDI: 6% calcium, 11% iron, 14% vit A, 23% vit C, 10% folate.

3	baking potatoes, peeled and cubed (about 1 lb/500 g total)	3
1	onion, chopped	1
1 cup	chopped fresh parsley	250 mL
1½ tsp	salt	7 mL
1	bunch collard greens (8 oz/250 g)	1
1	cured air-dried chorizo sausage, thinly sliced (7 oz/200 g)	1
1½ tsp	pepper	7 mL
2 tbsp	extra-virgin olive oil	25 mL

fridge NOTES

- **A member of the cabbage family, collard has an earthy flavour. To shred finely, roll several leaves tightly, then thinly cut roll crosswise.**

- **To avoid splatters when using an immersion blender, turn it on only after it is standing upright in the bottom of the pot.**

Soupe au Pistou

This gorgeous Provençale soup thickens as it sits, so if you're making it ahead, you may want to add a little water or stock when reheating. – Daphna

1¼ cups	dried white beans (such as cannellini or navy)	300 mL
1 tbsp	extra-virgin olive oil	15 mL
1	onion, finely chopped	1
3	cloves garlic, minced	3
6	carrots, diced	6
1	stalk celery, thinly sliced	1
½ tsp	each salt and pepper	2 mL
5 cups	chicken or vegetable stock	1.25 L
1	each bay leaf and sprig fresh thyme	1
4	small red potatoes, cubed	4
1	small bulb fennel, trimmed, cored and cubed	1
3	plum tomatoes, peeled, seeded and diced	3
1	zucchini, diced	1
4 oz	haricots verts or thin green beans	125 g
2 cups	shelled fresh or frozen peas	500 mL
¾ cup	broken vermicelli	175 mL

1 Rinse beans; sort if necessary, discarding any blemished ones and any grit.

2 In large saucepan, cover beans with 3 times their volume of water; bring to boil. Boil for 2 minutes. Remove from heat, cover and let stand for 1 hour. Drain; return soaked beans to pan along with 3 times their volume of fresh water. Bring to boil; reduce heat, cover and simmer until beans are tender, about 3 hours. (Or soak overnight, drain and cook with 3 times their volume of water until tender, about 2½ hours.) Drain; set aside.

3 Meanwhile, in Dutch oven, heat oil over medium heat; cook onion, garlic, carrots, celery, salt and pepper until onion is softened, about 6 minutes. Stir in 6 cups (1.5 L) water, stock, bay leaf and thyme sprig; bring to boil. Reduce heat, cover and simmer for 10 minutes. Add cooked beans, potatoes and fennel; return to boil. Reduce heat, cover and simmer until potatoes are almost tender, about 5 minutes.

4 Add tomatoes, zucchini, haricots verts, peas and vermicelli. (If using frozen peas, add during last minute of cooking.) Cover and simmer, stirring occasionally, until haricots verts and peas are tender, about 10 minutes. Discard bay leaf.

5 PISTOU: Meanwhile, in food processor, purée basil with cheese; gradually blend in oil in thin, steady stream. Transfer to bowl; stir in garlic. (MAKE-AHEAD: **Transfer to resealable plastic bag, press out air and refrigerate for up to 24 hours or freeze for up to 2 weeks.**)

6 To serve, ladle soup into warmed bowls. Top with generous dollop of pistou.

Makes 8 servings. PER SERVING: about 443 cal, 21 g pro, 14 g total fat (4 g sat. fat), 60 g carb, 12 g fibre, 10 mg chol, 949 mg sodium. % RDI: 28% calcium, 34% iron, 148% vit A, 37% vit C, 82% folate.

PISTOU:		
1½ cups	lightly packed fresh basil leaves	375 mL
1 cup	grated Parmigiano-Reggiano cheese	250 mL
¼ cup	extra-virgin olive oil	50 mL
4	large cloves garlic, minced	4

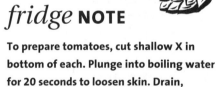

fridge NOTE

- **To prepare tomatoes, cut shallow X in bottom of each. Plunge into boiling water for 20 seconds to loosen skin. Drain, then plunge briefly into cold water to cool; peel. Cut in half crosswise; press out seeds and dice.**

Dee-Dee Peel puts final touches on the decoration of the set

Harira

This aromatic soup is traditionally served to break the fast during Ramadan, the ninth and holiest month of the Islamic calendar. – Daphna

1	each large bunch fresh coriander and parsley	1
8 cups	chicken or vegetable stock	2 L
1 cup	green or brown lentils	250 mL
1	can (19 oz/540 mL) chickpeas, drained and rinsed	1
2	cans (each 19 oz/540 mL) tomatoes, drained and chopped	2
2	onions, chopped	2
2 tsp	cinnamon	10 mL
1 tsp	each ground cumin, ground ginger, turmeric and pepper	5 mL
¼ cup	lemon juice	50 mL
2 tbsp	extra-virgin olive oil	25 mL
GARNISH:		
2 tsp	cinnamon	10 mL
1	lemon, thinly sliced	1
12	pitted dates, halved	12

1 Chop ¼ cup (50 mL) each of the coriander and parsley; set aside. Tie together remaining coriander and parsley; place in large saucepan. Add stock and bring to boil; reduce heat to low, cover and simmer for 15 minutes. Discard herb bundle. Add lentils; cover and simmer for 15 minutes.

2 Add chickpeas, tomatoes, onions, cinnamon, cumin, ginger, turmeric and pepper; cover and simmer for 30 minutes.

3 In food processor or blender, purée 3 cups (750 mL) of the soup. Return to pot and heat through. Stir in lemon juice, oil and reserved chopped herbs.

4 GARNISH: Ladle soup into bowls. Sprinkle with cinnamon; top with lemon slices and dates.

Makes 8 servings. PER SERVING: about 285 cal, 16 g pro, 6 g total fat (1 g sat. fat), 44 g carb, 7 g fibre, 0 mg chol, 1,031 mg sodium. % RDI: 8% calcium, 36% iron, 6% vit A, 27% vit C, 76% folate.

Gyoza

Serve lichee martinis with these dumplings: one shot lichee liqueur and two shots vodka shaken with ice. Strain and garnish with a lichee. – Emily

1 In bowl, toss cabbage with salt and let stand for 5 minutes. Squeeze out liquid. In fine sieve, press any liquid from shrimp. In large bowl, mix together cabbage, shrimp, pork, soy sauce, wine, onion, sesame oil, ginger and garlic.

2 Using 3-inch (8 cm) round cutter, cut wonton wrappers into circles, keeping covered with damp cloth to prevent drying out. Working with 4 wrappers at a time, brush edges lightly with water. On 1 half of each round, pinch four ¼-inch (5 mm) pleats. In rounded hollow of each wrapper, place 2 tsp (10 mL) filling; fold pleated side over filling, matching edges and pressing out all air. Press edges to seal.

3 Arrange, seam side up, on waxed paper–lined pan, curving into crescent and pressing to flatten bottom. (MAKE-AHEAD: **Cover and refrigerate for up to 8 hours. Or freeze in airtight container for up to 1 week; thaw in refrigerator.**) Cover with damp cloth.

4 In each of 2 large skillets, heat 1 tbsp (15 mL) oil over medium-high heat; fry 16 dumplings in each, flat side down, until golden on bottom, about 1 minute. Pour ¼ cup (50 mL) of the stock into each pan; reduce heat to low. Cover and simmer, without turning, until dumplings are translucent and most of the liquid is evaporated, about 7 minutes. Uncover and increase heat to medium; cook until liquid is evaporated and bottoms are dark brown, 5 to 7 minutes. Drain on paper towel. Transfer to dish; keep warm. Wipe pan; repeat with remaining oil, dumplings and stock.

5 DIPPING SAUCE: Stir together soy sauce, vinegar and ginger; serve with dumplings.

Makes 64 pieces. PER PIECE: about 54 cal, 3 g pro, 2 g total fat (1 g sat. fat), 5 g carb, trace fibre, 9 mg chol, 166 mg sodium. % RDI: 1% calcium, 3% iron, 1% vit A, 2% vit C, 5% folate.

2 cups	finely chopped napa or green cabbage	500 mL
1 tsp	salt	5 mL
8 oz	shrimp, peeled, deveined and finely chopped	250 g
1 lb	lean ground pork	500 g
2 tbsp	light-colour soy sauce	25 mL
2 tbsp	rice wine, sherry or white wine	25 mL
1 tbsp	chopped green onion	15 mL
1 tbsp	sesame oil	15 mL
2 tsp	minced gingerroot	10 mL
1	clove garlic, minced	1
64	wonton wrappers (2 pkg)	64
¼ cup	vegetable oil	50 mL
1 cup	chicken stock or water	250 mL
DIPPING SAUCE:		
2 tbsp	light-colour soy sauce	25 mL
1 tbsp	rice vinegar	15 mL
1 tsp	minced gingerroot	5 mL

Cod and Potato Ovals

Paula Tomas of J. & A. Botelho's in Cambridge, Ontario, gave Rose Murray and me her mother's version of this Portuguese appetizer. – Elizabeth

1¼ lb	salt cod	625 g
5 cups	riced or finely mashed mealy potatoes cooked without salt	1.25 L
½ cup	finely chopped onion	125 mL
⅓ cup	finely chopped fresh parsley	75 mL
4 tsp	lemon juice	20 mL
¼ tsp	nutmeg	1 mL
¼ tsp	pepper	1 mL
3	eggs, beaten	3
	Vegetable oil for deep-frying	

1 Rinse cod and soak for 12 hours or overnight in several changes of cold water.

2 Drain and rinse under cold water; place in large saucepan. Cover with cold water; bring to boil. Reduce heat and simmer until fish flakes easily when tested, about 15 minutes. Drain and let cool; remove skin and all bones. In food processor or by hand, chop cod very finely until no chunks remain.

3 In large bowl, combine cod, potatoes, onion, parsley, lemon juice, nutmeg and pepper; stir in eggs to form firm but malleable mixture. Using dessertspoon, scoop heaping spoonful of cod mixture. Using second dessertspoon cupped over first, press and form mixture into rounded oval, letting excess fall back into bowl. Place oval on large waxed paper–lined baking sheet. Repeat with remaining mixture.

4 In deep-fryer, heat 3 inches (8 cm) of oil to 375°F (190°C); fry ovals, about 8 at a time, until golden and crisp, about 2 minutes. Drain on paper towels. Serve immediately or keep warm until serving.

Makes about 60 pieces. PER PIECE: about 96 cal, 7 g pro, 6 g total fat (1 g sat. fat), 4 g carb, trace fibre, 24 mg chol, 601 mg sodium. % RDI: 2% calcium, 2% iron, 1% vit A, 3% vit C, 2% folate.

Crab Sui Mai

This Chinese dim sum snack is irresistible filled with shrimp, crab and a little pork. You can't stop at one! – Daphna

1 Peel and devein shrimp; transfer to food processor. Add pork, egg white, wine, oil, ginger, salt and pepper; pulse just until combined, scraping down side of bowl as necessary. Scrape into large bowl.

2 Drain crabmeat in sieve, pressing to remove as much liquid as possible; remove any cartilage. Add crabmeat to shrimp mixture along with water chestnuts, coriander and onions; stir gently to combine without breaking up crab.

3 Place 4 wonton wrappers on work surface, keeping remaining covered with damp cloth to prevent drying out; brush lightly with water. Place 1 tbsp (15 mL) crab mixture on centre of each; gather edges of wrapper and fold up around filling, leaving 1-inch (2.5 cm) opening at top. Holding dumpling between thumb and index finger, squeeze lightly to form "waist"; tap on counter to flatten bottom. Place 1 pea in centre of top opening of each. Repeat with remaining ingredients. (MAKE-AHEAD: **Transfer to cornstarch-dusted rimmed baking sheet; cover with damp towel and refrigerate for up to 6 hours. Or freeze on baking sheet until firm. Layer between waxed paper in airtight container and freeze for up to 2 weeks.**)

4 In wok or steamer, bring water to boil. Line 2 steamer trays with spinach leaves or waxed paper. Arrange sui mai, without touching, in single layer on spinach. Arrange stacked steamer trays over wok; cover and steam for 5 minutes. Reverse trays and steam until sui mai are firm and pink in centre, about 5 minutes. Repeat steaming for any remaining sui mai. Serve on spinach-lined platter.

Makes 46 pieces. PER PIECE: about 42 cal, 3 g pro, 1 g total fat (trace sat. fat), 5 g carb, trace fibre, 14 mg chol, 132 mg sodium. % RDI: 1% calcium, 4% iron, 1% vit A, 4% folate.

1 lb	medium shrimp	500 g
2 oz	ground pork	60 g
1	egg white	1
1 tbsp	Chinese cooking wine or sherry	15 mL
1 tbsp	sesame oil	15 mL
2 tsp	grated gingerroot	10 mL
1 tsp	salt	5 mL
½ tsp	white pepper	2 mL
1	pkg (7 oz/200 g) frozen crabmeat, thawed	1
½ cup	drained canned water chestnuts, finely diced	125 mL
¼ cup	chopped fresh coriander	50 mL
2	green onions, minced	2
46	very thin square wonton wrappers	46
46	fresh or frozen peas	46
	Large spinach leaves	

Falafels

Tahini – a light ivory-colour pure sesame paste – gives these crisp chickpea balls authentic Middle Eastern flavour. – Daphna

¼ cup	bulgur	50 mL
1	can (19 oz/540 mL) chickpeas, drained and rinsed	1
2	cloves garlic, minced	2
2	green onions, minced	2
2 tbsp	dry bread crumbs	25 mL
2 tbsp	chopped fresh parsley	25 mL
1	egg	1
1 tbsp	lemon juice	15 mL
1 tsp	ground cumin	5 mL
½ tsp	each ground coriander and salt	2 mL
¼ tsp	pepper	1 mL
¼ tsp	hot pepper sauce	1 mL
	Vegetable oil for deep-frying	
6	pita breads, warmed	6
	Tahini Sauce (recipe, page 119)	
TOPPINGS (OPTIONAL):		
	Dill pickles, chopped cabbage or lettuce, and chopped tomatoes	

1 Soak bulgur in 2 cups (500 mL) hot water for 20 minutes. Drain in sieve, pressing out excess moisture.

2 In food processor, combine bulgur and chickpeas; pulse until chickpeas are finely mashed but not puréed. Transfer to bowl; stir in garlic, onions, bread crumbs, parsley, egg, lemon juice, cumin, coriander, salt, pepper and hot pepper sauce.

3 In deep-fryer, deep pot or wok, heat oil to 350°F (180°C). Scoop mixture by level tablespoonfuls (15 mL) and form each into 1-inch (2.5 cm) ball. Fry, a few at a time, until browned, about 4 minutes. Transfer to paper towel–lined racks to drain.

4 Divide equally among pita breads. Top with Tahini Sauce and desired toppings.

Makes 6 servings. PER SERVING: about 509 cal, 15 g pro, 24 g total fat (3 g sat. fat), 61 g carb, 7 g fibre, 31 mg chol, 832 mg sodium. % RDI: 11% calcium, 33% iron, 3% vit A, 17% vit C, 60% folate.

> " Falafels represent what great street food is all about: messy, unpretentious, fun to personalize with condiments and wonderfully tasty. – *Daphna* "

Tahini Sauce

1 Stir ¼ cup (50 mL) water into lemon juice. Gradually stir enough of the lemon mixture into tahini to make very smooth, adding more if necessary (at first mixture will be stiff, then will thin out).

2 Stir in garlic, parsley and salt. Cover and refrigerate until chilled, about 1 hour. (**MAKE-AHEAD: Refrigerate for up to 4 hours.**) Let come to room temperature and stir before serving.

Makes about 1 cup (250 mL). PER 2 TBSP (25 mL): about 87 cal, 3 g pro, 8 g total fat (1 g sat. fat), 3 g carb, 1 g fibre, 0 mg chol, 74 mg sodium. % RDI: 2% calcium, 7% iron, 1% vit A, 5% vit C, 7% folate.

¼ cup	lemon juice	50 mL
½ cup	tahini	125 mL
1	clove garlic, finely minced	1
2 tbsp	chopped fresh Italian parsley	25 mL
¼ tsp	salt	1 mL

fridge NOTE

- **Look for tahini in Middle Eastern or Jewish grocery stores. Once opened, it must be stored in the refrigerator.**

Potato Gnocchi

There's nothing more comforting than freshly made dumplings, and every culture has its own delicious version. Here's my family's favourite. – Emily

6	Yukon Gold potatoes (unpeeled), 2½ lb (1.25 kg)	6
1	egg yolk	1
1 tbsp	salt	15 mL
2⅓ cups	all-purpose flour (approx)	575 mL
¼ cup	grated Parmesan cheese	50 mL
SAGE BUTTER SAUCE:		
10	fresh sage leaves	10
½ cup	butter	125 mL
¼ tsp	pepper	1 mL

fridge NOTE

- I use a fork or a special Italian basket my grandmother gave me for scoring gnocchi. You can leave them unscored if you find it easier.

1 In large saucepan of boiling water, cover and cook potatoes until tender, about 30 minutes. Drain and let cool until easy to handle, about 10 minutes. Peel and place in large bowl; refrigerate until cold, about 30 minutes.

2 Through medium disc of food mill or ricer, press potatoes into bowl to make 8 cups (2 L) unpacked. Mix in egg yolk and 1 tsp (5 mL) of the salt. Using wooden spoon, stir in 2 cups (500 mL) of the flour. Turn out onto unfloured surface. Knead to form soft, slightly sticky, spongy dough. Divide into 8 pieces. Roll each piece into 20-inch (50 cm) rope about ¾ inch (2 cm) thick. Cut each rope into ½-inch (1 cm) lengths. On work surface, toss with ¼ cup (50 mL) more flour.

3 Dip fork into remaining flour. Hold fork with tines facing down; with fingertips of other hand, lightly roll each piece down tines of fork to create ridges. Place gnocchi on floured baking sheet. (MAKE-AHEAD: **Freeze until firm, about 2 hours. Using metal spatula, transfer to freezer bags and freeze for up to 2 weeks.**)

4 Bring large pot of water to boil; add remaining salt. Cook half of the gnocchi, stirring gently, until tender and they float to surface, about 3 minutes. Using slotted spoon, transfer to warmed bowl. Repeat with remaining gnocchi.

5 SAGE BUTTER SAUCE: Meanwhile, chop 4 of the sage leaves. In large skillet, heat butter over medium heat; cook chopped and whole sage leaves and pepper until fragrant, about 1 minute. Pour over gnocchi; toss to coat. Sprinkle with Parmesan cheese.

Makes 4 to 6 servings. PER EACH OF 6 SERVINGS: about 467 cal, 10 g pro, 18 g total fat (11 g sat. fat), 66 g carb, 4 g fibre, 81 mg chol, 952 mg sodium. % RDI: 8% calcium, 19% iron, 32% folate, 17% vit A, 32% vit C.

Hot and Spicy Noodle Salad

I like to serve this salad on individually composed plates. It's such a feast for the eyes as well as the taste buds. – Daphna

1 SPICY PEANUT DRESSING: In bowl, whisk together peanut butter, stock, soy sauce, sesame oil, hot chili paste, sugar, ginger, black vinegar, garlic and rice wine vinegar. (MAKE-AHEAD: **Refrigerate in airtight container for up to 1 week.**)

2 Pull off and discard roots from bean sprouts. In large pot of boiling salted water, immerse carrots for 30 seconds. Transfer to colander; chill under cold water. Drain; shake off excess water. Set aside on towel-lined tray. Repeat with sprouts, blanching for 5 seconds.

3 In same pot of boiling water, cook noodles until tender but firm, about 8 minutes. Drain and rinse under cold water; shake off as much moisture as possible. Place on large platter; drizzle with sesame oil. Pour half of the peanut dressing over noodles; toss lightly. Top with bean sprouts. Cover and set aside.

4 Beat eggs lightly. Place 8- or 9-inch (20 or 23 cm) nonstick skillet over medium heat; brush lightly with some of the vegetable oil. Pour scant ¼ cup (50 mL) of the eggs into pan; fry until firm but not coloured on bottom, about 1 minute. Turn and fry, without stirring, until set, about 20 seconds. Lift out onto cutting board. Repeat with remaining eggs and oil to make 3 more omelettes. Let cool enough to handle; roll up and cut crosswise into ¼-inch (5 mm) thick slices. Sprinkle over sprouts along with carrot, sweet peppers and onions. (MAKE-AHEAD: **Cover and refrigerate for up to 2 hours.**)

5 Drizzle remaining dressing over salad; garnish with coriander. Toss just before serving.

Makes 4 servings. PER SERVING: about 742 cal, 28 g pro, 34 g total fat (6 g sat. fat), 87 g carb, 8 g fibre, 93 mg chol, 807 mg sodium. % RDI: 9% calcium, 38% iron, 57% vit A, 105% vit C, 120% folate.

5 cups	bean sprouts (12 oz/375 g)	1.25 L
1	carrot, julienned	1
12 oz	long flat pasta noodles (such as linguine or tagliatelle)	375 g
1 tbsp	sesame oil	15 mL
2	eggs	2
1 tsp	vegetable oil	5 mL
Half	each sweet red and yellow pepper, julienned	Half
3	green onions, thinly sliced	3
¼ cup	finely shredded fresh coriander	50 mL
SPICY PEANUT DRESSING:		
½ cup	chunky peanut butter	125 mL
½ cup	chicken or vegetable stock	125 mL
3 tbsp	each light soy sauce and sesame oil	50 mL
2 tbsp	hot chili paste or oil (or hot pepper sauce)	25 mL
1 tbsp	granulated sugar	15 mL
1 tbsp	minced gingerroot	15 mL
1 tbsp	Chinese black vinegar or Worcestershire sauce	15 mL
2	large cloves garlic, minced	2
2 tsp	rice wine vinegar	10 mL

Caldeirada

I dedicate this classic Portuguese fish stew to our two Portuguese angels at the magazine: Olga Goncalves and Teresa Sousa. – Emily

1 cup	extra-virgin olive oil	250 mL
2	onions, sliced	2
5	cloves garlic, minced	5
1	sweet green pepper, chopped	1
1	hot finger pepper, sliced	1
½ tsp	salt	2 mL
Pinch	each nutmeg and pepper	Pinch
1 lb	turbot or halibut fillets	500 g
1 lb	monkfish fillets	500 g
1½ lb	potatoes (about 3), peeled and thinly sliced	750 g
1½ lb	tomatoes, sliced	750 g
2 lb	littleneck clams, scrubbed	1 kg
⅓ cup	chopped fresh Italian parsley	75 mL
1 cup	dry white wine	250 mL
2	bay leaves	2

1 In large pot, heat 2 tbsp (25 mL) of the oil over medium heat. Add onions, garlic, green and hot peppers, salt, nutmeg and pepper; cook, stirring occasionally, until onions start to brown, about 8 minutes.

2 Meanwhile, cut turbot and monkfish fillets into 2-inch (5 cm) chunks; set aside. Layer half each of the potatoes and tomatoes over onion mixture. Top with fish and clams. Layer with remaining potatoes and tomatoes. Sprinkle with ¼ cup (50 mL) of the parsley. Pour in remaining oil, wine and bay leaves.

3 Cover and simmer for 20 minutes. Using spatula, gently push mixture down into liquid, adjusting heat as necessary to maintain simmer. Cook, covered, until potatoes are tender, about 20 minutes. Discard bay leaves and any clams that do not open. Sprinkle with remaining parsley.

Makes 6 to 8 servings. PER EACH OF 8 SERVINGS: about 451 cal, 25 g pro, 30 g total fat (4 g sat. fat), 21 g carb, 3 g fibre, 38 mg chol, 242 mg sodium. % RDI: 6% calcium, 29% iron, 16% vit A, 60% vit C, 14% folate.

Steamed Fish with Shiitake Mushrooms

Dried shiitakes taste even better than fresh in this dish. Reconstitute them in warm water and save the soaking liquid for a soup. – Elizabeth

1 Scatter cabbage in shallow serving dish or pasta bowl large enough to fit in steamer. Cut fish into serving-size pieces. Add fish; top with mushrooms, onions, ginger, salt and pepper. Cover and steam over high heat until fish flakes easily when tested, 16 to 18 minutes. Transfer to warmed serving platter.

2 Pour liquid from dish into saucepan; bring to boil over medium heat. In small bowl, blend soy sauce, cornstarch and 1 tbsp (15 mL) water; add to pan and return to boil. Stir in sesame oil; pour over fish. Garnish with coriander.

Makes 4 servings. PER SERVING: about 149 cal, 25 g pro, 3 g total fat (trace sat. fat), 4 g carb, 1 g fibre, 36 mg chol, 552 mg sodium. % RDI: 7% calcium, 11% iron, 8% vit A, 15% vit C, 17% folate.

1½ cups	shredded napa cabbage	375 mL
1 lb	halibut or salmon fillet	500 g
1 cup	finely sliced shiitake mushroom caps	250 mL
¼ cup	thinly sliced green onions	50 mL
1 tbsp	julienned gingerroot	15 mL
¼ tsp	salt	1 mL
Pinch	white pepper	Pinch
4 tsp	soy sauce	20 mL
1½ tsp	cornstarch	7 mL
½ tsp	sesame oil	2 mL
	Coriander sprigs	

Portuguese African Chicken

Africa adds the peanuts and coconut milk, and the New World provides the hot peppers and tomato to this irresistible dish. – Emily

4 lb	chicken pieces	2 kg
¾ tsp	each salt and pepper	4 mL
¼ cup	vegetable oil	50 mL
1	onion, chopped	1
4	cloves garlic, chopped	4
2 tbsp	minced hot red or jalapeño pepper	25 mL
3 tbsp	tomato paste	50 mL
2 tbsp	paprika	25 mL
½ tsp	ground ginger	2 mL
1 cup	coconut milk	250 mL
3 tbsp	peanut butter	50 mL
¼ cup	chopped fresh coriander or parsley	50 mL

1 Season chicken with ¼ tsp (1 mL) each of the salt and pepper; set aside.

2 In large skillet, heat half of the oil over medium-high heat; sauté onion, garlic and hot pepper, stirring occasionally, until softened, about 4 minutes.

3 Stir in tomato paste, paprika, 2 tbsp (25 mL) water, ginger and remaining salt and pepper; cook, stirring, for 1 minute. Stir in coconut milk and peanut butter; let cool slightly. Transfer to food processor and purée until smooth; set aside.

4 Wipe out skillet. Add remaining oil and heat over medium-high heat; brown chicken in batches. Transfer to roasting pan; cover with 1 cup (250 mL) of the sauce. Roast in 425°F (220°C) oven, basting twice, for 30 minutes.

5 Mix remaining sauce with coriander and pour over chicken; cook until juices run clear when chicken is pierced, about 12 minutes.

Makes 6 to 8 servings. PER EACH OF 8 SERVINGS: about 514 cal, 41 g pro, 36 g total fat (12 g sat. fat), 6 g carb, 1 g fibre, 149 mg chol, 399 mg sodium. % RDI: 4% calcium, 25% iron, 19% vit A, 15% vit C, 8% folate.

Chicken Saltimbocca

Nothing could be more impressive for company than these sautéed chicken breasts. Fresh sage and prosciutto add a touch of glamour. – Elizabeth

1 Between waxed paper, pound chicken to ¼-inch (5 mm) thickness. Sprinkle with pepper. Place 4 sage leaves on 1 side of each breast. Cover each breast with slice of prosciutto; press to adhere.

2 In very large skillet, heat oil over medium-high heat. Place flour in shallow dish; dredge breasts lightly in flour; gently shake off excess. Add chicken to pan; fry, turning once, until no longer pink inside, about 3 minutes per side. Transfer to serving platter; tent with foil to keep warm.

3 Add chicken stock, wine and Marsala to pan; bring to boil, scraping up any brown bits from bottom of pan. Boil until reduced to ½ cup (125 mL), about 4 minutes. Pour sauce over chicken.

Makes 4 servings. PER SERVING: about 317 cal, 34 g pro, 14 g total fat (2 g sat. fat), 7 g carb, trace fibre, 85 mg chol, 355 mg sodium. % RDI: 2% calcium, 9% iron, 1% vit A, 2% vit C, 5% folate.

4	boneless skinless chicken breasts (1 lb/500 g total)	4
¼ tsp	pepper	1 mL
16	fresh sage leaves	16
4	large thin slices prosciutto	4
3 tbsp	extra-virgin olive oil	50 mL
¼ cup	all-purpose flour	50 mL
½ cup	chicken stock	125 mL
¼ cup	dry white wine	50 mL
¼ cup	Marsala or Port	50 mL

" Chicken is like a canvas on which every country creates a delicious work of art. – *Elizabeth* "

Chicken Braised with Chestnuts and Shiitake Mushrooms

Chinese New Year begins with a feast full of auspicious, symbolic ingredients, such as carrot slices for gold coins to welcome a prosperous year. – Emily

1 lb	fresh chestnuts	500 g
16	large dried shiitake mushrooms	16
1	chicken (about 3 lb/1.5 kg)	1
3	green onions	3
1	piece (1½ inches/4 cm long) gingerroot	1
2 tbsp	vegetable oil	25 mL
2	carrots, sliced	2
¼ cup	soy sauce	50 mL
2 tbsp	granulated sugar	25 mL
2 tbsp	Chinese rice wine, sake (Japanese wine) or dry sherry	25 mL
½ tsp	Szechuan or black pepper	2 mL
¼ tsp	white pepper	1 mL
1 lb	baby bok choy or Shanghai bok choy, halved lengthwise	500 g
¼ tsp	sesame oil	1 mL

1 Cut X in flat side of each chestnut. In small saucepan of boiling water, cook chestnuts, 4 at a time, until skins can easily be peeled off, about 2 minutes. Place peeled nuts in saucepan and cover with water; bring to boil and cook until tender, about 5 minutes. Drain and set aside.

2 In bowl, soak shiitake mushrooms in 1½ cups (375 mL) warm water until tender, about 30 minutes. Drain, reserving liquid; remove stems and discard.

3 Meanwhile, using kitchen scissors, remove backbone from chicken. Cut off wing tips. Cut in half along breastbone. Cut each half between thigh and breast. Cut each breast in half crosswise. Cut each leg between drumstick and thigh.

4 Cut white and light green parts of onions into 1-inch (2.5 cm) lengths; finely chop dark green parts and set aside. Thinly slice ginger and stack slices; cut into diamond shapes and set aside.

5 In large shallow Dutch oven or deep skillet, heat oil over medium-high heat; brown chicken in batches. Transfer to plate. Drain all but 1 tbsp (15 mL) fat from pan. Add onion lengths and ginger; stir-fry for 30 seconds. Add mushrooms and carrots; stir-fry for 1 minute. Stir in reserved mushroom liquid, soy sauce, sugar and wine; bring to boil. Return chicken and any accumulated juices to pan; reduce heat, cover and simmer for 30 minutes.

6 Add chestnuts, Szechuan pepper and white pepper; simmer, uncovered, over medium heat until juices run clear when chicken is pierced, about 10 minutes.

7 Meanwhile, in large pot of boiling salted water, blanch bok choy until tender, about 2 minutes. Drain and toss with sesame oil; arrange on serving platter and keep warm. Using slotted spoon, arrange chicken on platter; surround with carrots, mushrooms and chestnuts. Add reserved chopped green onions to sauce; pour over chicken.

Makes 4 to 6 servings. PER EACH OF 6 SERVINGS: about 481 cal, 30 g pro, 25 g total fat (6 g sat. fat), 34 g carb, 7 g fibre, 105 mg chol, 1,037 mg sodium. % RDI: 12% calcium, 29% iron, 86% vit A, 65% vit C, 36% folate.

fridge NOTES

- If you prefer a thicker sauce, add 1 to 2 tsp (5 to 10 mL) cornstarch mixed with 1 tbsp (15 mL) water after removing chicken and vegetables; cook for 30 seconds.

- Chinese greens make a tasty and healthy side dish for many meals. Try blanching and sautéing napa and celery cabbage, bok choy (like the baby bok choy and Shang Hai varieties) and Chinese broccoli (also know as *gai lan* or *choy sam*).

Lamb Tagine with Artichokes and Mint

In Morocco, tagines, or stews, are cooked in a pottery dish called a tagine slaoui. *Its conical lid captures the moisture.* – Emily

3 lb	boneless lamb shoulder or leg roast	1.5 kg
2 tbsp	extra-virgin olive oil	25 mL
2	onions, sliced	2
1	carrot, diced	1
4	cloves garlic, minced	4
2 tsp	crumbled dried mint	10 mL
1 tsp	ground cumin	5 mL
¼ cup	dry white wine	50 mL
1½ cups	chicken stock	375 mL
1	bay leaf	1
½ tsp	salt	2 mL
¼ tsp	pepper	1 mL
1	can (19 oz/540 mL) chickpeas, drained and rinsed	1
1	can (14 oz/398 mL) artichokes, drained and quartered	1
¼ cup	raisins	50 mL
1 tsp	grated lemon rind	5 mL
1 tbsp	lemon juice	15 mL
¼ cup	pine nuts	50 mL

1 Trim lamb and cut into 1-inch (2.5 cm) cubes. In large Dutch oven, heat oil over medium-high heat; brown lamb in batches. Transfer to plate.

2 Drain any fat from pan and reduce heat to medium; cook onions, garlic, carrot, mint and cumin, stirring occasionally, until onions are softened, about 5 minutes. Add wine; cook, stirring, for 1 minute. Add chicken stock, bay leaf, salt and pepper.

3 Return lamb and any accumulated juices to pan; bring to boil. Cover and simmer over medium-low heat, or cover and cook in 350°F (180°C) oven, for 1 hour. Stir in chickpeas, artichokes, raisins, and lemon rind and juice; cover and cook until thickened and lamb is tender, about 30 minutes. Discard bay leaf.

4 Meanwhile, in small skillet, toast pine nuts over medium heat, shaking often, until golden, about 3 minutes; sprinkle over tagine.

Makes 6 to 8 servings. PER EACH OF 8 SERVINGS: about 369 cal, 30 g pro, 18 g total fat (4 g sat. fat), 24 g carb, 5 g fibre, 75 mg chol, 580 mg sodium. % RDI: 6% calcium, 27% iron, 24% vit A, 13% vit C, 30% folate.

Panforte

This was a big hit with viewers and readers. Many people told me how much this recipe reminded them of panforte they enjoyed in Tuscany. – Emily

1 Grease 8½-inch (2.25 L) springform pan. Line bottom and side with parchment paper; grease paper. Set aside.

2 Spread hazelnuts and almonds on rimmed baking sheet, keeping types separate; toast in 350°F (180°C) oven until fragrant and lightly browned, 8 to 10 minutes. Transfer hazelnuts to tea towel; rub off as much of the skins as possible. Let cool.

3 Coarsely chop nuts; place in large bowl. Add candied peel, candied citron, flour, orange and lemon rinds, cinnamon, pepper, nutmeg, coriander and cloves; stir to combine. Set aside.

4 In small heavy saucepan, stir sugar with honey; bring to boil over medium heat. Boil until at hard-ball stage of 265°F (129°C) or until ½ tsp (2 mL) syrup dropped into cold water forms hard but pliable ball, about 3 minutes. Quickly stir honey mixture into nut mixture, mixing well. Immediately scrape into prepared pan, spreading evenly with spatula.

5 Bake in 325°F (160°C) oven until slightly raised, golden brown and edge is firm, about 45 minutes. (Panforte will still be soft in centre.) Let cool in pan on rack until centre is firm to the touch, about 45 minutes.

6 Remove side of pan; invert onto second rack. Remove pan base; peel off paper. Invert panforte back onto first rack; let cool completely. Wrap in foil; let stand for 24 hours. (MAKE-AHEAD: **Store wrapped in foil in airtight container for up to 2 weeks.**)

Makes 20 servings. PER SERVING: about 205 cal, 3 g pro, 8 g total fat (1 g sat. fat), 33 g carb, 2 g fibre, 0 mg chol, 26 mg sodium. % RDI: 3% calcium, 6% iron, 2% vit C, 6% folate.

1 cup	hazelnuts	250 mL
1 cup	whole blanched almonds	250 mL
¾ cup	chopped candied mixed peel	175 mL
¾ cup	chopped candied citron	175 mL
½ cup	all-purpose flour	125 mL
1 tsp	each grated orange and lemon rind	5 mL
¾ tsp	each cinnamon and white pepper	4 mL
¼ tsp	each nutmeg and ground coriander	1 mL
Pinch	ground cloves	Pinch
⅔ cup	granulated sugar	150 mL
⅔ cup	liquid honey	150 mL

fridge **NOTE**

- **Be sure to wrap the panforte in foil; wrapping it in plastic wrap will cause it to soften.**

Traditional Mexican Flan

Flan remains one of the most enduringly popular desserts in Mexico, Latin American and Spain. Its French cousin is crème caramel. – Daphna

½ cup	granulated sugar	125 mL
CUSTARD:		
4 cups	milk	1 L
1	vanilla bean	1
½ cup	granulated sugar	125 mL
Pinch	salt	Pinch
4	eggs	4
6	egg yolks	6
1 tbsp	finely grated orange rind	15 mL
1 tbsp	finely grated lime rind	15 mL

fridge NOTE

- You can omit the vanilla bean and replace it with 2 tsp (10 mL) vanilla; whisk it into the milk and egg mixture just before pouring into the mould.

1 In deep heavy saucepan, stir sugar with 2 tbsp (25 mL) water over medium heat until dissolved, brushing down side of pan with pastry brush dipped in cold water. Bring to boil over medium-high heat; boil vigorously until dark amber, about 8 minutes. Immediately pour into flan mould or 4-cup (1 L) oval baking dish.

2 CUSTARD: In separate heavy saucepan, heat milk until tiny bubbles form around edge.

3 Meanwhile, using small knife, split vanilla bean in half lengthwise; scrape out seeds. Add seeds and pod to milk along with sugar and salt; simmer until reduced to 3½ cups (875 mL), about 15 minutes.

4 In bowl, combine eggs, egg yolks and orange and lime rinds. Pour milk mixture through cheesecloth-lined sieve into egg mixture, whisking to combine. Pour into caramel-coated mould.

5 Place mould in larger roasting pan; pour in enough hot water to come halfway up side of mould. Bake in centre of 350°F (180°C) oven until firm and knife inserted in centre comes out clean, about 1 hour. Transfer roasting pan to rack; let cool on rack until at room temperature. Remove mould from water and let cool completely. (MAKE-AHEAD: **Cover and refrigerate for up to 2 days. Place mould in warm water for 5 minutes before turning out.**)

6 Run knife around edge of mould; invert onto serving platter.

Makes 8 servings. PER SERVING: about 240 cal, 9 g pro, 9 g total fat (3 g sat. fat), 31 g carb, trace fibre, 255 mg chol, 97 mg sodium. % RDI: 16% calcium, 6% iron, 17% vit A, 3% vit C, 17% folate.

Spiced Coffee Granita

The whole point of a granita, unlike ice cream or sorbet, is the slightly granular texture you get by stirring it frequently as it freezes. – Daphna

1 In saucepan, combine sugar, lemon rind, star anise, cloves, cinnamon stick and ½ cup (125 mL) water; bring to boil, stirring to dissolve sugar. Remove from heat; pour in coffee. Let stand for 10 minutes. Strain through fine sieve into bowl; refrigerate until chilled completely.

2 Stir in liqueur. Pour into metal cake pan. Freeze for 1 hour. Stir with fork; repeat every 30 minutes until mixture forms small, even crystals, 3 to 4 hours. Serve immediately.

Makes 6 servings. PER SERVING: about 106 cal, 0 g pro, 0 g total fat (0 g sat. fat), 25 g carb, 0 g fibre, 0 mg chol, 2 mg sodium. % RDI: 1% iron.

⅔ cup	granulated sugar	150 mL
1	long strip lemon rind	1
1	star anise	1
4	whole cloves	4
1	cinnamon stick	1
2 cups	cold strong brewed coffee	500 mL
2 tbsp	coffee liqueur	25 mL

❝ Coffee is a such a global favourite that it runs the gastronomic gamut from sweet to savoury, flavouring everything from this granita to ribs to cakes. *– Daphna* **❞**

Kitchen Get-Togethers

*W*here do all the good parties end up?
In the kitchen. In my house, that's
where they start, too, with people congregat-
ing around the island. The fridge is handy
for refills, and there's a spot on the counter for
a helpful guest to whisk the salad dressing.
Being in the kitchen encourages no-fuss
entertaining, but that doesn't rule out a wee
bit of showmanship. After all, cooking is
part performance art, part practical, but
most of all a gesture of sharing. The dishes
we have chosen for our kitchen get-togethers
bear witness to our cooking: nothing is
complicated yet guests will revel in the lively
flavours, appealing colours and range of
textures when everyone sits down for the
best part: the eating. – Elizabeth

- Sirloin and Gorgonzola Pasta
- Clams and Pasta in White Wine Sauce
- Mussels and Sausage Simmer
- Seafood Risotto
- Beet Risotto with Rapini
- Chicken Gumbo
- Ginger Apricot Chicken
- Braised Chicken Breasts with Exotic and Wild Mushrooms
- Eggplant "Sandwiches"
- Free-Form Open-Faced Potato Tart

Sirloin and Gorgonzola Pasta

Emily created this recipe to combine three of her favourite ingredients: steak, pasta and gorgonzola. It's bliss in a dish! – Elizabeth

1 tbsp	vegetable oil	15 mL
8 oz	top sirloin grilling steak	250 g
2	onions, sliced	2
2 cups	sliced mushrooms (about 8 oz/250 g)	500 mL
2 tbsp	all-purpose flour	25 mL
½ tsp	salt	2 mL
¼ tsp	pepper	1 mL
1½ cups	milk	375 mL
5 cups	rigatoni pasta (12 oz/375 g)	1.25 L
3 oz	Gorgonzola or blue cheese, crumbled	90 g
1	plum tomato, seeded and chopped	1
Half	sweet yellow pepper, diced	Half
1	green onion, sliced (or about 8 chives, chopped)	1

1 In large nonstick skillet, heat oil over medium-high heat; fry steak, turning once, until browned outside and medium-rare inside, 8 to 10 minutes. Transfer to cutting board; cut across the grain into thin strips. Cover and keep warm.

2 Add onions and mushrooms to pan; cook, stirring often, until no liquid remains, about 8 minutes. Sprinkle with flour, salt and pepper; cook, stirring, for 1 minute.

3 Whisk milk into pan; bring to boil. Reduce heat and simmer, stirring often, until thick enough to coat back of spoon, about 5 minutes.

4 Meanwhile, in large pot of boiling salted water, cook pasta until tender but firm, 6 to 8 minutes. Drain and return to pot. Add sauce and cheese; toss to coat. Transfer to serving bowl. Top with reserved steak; sprinkle with tomato, yellow pepper and green onion. Toss to serve.

Makes 4 servings. PER SERVING: about 569 cal, 31 g pro, 16 g total fat (7 g sat. fat), 74 g carb, 5 g fibre, 55 mg chol, 938 mg sodium. % RDI: 26% calcium, 29% iron, 13% vit A, 57% vit C, 67% folate.

Clams and Pasta in White Wine Sauce

The name for these bivalves comes from the verb clam – *"to shut." They should be shut tight. Discard any that don't close after tapping.* – Daphna

1 In large deep heavy skillet, melt butter over medium-high heat. Add pancetta; stir-fry until starting to turn golden, about 5 minutes. Remove from pan; drain off all but 1 tbsp (15 mL) of the fat.

2 Add garlic, 2 tbsp (25 mL) of the parsley and hot pepper flakes; stir-fry for 1 minute. Pour in clam juice and wine; bring to boil. Add clams; cover and steam until clams open, about 5 minutes. Discard any that have not opened.

3 Meanwhile, in large pot of boiling salted water, cook pasta until tender but firm, 8 to 10 minutes. Drain and add to pan along with pancetta; toss to coat well. Serve sprinkled with remaining parsley.

Makes 4 servings. PER SERVING: about 461 cal, 17 g pro, 12 g total fat (5 g sat. fat), 66 g carb, 4 g fibre, 37 mg chol, 435 mg sodium. % RDI: 5% calcium, 51% iron, 11% vit A, 18% vit C, 59% folate.

2 tbsp	butter	25 mL
2 oz	thinly sliced pancetta or prosciutto, cut in thin strips	60 g
3	cloves garlic, minced	3
⅓ cup	chopped fresh parsley	75 mL
¼ tsp	hot pepper flakes	1 mL
½ cup	bottled clam juice	125 mL
½ cup	dry white wine	125 mL
2 lb	littleneck or manilla clams	1 kg
12 oz	linguine or fettuccine	375 g

> **"** My mother made this dish for special family dinners. It was my introduction to the divine pairing of clams and pasta. – *Daphna* **"**

fridge NOTE

- **For tasty seafood pasta when you don't have fresh clams, combine a jarred sun-dried tomato sauce with drained canned clams and toss with long, thin cooked pasta.**

Producer Holly Gillanders organizes the recipe segments on the storyboard

Mussels and Sausage Simmer

Nothing says hospitality like this robust entertaining dish. Serve with the proverbial salad and crusty bread. – Elizabeth

1 tbsp	extra-virgin olive oil	15 mL
2½ lb	mild Italian sausage, cut in chunks	1.25 kg
2	red onions, chopped	2
4	cloves garlic, minced	4
1 tbsp	paprika	15 mL
¼ tsp	hot pepper flakes	1 mL
1 cup	tomato juice	250 mL
¾ cup	dry red wine	175 mL
2½ lb	mussels	1.25 kg
¼ cup	sliced green onions	50 mL

1 In Dutch oven, heat oil over medium-high heat; brown sausage in batches. Transfer to plate.

2 Drain fat from pan. Add red onions, garlic, paprika and hot pepper flakes; cook until softened, about 5 minutes. Pour in tomato juice and wine; bring to boil. Return sausage to pan; reduce heat, cover and simmer for 45 minutes.

3 Meanwhile, scrub mussels under cool water; trim off any beards. Discard any that do not close when tapped. Add mussels to pan; cover and steam until mussels open, about 12 minutes. Discard any that have not opened. Serve sprinkled with green onions.

Makes 8 servings. PER SERVING: about 478 cal, 27 g pro, 34 g total fat (11 g sat. fat), 14 g carb, 2 g fibre, 86 mg chol, 1,174 mg sodium. % RDI: 6% calcium, 29% iron, 9% vit A, 22% vit C, 18% folate.

Seafood Risotto

Risotto refers to the cooking method that gives this rice dish such creaminess.
Risottos are so luscious – like Italy's answer to mashed potatoes. – Emily

1 In saucepan, bring stock, 2 cups (500 mL) water and saffron just to simmer over medium heat; reduce heat to low and keep warm.

2 In large shallow saucepan, heat half of the oil over medium heat; cook onion and garlic, stirring occasionally, until softened, about 3 minutes. Stir in rice until well coated.

3 Stir in ½ cup (125 mL) of the warm stock mixture; simmer, stirring constantly, until all liquid is absorbed. Stir in wine; simmer, stirring, until wine is absorbed. Continue to add stock, ½ cup (125 mL) at a time and stirring after each addition until completely absorbed, until rice is almost tender, about 15 minutes.

4 Meanwhile, scrub mussels; discard any that do not close when tapped. Cut squid into ½-inch (1 cm) rings. Add squid, mussels and shrimp to rice; cover and steam until mussels are open and shrimp are pink, about 7 minutes. Discard any mussels that have not opened. Uncover and stir in parsley. Serve sprinkled with pepper and drizzled with remaining oil.

Makes 6 servings. PER SERVING: about 429 cal, 29 g pro, 12 g total fat (2 g sat. fat), 45 g carb, 1 g fibre, 248 mg chol, 344 mg sodium. % RDI: 6% calcium, 21% iron, 4% vit A, 13% vit C, 19% folate.

3 cups	fish or chicken stock	750 mL
¼ tsp	saffron threads, crumbled	1 mL
¼ cup	extra-virgin olive oil (approx)	50 mL
1	onion, chopped	1
2	cloves garlic, minced	2
1½ cups	arborio rice	375 mL
¾ cup	dry white wine	175 mL
1 lb	mussels	500 g
1 lb	squid, cleaned	500 g
12 oz	large shrimp, peeled and deveined	375 g
2 tbsp	chopped fresh Italian parsley	25 mL
	Pepper	

Beet Risotto with Rapini

Bravo for beets! They may not be the prettiest vegetable in the garden, but here they tint risotto a stunning ruby red. – Emily

1 tbsp	extra-virgin olive oil	15 mL
1	onion, chopped	1
2	cloves garlic, minced	2
1½ cups	arborio rice or other short-grain Italian rice	375 mL
½ cup	white wine or chicken stock	125 mL
4	beets (1 lb/500 g), peeled and coarsely grated	4
3½ cups	hot chicken or vegetable stock	875 mL
2 cups	coarsely chopped rapini	500 mL
⅓ cup	grated Parmesan cheese	75 mL

1 In large saucepan, heat oil over medium heat; cook onion and garlic, stirring occasionally, until softened, about 5 minutes.

2 Add rice; cook, stirring, for 1 minute. Add wine; cook, stirring, until evaporated, about 2 minutes. Stir in beets and half of the stock; bring to boil. Reduce heat to medium-low, cover and simmer until rice is almost tender and most of the liquid is absorbed, about 10 minutes.

3 Stir in remaining stock and rapini; cook, covered, until rice and rapini are tender and most of the liquid is absorbed, about 12 minutes. Stir in Parmesan cheese.

Makes 4 servings. PER SERVING: about 439 cal, 16 g pro, 8 g total fat (3 g sat. fat), 73 g carb, 4 g fibre, 7 mg chol, 909 mg sodium. % RDI: 20% calcium, 16% iron, 10% vit A, 23% vit C, 38% folate.

" I grew up on rapini. My mom sautéed it in oil and made rapini sandwiches for me. All my schoolmates wondered what I was eating! – *Emily* **"**

Chicken Gumbo

For hearty, stewy chicken dishes like gumbo, choose thighs: they remain moist and pick up the heady creole flavours. – Elizabeth

1 Using kitchen scissors, trim off excess skin and fat from chicken thighs; place chicken in bowl. Sprinkle with cayenne pepper, salt and garlic; massage well to coat evenly. Cover and refrigerate for 30 minutes. (MAKE-AHEAD: **Refrigerate for up to 24 hours.**)

2 Pour flour into plastic bag; add chicken, a few pieces at a time, and shake to coat evenly. Reserve excess flour.

3 In large shallow Dutch oven, heat oil over medium-high heat; brown chicken, in batches if necessary. Transfer to platter.

4 Let pan cool slightly. Whisk reserved flour into cooled fat in pan to make smooth paste, scraping up any brown bits from bottom of pan. Cook over medium heat, stirring constantly, until roux is colour of melted dark chocolate and begins to smoke lightly, about 8 minutes.

5 Stir in onions, celery and green pepper; cook, stirring occasionally, until softened, about 8 minutes. Stir in stock. Return chicken to pan. Add sausage and bring to boil; reduce heat to medium-low, cover and simmer, turning chicken once, until juices run clear when chicken is pierced, about 30 minutes.

6 Meanwhile, trim okra. Blanch in boiling water until bright green, about 3 minutes. Drain and refresh under cold water; drain again. Add to gumbo; cook until okra is tender, about 8 minutes. Serve over rice.

Makes 6 servings. PER SERVING: about 985 cal, 53 g pro, 50 g total fat (11 g sat. fat), 77 g carb, 4 g fibre, 174 mg chol, 1,304 mg sodium. % RDI: 11% calcium, 35% iron, 8% vit A, 50% vit C, 36% folate.

4 lb	chicken thighs	2 kg
1 tsp	cayenne pepper	5 mL
½ tsp	salt	2 mL
4	large cloves garlic, minced	4
1 cup	all-purpose flour	250 mL
½ cup	vegetable oil	125 mL
2	large onions, chopped	2
1½ cups	thinly sliced celery	375 mL
1	large sweet green pepper, chopped	1
3 cups	chicken stock	750 mL
12 oz	andouille sausage	375 g
8 oz	fresh okra	250 g
2 cups	long-grain rice, cooked and hot	500 mL

fridge **NOTES**

- **You can replace the fresh okra with 1 pkg (250 g) frozen, omitting the blanching step.**

- **Try sausage with garlic and paprika if you can't find andouille sausage.**

Ginger Apricot Chicken

Ginger three ways: dried to season the chicken; fresh grated to blend with cardamom and cinnamon; and a shot of juice to freshen. – Elizabeth

1	air-chilled chicken (3½ lb/1.75 kg) or equivalent weight of thighs	1
1 tsp	each ground ginger and salt	5 mL
1½ cups	dried apricots	375 mL
1½ cups	boiling water	375 mL
1 tbsp	extra-virgin olive oil	15 mL
1 tbsp	butter	15 mL
1	large onion, finely chopped	1
1½ tsp	granulated sugar	7 mL
2 tbsp	finely grated gingerroot	25 mL
1	cinnamon stick, broken	1
8	green cardamom pods, lightly crushed	8
¼ tsp	each ground cloves and pepper	1 mL
1½ cups	finely chopped canned plum tomatoes	375 mL
⅔ cup	tomato juice	150 mL
⅓ cup	finely chopped fresh coriander	75 mL

1 Using kitchen scissors, cut along both sides of chicken backbone; cut off wing tips. Reserve for stock. Cut chicken in half along breastbone, then each side into 4 pieces: thigh, drumstick, and breast halved diagonally. Cut off wings if desired. Pull off skin, cutting drumsticks around joint to release skin easily; trim off excess fat. Place in bowl. Combine ground ginger and salt; sprinkle over chicken, rubbing well to coat evenly. Cover and refrigerate for 1 hour. (MAKE-AHEAD: **Refrigerate for up to 12 hours.**)

2 Meanwhile, in bowl, cover apricots with boiling water; let stand for 30 minutes.

3 In shallow Dutch oven or large deep skillet, heat oil over medium-high heat; brown chicken. Transfer to plate. Drain off any fat from pan; add butter and reduce heat to medium. Add onion, sugar, half of the grated ginger, the cinnamon, cardamom, cloves and pepper; cook, stirring often, until onion is golden, about 8 minutes.

4 Stir in tomatoes, tomato juice, apricots and soaking water; bring to boil over high heat, scraping up any brown bits from bottom of pan. Boil until tomatoes meld into liquid, about 5 minutes. Add all but 2 tbsp (25 mL) of the coriander. Return chicken to pan; reduce heat to medium-low, cover and simmer, turning chicken once, until juices run clear when chicken is pierced, about 20 minutes.

5 Place remaining ginger in fine sieve; press out juice. Sprinkle over chicken. Turn to distribute evenly. Arrange chicken and sauce on warmed platter; sprinkle with remaining coriander.

Makes 4 to 6 servings. PER EACH OF 6 SERVINGS: about 319 cal, 29 g pro, 11 g total fat (3 g sat. fat), 28 g carb, 4 g fibre, 96 mg chol, 683 mg sodium. % RDI: 5% calcium, 22% iron, 30% vit A, 25% vit C, 7% folate.

Braised Chicken Breasts with Exotic and Wild Mushrooms

This is a popular dish when the Test Kitchen entertains guests. Everyone enjoys the blend of mushrooms with oyster sauce and cream. – Daphna

1 In large skillet or shallow Dutch oven, heat half of the oil over medium heat; cook onion and garlic, stirring occasionally, until softened, about 3 minutes. Add mushrooms; cook, stirring often, until softened and slightly browned, about 5 minutes. Transfer to bowl.

2 Meanwhile, in shallow bowl, whisk together flour, oregano, herbes de Provence, salt and pepper; add chicken and turn to coat well. Set aside.

3 Add remaining oil to skillet and heat over medium-high heat; brown chicken. Drain off fat. Return mushroom mixture to pan.

4 In bowl, stir together stock, cream, oyster sauce and chili sauce; add to skillet and bring to boil. Reduce heat, cover and simmer until chicken is no longer pink inside, about 25 minutes. Transfer chicken to serving platter; tent with foil to keep warm.

5 Bring sauce to boil; boil until thick enough to coat back of spoon, about 5 minutes. Pour over chicken; sprinkle with chives and grated lemon rind.

Makes 6 servings. PER SERVING: about 346 cal, 36 g pro, 18 g total fat (6 g sat. fat), 10 g carb, 2 g fibre, 109 mg chol, 399 mg sodium. % RDI: 5% calcium, 14% iron, 8% vit A, 7% vit C, 13% folate.

⅓ cup	vegetable oil	75 mL
1	onion, chopped	1
3	cloves garlic, minced	3
1 lb	exotic mushrooms (shiitake caps, oyster, morel and chanterelle), trimmed	500 g
¼ cup	all-purpose flour	50 mL
2 tbsp	dried oregano	25 mL
1 tbsp	herbes de Provence	15 mL
¼ tsp	salt	1 mL
¼ tsp	pepper	1 mL
6	chicken breasts (3 lb/1.5 kg total)	6
1 cup	chicken stock	250 mL
½ cup	whipping cream	125 mL
1 tbsp	oyster sauce	15 mL
1 tsp	Asian chili sauce	5 mL
3 tbsp	chopped fresh chives	50 mL
1 tsp	grated lemon rind	5 mL

Eggplant "Sandwiches"

This attractive and easy side dish, or antipasto, is a Pusateri family trademark, available in their Toronto food emporium. – Emily

¾ cup	fresh bread crumbs	175 mL
½ cup	grated Parmesan cheese	125 mL
½ cup	finely chopped plum tomato	125 mL
¼ cup	extra-virgin olive oil	50 mL
2 tbsp	chopped fresh Italian parsley	25 mL
1	clove garlic, minced	1
½ tsp	salt	2 mL
¼ tsp	pepper	1 mL
12	slices (¼ inch/5 mm thick) 3-inch (8 cm) wide eggplant	12

1 In bowl, combine bread crumbs, Parmesan cheese, tomato, 2 tbsp (25 mL) of the oil, parsley, garlic, ¼ tsp (1 mL) of the salt and pepper; set aside.

2 Brush both sides of eggplant slices with remaining oil; sprinkle with remaining salt. Arrange half of the slices on rimmed baking sheet; top evenly with bread crumb mixture. Sandwich with remaining slices.

3 Bake in 450°F (230°C) oven, turning once, until browned, about 20 minutes.

Makes 6 servings. PER SERVING: about 151 cal, 5 g pro, 12 g total fat (3 g sat. fat), 8 g carb, 2 g fibre, 7 mg chol, 379 mg sodium. % RDI: 12% calcium, 5% iron, 4% vit A, 7% vit C, 7% folate.

" Guests will get a kick out of this casual, fun way to enjoy eggplant. It has a starring role as the 'bread' in this sandwich. – *Emily* **"**

Free-Form Open-Faced Potato Tart

I was born to make pies, and I especially enjoy rolling out this flaky pastry for a savoury tart. Serve for brunch and supper buffets. – Elizabeth

1 In bowl, whisk together flour, salt and cayenne; using pastry blender or 2 knives, cut in butter and shortening until mixture is in fine crumbs with a few larger pieces. Stirring with fork, pour in vinegar and enough of the water to make dough hold together. Press into ball; flatten into disc. Wrap in plastic wrap and refrigerate for 30 minutes.

2 FILLING: Meanwhile, line rimmed baking sheet with foil. Cut each tomato lengthwise into ½-inch (1 cm) thick slices; place on prepared pan. Sprinkle with pinch each of the salt and pepper; broil until slightly shrivelled and edges are blackened, 5 minutes per side. Set aside.

3 Meanwhile, in large saucepan of boiling salted water, cover and cook potatoes just until tender, about 20 minutes. Drain and let cool; slice thinly crosswise. Set aside.

4 Meanwhile, in skillet, heat oil over medium-high heat; sauté onions, garlic, rosemary and remaining salt and pepper, stirring occasionally, for 5 minutes. Reduce heat to medium; cook until onions are golden, about 5 minutes longer. Transfer to large bowl. Add potatoes, Asiago cheese and all but 1 tbsp (15 mL) of the eggs; toss gently to combine.

5 On lightly floured surface, roll out pastry into 16-inch (40 cm) circle; place on pizza pan. Spread potato mixture over pastry, leaving 2-inch (5 cm) border uncovered. Arrange tomatoes over filling; sprinkle with Parmesan cheese. Fold border over top, pleating to fit. Brush pastry with remaining egg. Bake in bottom third of 400°F (200°C) oven until pastry is golden, 40 to 45 minutes. Let stand on rack for 10 minutes before cutting.

Makes 6 servings. PER SERVING: about 542 cal, 14 g pro, 34 g total fat (16 g sat. fat), 46 g carb, 3 g fibre, 119 mg chol, 866 mg sodium. % RDI: 24% calcium, 17% iron, 24% vit A, 27% vit C, 28% folate.

1½ cups	all-purpose flour	375 mL
¼ tsp	salt	1 mL
Pinch	cayenne pepper	Pinch
⅓ cup	each cold butter and shortening	75 mL
1 tsp	vinegar	5 mL
¼ cup	cold water (approx)	50 mL
FILLING:		
6	plum tomatoes	6
1 tsp	salt	5 mL
½ tsp	pepper	2 mL
3	Yukon Gold potatoes (1¼ lb/625 g total), peeled	3
1 tbsp	extra-virgin olive oil	15 mL
2	onions, sliced	2
2	cloves garlic, minced	2
½ tsp	dried rosemary, crumbled, or crushed aniseed	2 mL
1½ cups	grated Asiago cheese	375 mL
2	eggs, beaten	2
1 tbsp	grated Parmesan cheese	15 mL

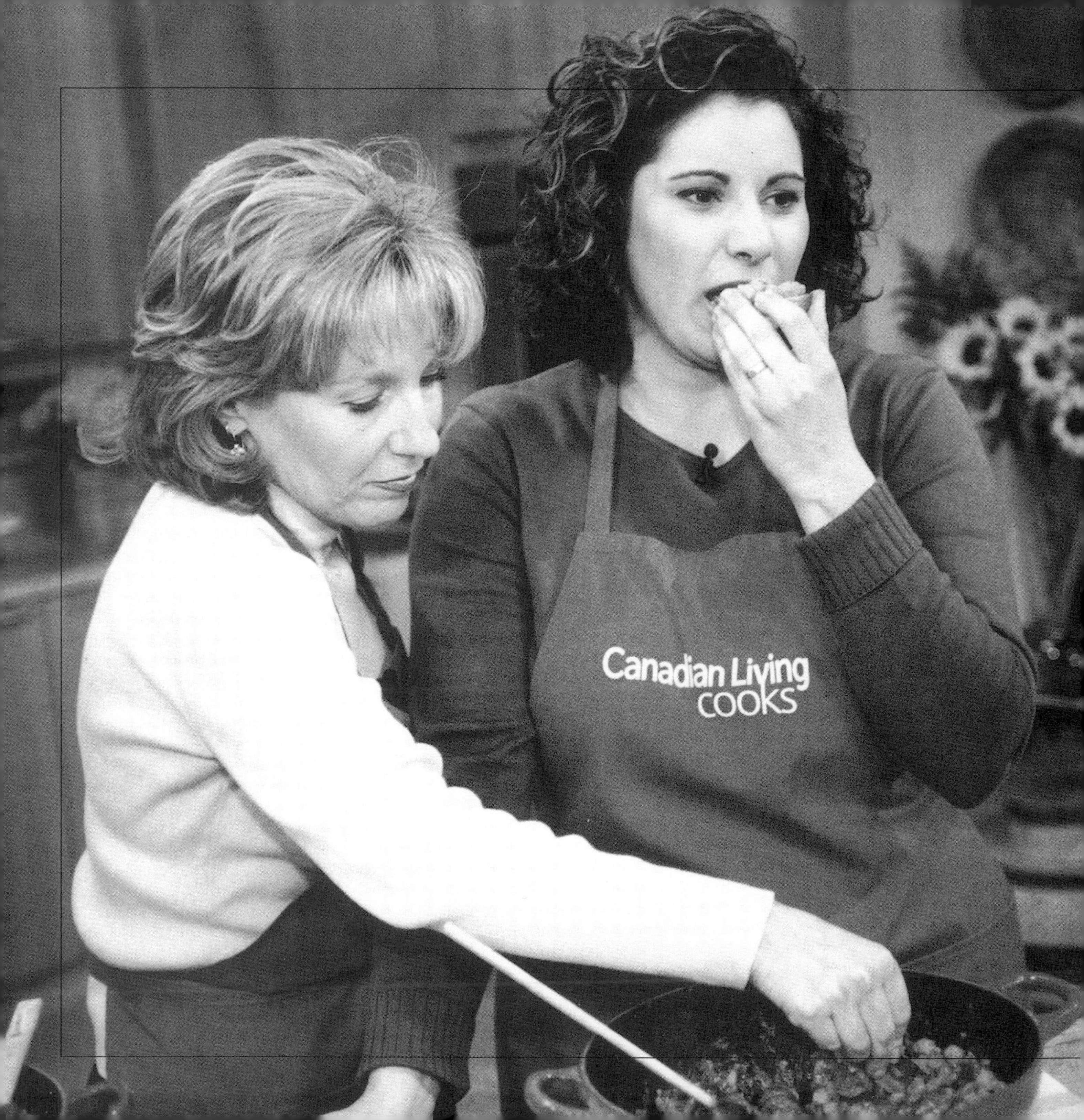
Canadian Living
COOKS

Coffee Break Treats

From classic peanut butter cookies to a stunning pear and anise loaf, nothing beats sharing treats with friends and family over a cup of coffee or tea. These recipes are so much fun to make, be sure to call the kids into the kitchen to help. The three of us feel like kids ourselves whenever we bake cookies to enjoy with a glass of cold milk. But these treats aren't just great with milk or coffee or tea. They're also perfect for contributing to bake sales and presenting as hostess gifts. The bonus is that most of them are freezer friendly, which comes in handy during those midnight snack attacks. Sneaking down to the freezer and popping a cold rugalah in my mouth makes everything all right. – Emily

- Brutti ma Buoni
- Peanut Butter Cookies
- Checkerboard Cookies
- Raspberry Pecan Rugalahs
- Irresistible Turtle Bars
- Chewy Double Ginger Bars
- Squirrelly Shortbread Bars
- Orange Cranberry White Chocolate Blondies
- Blueberry Cream Cheese Coffee Cake
- Orange Cardamom Mini-Loaves
- Dried Pear, Anise and Walnut Bread

Brutti ma Buoni

"Ugly but good" is the translation of the name of these Italian drop cookies, which are popular with my family and friends. – Emily

4	egg whites	4
1 cup	granulated sugar	250 mL
3 tbsp	all-purpose flour	50 mL
1 tsp	vanilla	5 mL
2 cups	coarsely chopped nougat milk chocolate bar (such as Toblerone)	500 mL
2 tbsp	icing sugar	25 mL

fridge NOTE

- **The Swiss meringue method – cooking the egg whites with sugar – gives Brutti ma Buoni their distinctively crisp exterior and chewy interior.**

1 Line 2 rimless baking sheets with parchment paper or foil; grease foil. Set aside.

2 In large heatproof bowl over saucepan of gently simmering water, cook egg whites with granulated sugar, whisking occasionally, until opaque, about 10 minutes. Remove from heat; beat until cool, thickened and glossy, about 7 minutes. Fold in flour and vanilla; fold in chopped chocolate bar. Drop by heaping tablespoonfuls (15 mL) onto prepared pans.

3 Bake in top and bottom thirds of 350°F (180°C) oven, rotating and switching pans halfway through, until light brown, 25 to 30 minutes. Let cool on pans on racks. Dust with icing sugar. (**MAKE-AHEAD: Store in airtight container at room temperature for up to 3 days.**)

Makes 24 cookies. PER COOKIE: about 110 cal, 1 g pro, 2 g total fat (1 g sat. fat), 22 g carb, trace fibre, 1 mg chol, 43 mg sodium. % RDI: 2% calcium, 1% iron, 1% folate.

VARIATION

Ginger Brutti ma Buoni: Substitute 1 tsp (5 mL) ground ginger for the vanilla and 1 cup (250 mL) chopped crystallized ginger for the chopped chocolate bar.

Peanut Butter Cookies

When test kitchen manager Heather Howe makes these at home, she always gets help from daughters Rebecca and Olivia. – Emily

1 Grease 2 rimless baking sheets or line with parchment paper; set aside.

2 In large bowl, beat butter until light and fluffy. Beat in brown and granulated sugars, then peanut butter.

3 Beat in eggs, 1 at a time, beating well after each addition. Beat in vanilla. In separate bowl, whisk together flour, baking soda, baking powder and salt. Using wooden spoon, stir into butter mixture in 2 additions until combined.

4 Shape by rounded tablespoonfuls (15 mL) into balls; place 2 inches (5 cm) apart on prepared pans. Dip fork into flour; press balls to make crisscross pattern and flatten to ½-inch (1 cm) thickness.

5 Bake, 1 sheet at a time, in centre of 350°F (180°C) oven until firm and bottoms are golden, 10 to 12 minutes. Let cool on pan on rack for 2 minutes. Transfer to racks and let cool completely.

Makes about 44 cookies. PER COOKIE: about 128 cal, 3 g pro, 7 g total fat (3 g sat. fat), 14 g carb, 1 g fibre, 21 mg chol, 119 mg sodium. % RDI: 1% calcium, 4% iron, 4% vit A, 6% folate.

1 cup	butter, softened	250 mL
¾ cup	each packed brown sugar and granulated sugar	175 mL
1 cup	peanut butter	250 mL
2	eggs	2
1 tsp	vanilla	5 mL
2½ cups	all-purpose flour	625 mL
1 tsp	each baking soda and baking powder	5 mL
¼ tsp	salt	1 mL

fridge NOTES

- Let the cookie sheet cool completely between batches so that the dough doesn't melt.

- For Thumb-Print Peanut Butter Cookies, press your thumb into the flattened balls of raw dough to make an indent; fill with jam or jelly and bake.

- Store cookies in an airtight container for up to five days or freeze for up to one month.

COFFEE BREAK TREATS

Checkerboard Cookies

These two-tone cookies look so impressive yet they're simple and fun to make with two doughs: vanilla and chocolate. – Emily

4 oz	unsweetened chocolate, chopped	125 g
1 cup	butter, softened	250 mL
2 cups	granulated sugar	500 mL
3	eggs	3
2 tbsp	vanilla	25 mL
4 cups	all-purpose flour	1 L
1 tsp	baking soda	5 mL
1 tsp	salt	5 mL

1 Line rimless baking sheets with parchment paper or grease; set aside.

2 In bowl over saucepan of hot (not boiling) water, melt chocolate, stirring often. Let cool to room temperature.

3 In large bowl, beat butter with sugar until light and fluffy. Beat in 2 of the eggs, 1 at a time; beat in vanilla. In separate bowl, whisk together flour, baking soda and salt; stir into butter mixture one-third at a time, using hands if too stiff to stir.

4 Remove half of the dough for vanilla dough. Stir chocolate into remaining dough, using hands to blend thoroughly.

5 Divide vanilla dough in half; flatten each half into square. Place dough, 1 square at a time, between 2 sheets of waxed paper and roll out into 7-inch (18 cm) square, shaping edges neatly. Repeat with chocolate dough. Refrigerate until firm, about 30 minutes. Using ruler and sharp knife, cut each square into nine ¾-inch (2 cm) wide strips.

6 Place 12-inch (30 cm) long piece of plastic wrap on work surface. Alternating vanilla and chocolate strips, place 3 strips of dough side by side (close but not touching) on plastic wrap. Whisk remaining egg; brush over sides and tops of strips. Gently press long edges of strips together to adhere. Repeat, forming second and third layers and alternating flavours of strips, which will create checkerboard effect when cut. Pull plastic wrap up and cover log. Repeat to make 3 more logs. (If desired, you can reverse the pattern for some logs.) Refrigerate for 30 minutes. (**MAKE-AHEAD: Refrigerate for up to 4 days.**)

> " I like to keep cookie dough in the freezer ready to slice and pop in the oven. That way, I can have fresh-baked treats whenever I want. – *Emily* "

7 Using sharp knife, trim ends of each log even; cut into ¼-inch (5 mm) thick slices. Arrange, about 1 inch (2.5 cm) apart, on prepared pans. Bake, 1 sheet at a time, in centre of 350°F (180°C) oven until set and very light golden, about 12 minutes. Let cool on pan on rack for 3 minutes. Transfer to racks and let cool completely. (**MAKE-AHEAD: Layer between waxed paper in airtight container and store at room temperature for up to 2 weeks or freeze for up to 1 month.**)

Makes about 86 cookies. PER COOKIE: about 68 cal, 1 g pro, 3 g total fat (2 g sat. fat), 9 g carb, trace fibre, 13 mg chol, 65 mg sodium. % RDI: 3% iron, 2% vit A, 4% folate.

Raspberry Pecan Rugalahs

Making the same cookie over and over? Take your cookie jar from tired to inspired with my family's favourite cookie. – Daphna

1	pkg (8 oz/250 g) cream cheese, softened	1
1 cup	butter, softened	250 mL
2 tbsp	granulated sugar	25 mL
2 cups	all-purpose flour	500 mL
FILLING:		
1 cup	toasted coarsely chopped pecans	250 mL
½ cup	golden raisins (optional)	125 mL
¼ cup	granulated sugar	50 mL
¼ cup	packed brown sugar	50 mL
¾ tsp	cinnamon	4 mL
¾ cup	raspberry jam	175 mL
GLAZE:		
1	egg, lightly beaten	1
2 tbsp	coarse or granulated sugar	25 mL

1 Line rimless baking sheets with parchment paper; set aside.

2 In bowl, beat cream cheese with butter until fluffy; beat in granulated sugar. Using wooden spoon, stir in flour, ½ cup (125 mL) at a time. Form dough into ball; cut into quarters and shape into discs. Wrap each in plastic wrap; refrigerate for 2 hours. (MAKE-AHEAD: **Refrigerate for up to 24 hours; let stand at room temperature for 15 minutes before rolling out.**)

3 FILLING: In small bowl, stir together pecans, raisins (if using), granulated and brown sugars, and cinnamon. In separate bowl, stir jam with 1 tsp (5 mL) water until spreadable.

4 On lightly floured surface, roll out 1 dough disc into 11-inch (28 cm) circle. Spread 3 tbsp (50 mL) of the jam evenly over top. Sprinkle with one-quarter of the filling. Using sharp knife, cut circle into 12 pie-shaped wedges. Starting from wide end, roll up each wedge to form crescent shape. Place on prepared pans; refrigerate for 30 minutes. Repeat with remaining dough and filling.

5 GLAZE: Brush egg over tops of chilled cookies; sprinkle with sugar.

6 Bake, 1 sheet at a time, in centre of 350°F (180°C) oven until golden, about 25 minutes. Let cool on pans on racks. (MAKE-AHEAD: **Store in airtight container at room temperature for up to 5 days or freeze for up to 1 month.**)

Makes 48 cookies. PER COOKIE: about 116 cal, 1 g pro, 8 g total fat (4 g sat. fat), 11 g carb, 1 g fibre, 22 mg chol, 58 mg sodium. % RDI: 1% calcium, 3% iron, 6% vit A, 5% folate.

Irresistible Turtle Bars

This combination of nuts, caramel and chocolate will definitely have you salivating for snack time. – Elizabeth

1 Line 13- x 9-inch (3.5 L) metal cake pan with parchment paper; set aside.

2 In bowl, beat butter with granulated sugar until fluffy. Sift flour and cocoa powder over top; stir until combined. Press into prepared pan. Bake in centre of 350°F (180°C) oven until firm, about 15 minutes. Let cool in pan on rack.

3 FILLING: In saucepan, bring butter, brown sugar, corn syrup and whipping cream to boil, stirring; boil, without stirring, until thickened, about 1 minute. Remove from heat; stir in pecans. Spread over prepared crust.

4 Bake in centre of 350°F (180°C) oven until bubbling and edges are light golden, about 20 minutes. Let cool in pan on rack. Drizzle with melted chocolate. Let stand until chocolate is set. Cut into bars. (MAKE-AHEAD: **Layer between waxed paper in airtight container and refrigerate for up to 1 week or freeze for up to 1 month.**)

Makes 40 bars. PER BAR: about 140 cal, 1 g pro, 9 g total fat (5 g sat. fat), 14 g carb, 1 g fibre, 19 mg chol, 73 mg sodium. % RDI: 1% calcium, 4% iron, 6% vit A, 4% folate.

¾ cup	butter, softened	175 mL
½ cup	granulated sugar	125 ml
1¾ cups	all-purpose flour	425 mL
½ cup	cocoa powder	125 mL
2 oz	semisweet chocolate, melted	60 g
FILLING:		
⅔ cup	butter	150 mL
½ cup	packed brown sugar	125 mL
½ cup	corn syrup	125 mL
2 tbsp	whipping cream	25 mL
1 cup	chopped pecans, toasted	250 mL

VARIATION

Irresistible Black Forest Bars: Omit filling. Spread cooled crust with ¾ cup (175 mL) sour cherry jam. Whisk together ½ cup (125 mL) all-purpose flour, ⅓ cup (75 mL) granulated sugar and 2 tbsp (25 mL) cocoa powder. Using pastry blender or 2 knives, cut in ⅓ cup (75 mL) cold butter until crumbly. Sprinkle over jam. Bake in centre of 350°F (180°C) oven until firm to the touch, about 30 minutes. Let cool in pan on rack. Dust with 1 tbsp (15 mL) icing sugar.

fridge **NOTE**

- **One trick we use in The Canadian Living Test Kitchen when making bars and squares is to line the pan with parchment paper. When bars are baked and cooled, we use the edges of the paper to lift them from the pan onto a cutting board. Then they're easy to cut neatly.**

Chewy Double Ginger Bars

Crystallized ginger is available in bulk-food stores and in the baking aisle of your grocery store. Here, it adds chewiness and a wallop of flavour. – Emily

1 cup	packed brown sugar	250 mL
½ cup	fancy molasses	125 mL
¼ cup	butter, melted	50 mL
2	eggs	2
1 tsp	vanilla	5 mL
2 cups	all-purpose flour	500 mL
1 tsp	ground ginger	5 mL
½ tsp	each baking soda and cinnamon	2 mL
¼ tsp	ground cloves	1 mL
Pinch	salt	Pinch
½ cup	chopped crystallized ginger	125 mL
GLAZE:		
1 cup	icing sugar	250 mL
¼ cup	butter, melted	50 mL
2 tbsp	lemon juice	25 mL

1 Line 13- x 9-inch (3.5 L) metal cake pan with parchment paper; set aside.

2 In bowl, whisk together brown sugar, molasses, butter, eggs and vanilla. In separate bowl, whisk together flour, ground ginger, baking soda, cinnamon, cloves and salt; stir into butter mixture in 2 batches. Stir in crystallized ginger; scrape into prepared pan.

3 Bake in centre of 350°F (180°C) oven until tester inserted in centre comes out clean, about 40 minutes. Let cool in pan on rack for 45 minutes.

4 GLAZE: Stir together icing sugar, butter and lemon juice; spread over bars. Let cool completely. Cut into bars. (MAKE-AHEAD: **Layer between waxed paper in airtight container and store at room temperature for up to 4 days or freeze for up to 1 month.**)

Makes 40 bars. PER BAR: about 98 cal, 1 g pro, 3 g total fat (2 g sat. fat), 18 g carb, trace fibre, 17 mg chol, 47 mg sodium. % RDI: 2% calcium, 9% iron, 3% vit A, 2% vit C, 4% folate.

Squirrelly Shortbread Bars

Crazy for nuts? These bars, with their caramel-coated peanuts and almonds on top of melt-in-your-mouth shortbread, are for you. – Daphna

1 Line 13- x 9-inch (3.5 L) metal cake pan with parchment paper; set aside.

2 In bowl, beat butter with sugar until fluffy. Using wooden spoon, stir in flour, ½ cup (125 mL) at a time, until combined. Press evenly into prepared pan. Bake in centre of 350°F (180°C) oven until golden, about 25 minutes. Let cool in pan on rack.

3 TOPPING: Meanwhile, in saucepan, bring butter, brown sugar, corn syrup and cream to boil, stirring; boil, without stirring, until thickened slightly, about 1 minute. Remove from heat; stir in peanuts and almonds. Spread over prepared crust.

4 Bake in centre of 350°F (180°C) oven until golden, about 25 minutes. Let cool in pan on rack. Cut into bars. (MAKE-AHEAD: **Layer between waxed paper in airtight container and store for up to 5 days or freeze for up to 1 month.**)

Makes 40 bars. PER BAR: about 174 cal, 3 g pro, 12 g total fat (5 g sat. fat), 15 g carb, 1 g fibre, 19 mg chol, 104 mg sodium. % RDI: 2% calcium, 4% iron, 6% vit A, 8% folate.

¾ cup	butter, softened	175 mL
½ cup	granulated sugar	125 mL
2 cups	all-purpose flour	500 mL
TOPPING:		
⅔ cup	butter	150 mL
½ cup	packed dark brown sugar	125 mL
½ cup	corn syrup	125 mL
2 tbsp	whipping cream	25 mL
2 cups	salted peanuts	500 mL
1 cup	slivered almonds	250 mL

" Is it a bar, or can we call it a square? It's up to you and your knife – the only distinction is in how you cut them. Remember, diamonds can be a girl's best friend. – *Daphna* **"**

Production coordinator Sheri Kowall

Orange Cranberry White Chocolate Blondies

*Blondies are close cousins of brownies but are made without cocoa powder
or chocolate. The great thing is that they're a one-pot treat.* – Daphna

1 cup	butter, softened	250 mL
10 oz	white chocolate, chopped	300 g
1¼ cups	granulated sugar	300 mL
4	eggs	4
2 cups	all-purpose flour	500 mL
1 cup	dried cranberries	250 mL
1 tbsp	grated orange rind	15 mL
1 tbsp	vanilla	15 mL
½ tsp	salt	2 mL

1 Line 13- x 9-inch (3.5 L) metal cake pan with parchment paper; set aside.

2 In saucepan over low heat, melt butter with white chocolate, stirring occasionally, until smooth. Let cool for 10 minutes.

3 Using wooden spoon, stir in sugar, then eggs, 1 at a time, stirring well after each addition. Stir in flour, cranberries, orange rind, vanilla and salt. Spread in prepared pan.

4 Bake in centre of 325°F (160°C) oven until tester inserted in centre comes out clean, 30 to 35 minutes. Let cool in pan on rack. Cut into bars. (MAKE-AHEAD: **Layer between waxed paper in airtight container and refrigerate for up to 1 week or freeze for up to 1 month.**)

Makes 40 bars. PER BAR: about 142 cal, 2 g pro, 7 g total fat (4 g sat. fat), 17 g carb, trace fibre, 33 mg chol, 88 mg sodium. % RDI: 2% calcium, 2% iron, 5% vit A, 2% vit C, 5% folate.

Blueberry Cream Cheese Coffee Cake

This moist cake is best eaten the same day, so for a brunch, set out the ingredients the night before to speed up assembly the next morning. – Daphna

1 Grease 9-inch (2.5 L) springform pan; set aside.

2 CRUMB TOPPING: In small bowl, whisk together flour, brown and granulated sugars, and cinnamon. Drizzle butter evenly over top; toss with fork until moistened. Set aside.

3 CREAM CHEESE FILLING: In separate bowl, beat cream cheese with sugar until light and fluffy, scraping down side of bowl occasionally. Beat in egg and lemon rind just until smooth; set aside.

4 In large bowl, beat butter with sugar until combined. Beat in eggs, 1 at a time, beating well after each addition. Beat in vanilla. In separate bowl, whisk together flour, baking powder, baking soda and salt. Using wooden spoon, stir into butter mixture alternately with sour cream, making 3 additions of flour mixture and 2 of sour cream.

5 Spread in prepared pan, mounding slightly in centre. Sprinkle 1 cup (250 mL) of the blueberries over top. Gently spread cream cheese filling over blueberries; sprinkle with remaining blueberries. Sprinkle evenly with crumb topping.

6 Bake in centre of 350°F (180°C) oven until edge is set and just beginning to come away from pan, about 1¼ hours. Let cool in pan on rack for 30 minutes. Serve warm or at room temperature.

Makes 12 servings. PER SERVING: about 396 cal, 6 g pro, 20 g total fat (12 g sat. fat), 48 g carb, 1 g fibre, 108 mg chol, 307 mg sodium. % RDI: 5% calcium, 12% iron, 22% vit A, 3% vit C, 6% folate.

⅓ cup	butter, softened	75 mL
⅔ cup	granulated sugar	150 mL
2	eggs	2
2 tsp	vanilla	10 mL
1½ cups	all-purpose flour	375 mL
1 tsp	baking powder	5 mL
½ tsp	baking soda	2 mL
¼ tsp	salt	1 mL
½ cup	sour cream	125 mL
1½ cups	fresh or frozen wild blueberries	375 mL

CRUMB TOPPING:

1 cup	all-purpose flour	250 mL
¼ cup	packed brown sugar	50 mL
¼ cup	granulated sugar	50 mL
½ tsp	cinnamon	2 mL
⅓ cup	butter, melted	75 mL

CREAM CHEESE FILLING:

1	pkg (8 oz/250 g) cream cheese, softened	1
¼ cup	granulated sugar	50 mL
1	egg	1
1 tsp	finely grated lemon rind	5 mL

Orange Cardamom Mini-Loaves

One batch makes three mini-loaves. I like to wrap them in cellophane, tie with a bow and offer as host or hostess gifts. – Elizabeth

½ cup	butter, softened	125 mL
1 cup	granulated sugar	250 mL
2	eggs	2
1 tbsp	grated orange rind	15 mL
¼ tsp	almond extract	1 mL
2 cups	all-purpose flour	500 mL
2 tsp	baking powder	10 mL
½ tsp	salt	2 mL
½ tsp	ground cardamom or nutmeg	2 mL
½ cup	milk	125 mL
¼ cup	orange juice	50 mL
¾ cup	chopped toasted almonds	175 mL

1 Grease three 5¾- x 3¼-inch (625 mL) mini-loaf pans; line bottoms with waxed paper. Set aside.

2 In large bowl, beat butter with sugar until fluffy; beat in eggs, 1 at a time. Stir in orange rind and almond extract.

3 In separate bowl, whisk together flour, baking powder, salt and cardamom. Stir into butter mixture alternately with milk and orange juice, making 3 additions of dry ingredients and 2 of wet. Fold in almonds. Divide batter evenly among prepared pans.

4 Bake in centre of 350°F (180°C) oven until golden and cake tester inserted in centre comes out clean, about 35 minutes. Let cool in pans on racks for 10 minutes. Remove from pans; let cool completely. (MAKE-AHEAD: **Wrap in foil or plastic wrap and store in airtight container for up to 3 days or freeze for up to 1 month.**)

Makes 3 mini-loaves, each 8 slices. PER SLICE: about 274 cal, 5 g pro, 13 g total fat (5 g sat. fat), 36 g carb, 2 g fibre, 56 mg chol, 235 mg sodium. % RDI: 5% calcium, 10% iron, 9% vit A, 3% vit C, 15% folate.

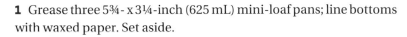

fridge NOTE

- **Look for foil mini-loaf pans at the grocery store. You can leave the loaves in the pans to cool, then wrap for gift giving.**

Dried Pear, Anise and Walnut Bread

A slice of fruit bread adds satisfaction to teatime. You may not have thought of pears and anise together, but they are a divine couple. – Elizabeth

1 Line 8- x 4-inch (1.5 L) loaf pan with parchment paper; set aside.

2 Place pears in large bowl; pour in 1 cup (250 mL) boiling water. Stir in sugar and butter until sugar is dissolved and butter is melted. Let cool. Stir in egg and vanilla.

3 Meanwhile, in large bowl, whisk together flour, baking soda, aniseed, baking powder and salt; stir in walnuts. Using wooden spoon, stir in pear mixture just until combined. Spread in prepared pan.

4 Bake in centre of 350°F (180°C) oven until cake tester inserted in centre comes out clean, about 1 hour and 10 minutes. Let cool in pan on rack for 15 minutes. Invert loaf onto rack and let cool completely. Wrap in plastic wrap and store for at least 24 hours before serving.

Makes 1 loaf, 12 slices. PER SLICE: about 302 cal, 5 g pro, 11 g total fat (3 g sat. fat), 48 g carb, 4 g fibre, 26 mg chol, 212 mg sodium. % RDI: 3% calcium, 14% iron, 5% vit A, 3% vit C, 19% folate.

1½ cups	diced dried pears	375 mL
¾ cup	granulated sugar	175 mL
¼ cup	unsalted butter	50 mL
1	egg	1
1 tsp	vanilla	5 mL
2¼ cups	all-purpose flour	550 mL
1 tsp	baking soda	5 mL
1 tsp	aniseed, crushed	5 mL
½ tsp	baking powder	2 mL
½ tsp	salt	2 mL
1 cup	coarsely chopped walnuts	250 mL

Picnics and Potlucks

During the show's first season, we knew we were on to something when we learned that the potluck dishes had scored the most hits of any recipes on our Web site. That's potluck as in make-ahead, crowd-pleasing and affordable, a smart solution to the challenge of getting a gang together without bankrupting – or exhausting – the hosts. For the show, we've chosen the dishes that travel well, from satisfying salads and crispy chicken to baked pastas and delectable desserts. And while we think of many of these as stars of the potluck world, choice among them are the kinds of dishes we most like to pack into a picnic basket before heading out to the park or beach. Moveable feasts, any way you look at it. – Elizabeth

- Baby Bow Tie and Walnut Pasta Salad
- Easy Layered Lunch Salad
- Tomato Basil Wheat Berry Salad
- Potato and Leek Salad
- Creamy Coleslaw
- Buttermilk Fried Chicken
- Chicken Zarzuela Casserole
- Chunky Chili with Corn Bread Cobbler
- Sweet-and-Sour Braised Beef with Prunes
- Eggplant and Pasta Charlotte
- Mediterranean Vegetable Pie
- Frozen Cappuccino Charlotte
- Raspberry Chocolate Chip Bundt Cake

◄ The cameramen are ready to roll tape

Baby Bow Tie and Walnut Pasta Salad

Toasting some of the pasta boosts the flavour beautifully. Besides miniature bow-ties, other small pasta shapes are also suitable for this salad. – Daphna

1½ cups	farfallini pasta	375 mL
1 tbsp	vegetable oil	15 mL
Half	onion, chopped	Half
¾ cup	chopped walnuts	175 mL
½ cup	chopped sweet green pepper	125 mL
2 tbsp	extra-virgin olive oil	25 mL
1 tbsp	cider vinegar	15 mL
¼ tsp	salt	1 mL
Pinch	pepper	Pinch
2 tbsp	chopped fresh coriander	25 mL
1 cup	cherry tomatoes, quartered, or chopped tomatoes	250 mL
	Fresh coriander sprigs	

1 In skillet, toast ½ cup (125 mL) of the pasta over medium heat, stirring often, until light brown, about 5 minutes.

2 In saucepan of boiling salted water, cook toasted and remaining pasta until tender but firm, 7 to 8 minutes. Drain and rinse under cold water; drain well and set aside in large bowl.

3 In skillet, heat vegetable oil over medium heat; cook onion, stirring often, just until slightly softened, about 2 minutes. Add walnuts; cook for 2 minutes. Stir in green pepper; cook for 1 minute. Pour over pasta; let cool.

4 In small bowl, whisk together olive oil, vinegar, salt and pepper; pour over pasta mixture. Add chopped coriander and toss to combine. (MAKE-AHEAD: **Cover and refrigerate for up to 24 hours.**) Garnish with tomatoes and coriander sprigs.

Makes 8 servings. PER SERVING: about 223 cal, 5 g pro, 13 g total fat (2 g sat. fat), 22 g carb, 2 g fibre, 0 mg chol, 144 mg sodium. % RDI: 2% calcium, 7% iron, 2% vit A, 17% vit C, 23% folate.

fridge NOTE

- When making a pasta salad, be sure to rinse the pasta under a spray of cold water. When the pasta dish is hot and sauced, skip the rinse so that the sauce will cling better.

Easy Layered Lunch Salad

Pack salads into individual plastic containers or jars and you won't need to include serving plates. – Daphna

1 LIME CHILI DRESSING: In jar with tight-fitting lid, shake together oil, chili powder, 2 tbsp (25 mL) water, sugar, lime rind and juice, and salt. Set aside.

2 In bowl, pour 1½ cups (375 mL) boiling water over couscous; cover and let stand for 5 minutes. Fluff with fork. Refrigerate until chilled. Using fork, stir in lentils, basil and salt. Divide among eight 2-cup (500 mL) plastic containers with tight-fitting lids.

3 In bowl, combine carrots, radishes, cauliflower, celery and red pepper. Layer evenly over couscous.

4 Drizzle with Lime Chili Dressing. Sprinkle with cucumber, tomatoes, feta and onion. Top with lids. Chill and serve within 4 hours.

Makes 8 servings. PER SERVING: about 400 cal, 10 g pro, 23 g total fat (3 g sat. fat), 41 g carb, 6 g fibre, 7 mg chol, 611 mg sodium. % RDI: 8% calcium, 21% iron, 130% vit A, 110% vit C, 65% folate.

1 cup	couscous	250 mL
1	can (19 oz/540 mL) lentils, drained and rinsed	1
¼ cup	chopped fresh basil or coriander	50 mL
½ tsp	salt	2 mL
4	carrots, grated	4
4	radishes, halved and sliced	4
2 cups	chopped cauliflower florets	500 mL
2	stalks celery, sliced	2
1	sweet red pepper, chopped	1
1½ cups	chopped English cucumber	375 mL
2 cups	cherry tomatoes, halved	500 mL
½ cup	crumbled feta cheese	125 mL
1	green onion, chopped	1
LIME CHILI DRESSING:		
1 cup	vegetable oil	250 mL
2 tbsp	chili powder	25 mL
4 tsp	granulated sugar	20 mL
1 tbsp	grated lime or lemon rind	15 mL
⅔ cup	lime or lemon juice	150 mL
1 tsp	salt	5 mL

Tomato Basil Wheat Berry Salad

Wheat berries take a while to cook, but their nutty flavour and al dente texture are worth the time. Or you can cook them a day ahead. – Emily

1½ cups	wheat berries	375 mL
¼ cup	extra-virgin olive oil	50 mL
2 tbsp	white wine vinegar	25 mL
½ tsp	each salt and pepper	2 mL
2	tomatoes, chopped	2
2	green onions, chopped	2
¼ cup	chopped fresh basil	50 mL

1 In large saucepan, cover wheat berries with about 2 inches (5 cm) cold water; bring to boil. Reduce heat and simmer until tender but firm, 1 to 1½ hours. Drain well and transfer to large bowl; let cool completely.

2 In small bowl, whisk together oil, vinegar, salt and pepper; pour over wheat berries. Add tomatoes, onions and basil; toss to coat.

Makes 4 servings. PER SERVING: about 346 cal, 7 g pro, 15 g total fat (2 g sat. fat), 51 g carb, 9 g fibre, 0 mg chol, 295 mg sodium. % RDI: 3% calcium, 19% iron, 4% vit A, 22% vit C, 15% folate.

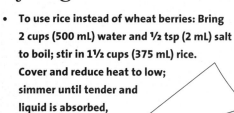

fridge **NOTE**

- **To use rice instead of wheat berries:** Bring 2 cups (500 mL) water and ½ tsp (2 mL) salt to boil; stir in 1½ cups (375 mL) rice. Cover and reduce heat to low; simmer until tender and liquid is absorbed, about 20 minutes.

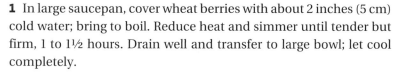 Wheat berries are one of my favourite grains. I boil up large batches and freeze them in bags. When thawed, they're ready to serve in a salad or a hot side dish. *– Emily*

Potato and Leek Salad

This potato salad is ideal for picnics, especially when there are guests who don't like raw onions. – Elizabeth

1 In large pot of boiling salted water, cover and cook potatoes until tender, 25 to 30 minutes. Using slotted spoon, remove and let cool; peel and cut into ¾-inch (2 cm) cubes. Place in large bowl.

2 Meanwhile, blanch leeks and celery in same boiling water for 20 seconds; drain in colander. Chill under cold water; drain well and add to potatoes.

3 In small bowl, whisk together mayonnaise, parsley, oil, lemon juice, salt and pepper; pour over vegetables and mix well. Sprinkle with feta cheese and olives.

Makes 8 servings. PER SERVING: about 167 cal, 4 g pro, 9 g total fat (3 g sat. fat), 19 g carb, 3 g fibre, 13 mg chol, 553 mg sodium. % RDI: 8% calcium, 9% iron, 3% vit A, 22% vit C, 12% folate.

4	new potatoes (about 1½ lb/750 g)	4
3	leeks (white and light green parts), sliced	3
1 cup	sliced celery	250 mL
¼ cup	light mayonnaise	50 mL
2 tbsp	chopped fresh parsley	25 mL
2 tbsp	extra-virgin olive oil	25 mL
4 tsp	lemon juice	20 mL
¼ tsp	each salt and pepper	1 mL
¾ cup	cubed or crumbled feta cheese	175 mL
½ cup	black olives	125 mL

Creamy Coleslaw

This cooked salad dressing, sometimes called a mustard custard, is the base of old-fashioned potato and cabbage salads. – Elizabeth

4 cups	very finely shredded green cabbage	1 L
4	green onions, thinly sliced	4
2	tender stalks celery, thinly sliced	2
1	large carrot, finely diced or julienned	1
Half	bulb fennel, thinly shaved	Half
Half	sweet red pepper, thinly sliced	Half
DRESSING:		
⅓ cup	Homemade Salad Dressing (recipe, page 165) or light mayonnaise	75 mL
⅓ cup	light sour cream	75 mL
1 tbsp	each Dijon mustard and cider vinegar	15 mL
2 tsp	granulated sugar	10 mL
½ tsp	celery or mustard seeds	2 mL
½ tsp	each salt and pepper	2 mL

1 In large bowl, toss together cabbage, onions, celery, carrot, fennel and red pepper. (MAKE-AHEAD: **Cover with damp tea towel and plastic wrap. Refrigerate for up to 8 hours.**)

2 DRESSING: In small bowl, stir together Homemade Salad Dressing, sour cream, mustard, vinegar, sugar, celery seeds, salt and pepper; pour over cabbage mixture and toss to coat. (MAKE-AHEAD: **Cover and refrigerate for up to 2 hours.**)

Makes 8 servings. PER SERVING: about 69 cal, 2 g pro, 2 g total fat (1 g sat. fat), 13 g carb, 2 g fibre, 11 mg chol, 262 mg sodium. % RDI: 6% calcium, 6% iron, 42% vit A, 52% vit C, 15% folate.

Floor director David Berube offers a last-minute word of encouragement

> **"** Here's the quintessential Canadian picnic salad. It takes me back to my childhood and Aunt Helen's paper-thin cabbage mixed with this tangy dressing. – *Elizabeth* **"**

Homemade Salad Dressing

1 In top of double boiler or in small heavy saucepan, whisk together sugar, flour, mustard, salt and turmeric. Whisk in egg yolk, vinegar and milk.

2 Cook over saucepan of simmering water or over medium-low heat, stirring constantly, until thick enough to coat back of spoon, about 10 minutes. Stir in butter. Let cool, stirring often. (Dressing will continue to thicken as it cools.) (MAKE-AHEAD: **Refrigerate in airtight container for up to 1 week.**)

Makes about 1 cup (250 mL). PER 1 TBSP (15 mL): about 39 cal, 1 g pro, 1 g total fat (1 g sat. fat), 8 g carb, 0 g fibre, 15 mg chol, 85 mg sodium. % RDI: 1% calcium, 1% iron, 1% vit A, 1% folate.

½ cup	granulated sugar	125 mL
1 tbsp	all-purpose flour	15 mL
1 tsp	dry mustard	5 mL
½ tsp	salt	2 mL
Pinch	turmeric	Pinch
1	egg yolk	1
½ cup	cider vinegar	125 mL
½ cup	milk	125 mL
2 tsp	butter	10 mL

fridge **NOTE**

- **Use a mandoline (Japanese ones are inexpensive) to finely shred the cabbage and fennel.**

Buttermilk Fried Chicken

Pack the picnic basket and a blanket and head outdoors for a day of fun.
This crispy-skinned chicken is the perfect picnic pleasure food. – Daphna

1	whole chicken (3 lb/1.5 kg) or equivalent weight of thighs or parts	1
1	onion, chopped	1
6	sprigs fresh thyme (or 1 tsp/5 mL dried)	6
1 cup	buttermilk	250 mL
1 cup	all-purpose flour	250 mL
1 tbsp	finely chopped fresh thyme (or 1 tsp/5 mL dried)	15 mL
1 tsp	salt	5 mL
½ tsp	each cayenne pepper and coarsely ground black pepper	2 mL
2 cups	shortening or canola oil	500 mL

fridge NOTE

- Choose air-chilled chicken when making fried chicken; it will have less water content, reducing the splattering when frying and resulting in a crispier skin.

1 Using kitchen scissors and holding chicken on cutting board breast side down, cut off wing tips at first joint. Cut along both sides of backbone. Turn over; flatten with heels of hands. Turn chicken over; with chef's knife, cut along centre of breast. Cut off each leg; at joint, cut into thigh and drumstick pieces. Cut off wings; cut breast diagonally into 2 pieces. Trim excess fat and loose skin.

2 Place pieces in 8-inch (2 L) square glass baking dish. Add onion, thyme sprigs and buttermilk; turn to coat chicken evenly. Cover and marinate in refrigerator for 2 hours. (MAKE-AHEAD: **Refrigerate for up to 24 hours.**) Remove from marinade, shaking off excess. Set chicken aside on large plate. Discard marinade.

3 In large bowl, whisk together flour, chopped thyme, salt, cayenne and pepper. Press chicken, 1 piece at a time, into flour mixture, turning to coat. Place on waxed paper–lined rimmed baking sheet. Refrigerate for 15 minutes.

4 Heat 2 large (10- or 12-inch/25 or 30 cm) cast-iron skillets over medium heat. Divide shortening between skillets; heat until pinch of flour mixture dropped in skillet sizzles and browns. Place breast and wings in 1 skillet in single layer, fleshiest side down; place dark meat thighs and drumsticks in other skillet. Cover and fry, adjusting heat as necessary to avoid burning, until crisp and brown on bottom, about 9 minutes. Turn, cover and fry until crisp and brown on all sides and juices run clear when pierced, about 9 minutes. Drain on paper towel–lined platter.

Makes 4 to 6 servings. PER EACH OF 6 SERVINGS: about 352 cal, 24 g pro, 21 g total fat (6 g sat. fat), 15 g carb, 1 g fibre, 80 mg chol, 385 mg sodium. % RDI: 5% calcium, 12% iron, 5% vit A, 5% vit C, 13% folate.

Chicken Zarzuela Casserole

Ground almonds thicken this Spanish tomato sauce. You can add cooked potatoes to the casserole before heating through. – Elizabeth

1 Sprinkle chicken with ½ tsp (2 mL) of the salt and pepper. In large nonstick skillet, heat vegetable oil over medium-high heat; brown chicken in batches. Transfer to 13- x 9-inch (3 L) glass baking dish. Drain off any fat from pan. Add wine; bring to boil, scraping up any brown bits from bottom of pan. Pour over chicken.

2 Wipe out skillet. Add olive oil; heat over medium heat. Cook onions and two-thirds of the garlic until golden, about 4 minutes. Add tomatoes, paprika, marjoram and remaining salt, breaking up tomatoes with wooden spoon; bring to boil and pour over chicken. Cover loosely with foil; bake in 375°F (190°C) oven until juices run clear when chicken is pierced, about 40 minutes.

3 Meanwhile, crumble saffron into bowl; pour in 2 tbsp (25 mL) hot water and let stand for 5 minutes. Add almonds, lemon juice and remaining garlic to saffron; stir into chicken mixture along with olives. Bake until heated through, about 10 minutes. (**MAKE-AHEAD: Let cool for 30 minutes. Transfer to airtight container. Refrigerate, uncovered, until cold. Cover and refrigerate for up to 24 hours. Or freeze for up to 2 weeks; thaw in refrigerator for 24 hours. Reheat in 375°F/190°C oven until hot, about 40 minutes.**) Stir in parsley.

Makes 8 servings. PER SERVING: about 356 cal, 35 g pro, 17 g total fat (3 g sat. fat), 16 g carb, 4 g fibre, 138 mg chol, 1,040 mg sodium. % RDI: 9% calcium, 26% iron, 17% vit A, 35% vit C, 15% folate.

16	skinless chicken thighs (about 4 lb/2 kg)	16
1 tsp	salt	5 mL
½ tsp	pepper	2 mL
1 tbsp	vegetable oil	15 mL
½ cup	dry white wine	125 mL
1 tbsp	extra-virgin olive oil	15 mL
2	Spanish onions, chopped	2
6	cloves garlic, minced	6
1	can (28 oz/796 mL) tomatoes	1
4 tsp	sweet paprika	20 mL
1 tsp	dried marjoram or oregano	5 mL
¼ tsp	saffron threads	1 mL
⅓ cup	ground almonds	75 mL
1 tbsp	lemon juice	15 mL
1 cup	large green olives, pitted and halved	250 mL
¼ cup	chopped fresh parsley	50 mL

Chunky Chili with Corn Bread Cobbler

*Inside round or sirloin tip oven roasts are perfect for chili because they're
lean and tenderize beautifully when simmered.* – Daphna

2 lb	inside round or sirloin tip oven roast, trimmed	1 kg
2 tbsp	vegetable oil	25 mL
1	onion, chopped	1
2	cloves garlic, minced	2
1	stalk celery, chopped	1
1	carrot, chopped	1
2 tbsp	chili powder	25 mL
1 tsp	dried oregano	5 mL
¼ tsp	pepper	1 mL
1	can (19 oz/540 mL) chili-style stewed tomatoes	1
1	can (14 oz/398 mL) tomato sauce	1
1	can (19 oz/540 mL) red kidney beans, drained and rinsed	1
¼ cup	chopped fresh coriander	50 mL

1 Cut beef into ½-inch (1 cm) cubes. In large shallow Dutch oven, heat oil over medium-high heat; brown beef in batches. Transfer to bowl; set aside.

2 Reduce heat to medium; add onion, garlic, celery, carrot, chili powder, oregano and pepper to pan. Cook, stirring occasionally, until onion is softened, about 5 minutes.

3 Return beef and any accumulated juices to pan. Add tomatoes, tomato sauce and kidney beans; bring to boil. Reduce heat, cover and simmer until beef is tender, about 1½ hours. (MAKE-AHEAD: **Let cool for 30 minutes. Refrigerate until cold. Freeze in airtight container for up to 2 weeks. Thaw in refrigerator for 24 hours. To reheat, transfer to 13- x 9-inch/3 L glass baking dish, cover with foil and heat in 400°F/200°C oven until bubbling, about 30 minutes. Continue with recipe.**) Transfer to 13- x 9-inch (3 L) glass baking dish. Stir in coriander.

4 CORN BREAD COBBLER: In bowl, whisk together flour, cornmeal, baking powder, baking soda and salt. In separate bowl, whisk together buttermilk, butter and egg; pour over flour mixture. Sprinkle with corn; stir just until combined. Spoon in 8 dollops over filling. Sprinkle with cheese. Bake in 400°F (200°C) oven until topping is golden and no longer doughy underneath, 30 to 35 minutes. Let stand for 10 minutes before serving.

Makes 8 servings. PER SERVING: about 492 cal, 41 g pro, 15 g total fat (6 g sat. fat), 51 g carb, 8 g fibre, 97 mg chol, 1,171 mg sodium. % RDI: 22% calcium, 38% iron, 47% vit A, 27% vit C, 35% folate.

CORN BREAD COBBLER:

1 cup	all-purpose flour	250 mL
½ cup	cornmeal	125 mL
2 tsp	baking powder	10 mL
½ tsp	each baking soda and salt	2 mL
1 cup	buttermilk	250 mL
2 tbsp	butter, melted	25 mL
1	egg	1
2 cups	corn kernels	500 mL
1 cup	shredded Monterey Jack or Cheddar cheese	250 mL

Set stylist Robert James gives a new look to the set for each show

fridge NOTE

- Keep the potluck line moving with a one-stop pickup of cutlery, napkins and glasses – and make sure you place them at the end of the table, right after the food.

Sweet-and-Sour Braised Beef with Prunes

Dried fruits are a delicious part of holiday cooking. Here's a tip: if you use beef stock instead of beer, reduce the salt by half. – Emily

2 tbsp	vegetable oil	25 mL
3 lb	lean stewing beef cubes	1.5 kg
2	onions, thinly sliced	2
2	stalks celery, thinly sliced	2
2	cloves garlic, minced	2
2 cups	dark beer or beef stock	500 mL
2 cups	beef stock	500 mL
½ cup	cider vinegar	125 mL
2 tbsp	packed brown sugar	25 mL
2	bay leaves	2
1 tsp	each salt and ground ginger	5 mL
½ tsp	each ground allspice, cinnamon and nutmeg	2 mL
½ tsp	pepper	2 mL
¼ tsp	ground cloves	1 mL
6	carrots, cut in chunks	6
24	pitted prunes	24
¼ cup	all-purpose flour	50 mL
¼ cup	butter, softened	50 mL
2 tbsp	chopped fresh parsley	25 mL

1 In Dutch oven, heat half of the oil over medium-high heat; brown beef in 3 batches. Using slotted spoon, transfer to bowl; set aside.

2 Reduce heat to medium; add remaining oil to pan. Cook onions, celery and garlic, stirring occasionally, until onions are softened, about 4 minutes. Return beef and any accumulated juices to pan; add beer, stock, vinegar, sugar, bay leaves, salt, ginger, allspice, cinnamon, nutmeg, pepper and cloves. Bring to boil; reduce heat, cover and simmer for 1 hour. Stir in carrots and prunes; cook until beef is tender, about 1 hour. Discard bay leaves.

3 Mix flour with butter until smooth; add to beef mixture, 1 tbsp (15 mL) at a time, stirring until slightly thickened. Bring to boil; reduce heat and simmer for 5 minutes. (**MAKE-AHEAD: Let cool for 30 minutes. Transfer to airtight container. Refrigerate, uncovered, until cold. Cover and refrigerate for up to 3 days. Or freeze for up to 2 weeks; thaw in refrigerator for 24 hours. Reheat over medium heat, stirring occasionally, until hot.**) Sprinkle with parsley.

Makes 8 servings. PER SERVING: about 513 cal, 41 g pro, 22 g total fat (8 g sat. fat), 39 g carb, 6 g fibre, 99 mg chol, 695 mg sodium. % RDI: 7% calcium, 38% iron, 145% vit A, 10% vit C, 14% folate.

Eggplant and Pasta Charlotte

What a creative use for eggplant! Thin slices form the covering for a robust tomato-sauced baked pasta. – Elizabeth

1 Cut eggplant lengthwise into ¼-inch (5 mm) thick slices. Layer in colander, sprinkling each with salt. Let stand for 30 minutes. Rinse each layer well to remove salt; pat dry.

2 In skillet, heat some of the oil over medium heat; fry eggplant slices, a few at a time, until golden brown, about 3 minutes per side, adding more oil as necessary. Drain well on paper towels.

3 Meanwhile, in large pot of boiling salted water, cook rigatoni until tender but still quite firm, about 7 minutes. Drain well and return to pot. Add pasta sauce and mozzarella, Asiago and Romano cheeses; stir to combine. Stir in thyme, pepper and rosemary; set aside.

4 Lightly brush 8½-inch (2.25 L) springform pan with olive oil. Sprinkle with half of the bread crumbs. Line side of pan with overlapping pieces of eggplant, making sure each extends to rim of pan and leaving no gaps. Cover bottom with overlapping slices of eggplant. Spoon pasta mixture into pan, pressing down lightly. Sprinkle with remaining bread crumbs. Cover with foil.

5 Bake in centre of 375°F (190°C) oven until steaming, about 30 minutes. Let stand for 15 minutes. Run tip of knife around edge of pan to loosen charlotte. Invert onto serving platter and unmould.

Makes 8 to 10 servings. PER EACH OF 10 SERVINGS: about 330 cal, 13 g pro, 16 g total fat (6 g sat. fat), 34 g carb, 4 g fibre, 28 mg chol, 585 mg sodium. % RDI: 22% calcium, 11% iron, 11% vit A, 10% vit C, 26% folate.

2	eggplants (each about 8 oz/250 g)	2
1 tsp	salt	5 mL
¼ cup	extra-virgin olive oil (approx)	50 mL
5 cups	rigatoni pasta	1.25 L
1	jar (3 cups/750 mL) herbed pasta sauce	1
2 cups	shredded mozzarella cheese (8 oz/250 g)	500 mL
½ cup	shredded Asiago cheese	125 mL
⅓ cup	grated Romano cheese	75 mL
½ tsp	each dried thyme and pepper	2 mL
¼ tsp	dried rosemary, crumbled	1 mL
2 tbsp	dry bread crumbs	25 mL

Mediterranean Vegetable Pie

Looking for something different to take to a potluck? The bonus of this free-form pie is that it's a delicious vegetarian option for any gathering. – Emily

1¾ cups	all-purpose flour	425 mL
1 tsp	salt	5 mL
1 tsp	baking powder	5 mL
⅓ cup	extra-virgin olive oil	75 mL
⅓ cup	milk	75 mL
2	eggs	2
FILLING:		
¼ cup	extra-virgin olive oil	50 mL
2	zucchini	2
2	onions	2
1	eggplant	1
1 tsp	salt	5 mL
1	head garlic	1
3	roasted red peppers, peeled and sliced	3
1 cup	shredded Fontina or mozzarella cheese	250 mL
¼ cup	chopped fresh oregano (or 2 tsp/10 mL dried)	50 mL
½ tsp	pepper	2 mL

1 In large bowl, whisk together flour, salt and baking powder. In separate bowl, whisk together oil, milk and 1 of the eggs; add to dry ingredients all at once. Using fingers or in mixer using dough hook, blend until liquid is absorbed and dough is smooth. Turn out onto lightly floured surface; knead until smooth, about 2 minutes. Transfer to bowl; cover and refrigerate for 30 minutes. (MAKE-AHEAD: **Wrap in plastic wrap and refrigerate for up to 5 days.**)

2 FILLING: Brush 2 large rimmed baking sheets with 2 tsp (10 mL) of the oil. Cut zucchini, onions and eggplant crosswise into ½-inch (1 cm) thick slices; place in single layer on prepared sheets. Brush with 2 tbsp (25 mL) of the oil; sprinkle with ½ tsp (2 mL) of the salt. Without peeling, separate garlic into cloves and place in small bowl; add remaining oil and toss to coat. Add garlic to sheets, reserving oil in bowl.

3 Roast in top and bottom thirds of 425°F (220°C) oven, rotating and switching pans once, until vegetables are tender and garlic is softened, about 40 minutes. Let cool. (MAKE-AHEAD: **Refrigerate in airtight container for up to 12 hours.**) Squeeze garlic from skins into reserved oil in bowl; mash with fork and set aside.

> " Anytime anyone asks me for a potluck recipe, this is the one I recommend. It's a fantastic departure from the usual casserole fare. – *Emily* "

4 On lightly floured surface or pastry cloth, roll out pastry to 18-inch (45 cm) circle; transfer to large rimmed baking sheet. Spread garlic in 9-inch (23 cm) circle in centre of pastry. Top with one-third each of the vegetable mixture and the red peppers; sprinkle with one-third of the cheese, the oregano, pepper and remaining salt. Repeat vegetable, red pepper and cheese layers twice. Fold pastry border over filling to form attractive irregular edge, leaving 2-inch (5 cm) opening on top. Lightly beat remaining egg; brush over pastry to seal folds.

5 Bake in bottom third of 375°F (190°C) oven until pastry is golden and filling is steaming, about 30 minutes. Let stand on sheet on rack for about 5 minutes before cutting into wedges.

Makes 6 servings. PER SERVING: about 490 cal, 13 g pro, 29 g total fat (7 g sat. fat), 45 g carb, 5 g fibre, 85 mg chol, 993 mg sodium. % RDI: 18% calcium, 21% iron, 24% vit A, 117% vit C, 39% folate.

fridge **NOTE**

- **Instead of roasting your own peppers, you can use 1 jar (340 mL) roasted red peppers, drained.**

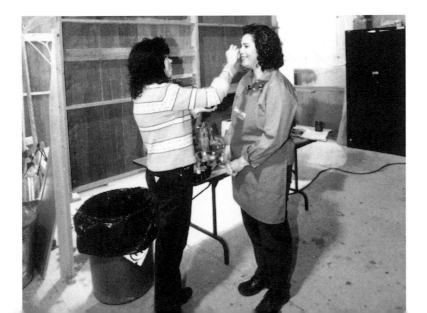

Emily gets a touch-up
from makeup artist
Sue Timewell-Jeffs

Frozen Cappuccino Charlotte

*This fancy dessert contains a surprise crunch of chocolate bars folded into
a caramel and coffee mousse, surrounded by soft ladyfingers.* – Daphna

1½ cups	granulated sugar	375 mL
¾ cup	strong coffee	175 mL
1	pkg (7 g) unflavoured gelatin	1
1	pkg (3 oz/85 g) soft ladyfinger cookies	1
3 cups	whipping cream	750 mL
1 tbsp	coffee liqueur	15 mL
2 tsp	vanilla	10 mL
4	bars (each 44 g) milk chocolate–covered sponge toffee, chopped	4

fridge NOTE

- **When serving creamy chilled desserts, get set with a tall pitcher of hot water, a long knife and a clean cloth. Before each slice, plunge the knife into the water, wipe dry and make a clean cut. That's how the pros plate their fancy desserts.**

1 In large saucepan over medium-high heat, bring sugar and ¼ cup (50 mL) water to boil, stirring until dissolved; boil, without stirring but occasionally brushing down side of pan with brush dipped in cold water, until dark amber, about 10 minutes. Remove from heat.

2 Standing back and averting face to avoid splatters, slowly stir in ½ cup (125 mL) of the coffee; simmer over low heat, stirring constantly, just until smooth, about 1 minute. Let cool slightly.

3 Sprinkle gelatin over remaining coffee; let stand for 1 minute. Stir into caramel mixture until gelatin is dissolved. Pour into bowl; refrigerate, stirring often, until cooled and thickened, about 1 hour.

4 Line side of 8-inch (2 L) springform pan with parchment or waxed paper. Trim 1 end of each ladyfinger to make 2½-inch (6 cm) length. Place tightly together, with rounded side facing outward and trimmed end down, to line side of pan; set aside.

5 In bowl, whip cream; beat in liqueur and vanilla. Fold one-third into coffee mixture; fold in remaining whipped cream mixture. Fold in three-quarters of the chopped chocolate bars. Pour into prepared pan, swirling top; sprinkle with remaining chocolate bar. Cover with plastic wrap and freeze until firm, about 6 hours. (MAKE-AHEAD: **Freeze in airtight container for up to 2 weeks.**) To serve, unmould and peel off paper; cut into wedges.

Makes 12 servings. PER SERVING: about 390 cal, 3 g pro, 24 g total fat (13 g sat. fat), 42 g carb, 0 g fibre, 102 mg chol, 34 mg sodium. % RDI: 4% calcium, 2% iron, 24% vit A, 2% folate.

Raspberry Chocolate Chip Bundt Cake

Here's a chocolate-rich berry dessert you can make year-round thanks to frozen raspberries. It's ideal for brunch. – Daphna

1 Grease 10-inch (3 L) Bundt pan; set aside.

2 Thaw 1 cup (250 mL) of the raspberries in sieve over bowl, reserving juice. Thaw remaining berries; purée in food processor, adding reserved juice. Press through sieve into bowl to remove seeds; add icing sugar. Set raspberry sauce aside.

3 In bowl, beat butter with granulated sugar until fluffy. Beat in eggs, 1 at a time, beating well after each; beat in vanilla. Whisk together flour, baking powder, baking soda and salt; stir half into butter mixture. Stir in sour cream; stir in remaining flour mixture and 1 cup (250 mL) of the chocolate chips. Spread half in prepared pan; sprinkle with reserved drained berries. Spread with remaining batter.

4 Bake in centre of 350°F (180°C) oven until cake springs back when lightly touched, about 40 minutes. Let cool for 10 minutes. Invert onto rack to let cool completely. Transfer to plate; slip strips of waxed paper under cake. Melt remaining chocolate chips with cream. Pour over cake, drizzling down side. Remove waxed paper strips. Serve cake with raspberry sauce.

Makes 12 servings. PER SERVING: about 442 cal, 6 g pro, 23 g total fat (14 g sat. fat), 53 g carb, 2 g fibre, 96 mg chol, 433 mg sodium. % RDI: 7% calcium, 14% iron, 17% vit A, 5% vit C, 20% folate.

2	pkg (each 300 g) frozen unsweetened raspberries	2
3 tbsp	icing sugar	50 mL
¾ cup	butter	175 mL
1 cup	granulated sugar	250 mL
3	eggs	3
2 tsp	vanilla	10 mL
2¼ cups	all-purpose flour	550 mL
2 tsp	baking powder	10 mL
1½ tsp	baking soda	7 mL
½ tsp	salt	2 mL
1½ cups	sour cream	375 mL
1½ cups	chocolate chips	375 mL
¼ cup	10% cream	50 mL

Great Grilling

Canadians love to grill – indoors or outdoors, summer or winter, meat or poultry, or anything in between. Grilling ranks as one of the top choices for cooking because it makes food taste great. It's easy to boot, as long as you follow certain guidelines. Grill tender cuts over medium to medium-high heat; they don't need to be marinated unless you're doing it for flavour. Marinate less tender cuts to transform them into marvellous morsels. Whatever type of meat you're grilling, be sure to let it stand for five to 10 minutes after cooking to allow the juices to redistribute evenly. Tutorial's over. Go forth and grill! – Daphna

◄ Food stylist Wendy Trusler with Daphna

- Chicken and Prosciutto Brochettes
- Chicken Under Bricks
- Latin American Mojo Chicken
- Asian Beef Salad
- Grilled T-Bone Steak with Zesty Barbecue Sauce
- Devilled Beef Ribs
- Indian Spiced Beef Koftas
- Slow and Easy Java Ribs
- Italian Sausage and Tomato Kabobs
- Grilled Vegetable Panini

Chicken and Prosciutto Brochettes

Here's an unexpected twist on grilled chicken breasts. In The Canadian Living Test Kitchen, we love the salty kick prosciutto adds. – Elizabeth

½ cup	lightly packed fresh basil leaves	125 mL
2 tbsp	extra-virgin olive oil	25 mL
2	cloves garlic	2
¼ tsp	salt	1 mL
2	boneless skinless chicken breasts (8 oz/250 g total)	2
4	large thin slices prosciutto	4
4	slices (½ inch/1 cm thick) yellow zucchini, halved	4

1 In food processor, pulse together basil, half of the oil, the garlic and salt until in rough paste; set aside. Starting at right side with knife parallel to board, slice each chicken breast in half; between waxed paper, pound each to ¼-inch (5 mm) thickness.

2 Place each prosciutto slice on work surface; top with chicken. Spread generous 1 tsp (5 mL) basil mixture over chicken; roll up and cut in half crosswise.

3 Alternately thread 2 chicken rolls and 2 pieces zucchini onto each of 4 metal or soaked wooden skewers; brush with remaining oil. (MAKE-AHEAD: **Cover and refrigerate for up to 4 hours.**)

4 Place on greased grill over medium-high heat; close lid and grill, turning once, until chicken is no longer pink inside, about 10 minutes.

Makes 4 brochettes. PER BROCHETTE: about 154 cal, 18 g pro, 8 g total fat (1 g sat. fat), 1 g carb, trace fibre, 45 mg chol, 270 mg sodium. % RDI: 1% calcium, 4% iron, 3% vit A, 2% vit C, 3% folate.

fridge NOTE

- **If using wooden or bamboo skewers, soak them for at least 30 minutes so they won't char on the grill. We like to soak them in a 13- x 9-inch (3 L) baking dish.**

Chicken Under Bricks

Here's a convenient marinate-ahead dish for weekends at the cottage. Bricks ensure even grilling – and provoke lots of comments! – Emily

1 In small bowl, stir together oil, garlic, oregano, salt, pepper and hot pepper flakes; set aside. Using kitchen scissors, cut chicken down each side of backbone; remove backbone. Turn chicken breast side up; press firmly on breastbone to flatten. Tuck wings behind back. Place in shallow dish. Brush oil mixture all over chicken. Cover and refrigerate for 4 hours. (MAKE-AHEAD: **Refrigerate for up to 24 hours.**)

2 Wrap 2 bricks in foil. Place chicken, skin side down, on greased grill over medium heat. Place bricks on chicken; close lid and grill for 20 minutes.

3 Wearing oven mitts, remove bricks. Using tongs, turn chicken over. Replace bricks; grill until juices run clear when thigh is pierced, about 20 minutes. Transfer to cutting board and tent with foil; let stand for 10 minutes. Using chef's knife or clean kitchen scissors, cut into 2 breast and 2 leg portions.

Makes 4 servings. PER SERVING: about 452 cal, 41 g pro, 31 g total fat (7 g sat. fat), 1 g carb, trace fibre, 132 mg chol, 552 mg sodium. % RDI: 3% calcium, 15% iron, 8% vit A, 2% vit C, 4% folate.

¼ cup	extra-virgin olive oil	50 mL
4	cloves garlic, minced	4
2 tbsp	finely chopped fresh oregano (or 1 tsp/5 mL dried)	25 mL
1 tsp	salt	5 mL
1 tsp	pepper	5 mL
½ tsp	hot pepper flakes	2 mL
1	chicken (about 3 lb/1.5 kg)	1

fridge NOTE

- **If wings start to brown too quickly on the barbecue, wrap them in foil.**

VARIATIONS

Cornish Hens Under Bricks: Use two 1½-lb (750 g) Cornish hens; reduce cooking time by about 10 minutes, watching carefully to avoid flare-ups. Cut each in half to serve.

Herbed Chicken Under Bricks: Omit oregano and hot pepper flakes. Use 2 tbsp (25 mL) chopped fresh sage (or 2 tsp/10 mL dried) and 1 tbsp (15 mL) chopped fresh rosemary (or 1 tsp/5 mL dried).

Latin American Mojo Chicken

Lime juice, cumin and hot peppers contribute a vigorous Latin touch to tried-and-true chicken. – Emily

¼ cup	extra-virgin olive oil	50 mL
4	cloves garlic, minced	4
1	jalapeño pepper, seeded and minced	1
2 tsp	ground cumin	10 mL
¼ tsp	each salt and pepper	1 mL
3 tbsp	lime juice	50 mL
1 tbsp	sherry or wine vinegar	15 mL
4	boneless skinless chicken breasts (1 lb/500 g total)	4

1 In small saucepan, heat oil over medium heat just until hot and oil begins to move on its own, about 3 minutes.

2 Meanwhile, in bowl, stir together garlic, jalapeño pepper, cumin, salt and pepper. Pour in hot oil. Whisk in lime juice and sherry. Let stand for 5 minutes. Add chicken, turning to coat. Let stand for 5 minutes. (MAKE-AHEAD: **Cover and refrigerate for up to 24 hours.**)

3 Reserving marinade, place chicken on greased grill over medium-high heat; brush with reserved marinade. Close lid and grill, turning once, until no longer pink inside, 10 to 12 minutes. Discard any remaining marinade.

Makes 4 servings. PER SERVING: about 262 cal, 33 g pro, 13 g total fat (2 g sat. fat), 2 g carb, trace fibre, 84 mg chol, 193 mg sodium. % RDI: 2% calcium, 9% iron, 3% vit A, 8% vit C, 2% folate.

Asian Beef Salad

*Make this winner salad with beef, pork tenderloin or chicken breasts. I
highly recommend it for warm-weather entertaining.* – Elizabeth

1 Place steak in large shallow dish. Whisk together fish sauce, lime
juice, hoisin sauce, ginger, sherry, garlic, chili paste and sesame oil;
pour half over meat, turning to coat. Cover and refrigerate fish and
reserved marinade separately for 8 hours. (MAKE-AHEAD: **Refrigerate
for up to 24 hours.**)

2 Place lettuce in large bowl. In saucepan of boiling water, cook snow
peas until tender-crisp, about 2 minutes. Drain and chill under cold
water; drain again and pat dry. Add to bowl along with red pepper.

3 Slice cucumber in half lengthwise; slice thinly crosswise and add
to bowl along with bean sprouts. Place steak on foil-lined rimmed
baking sheet. Spoon marinade from dish over steak. Broil, 6 inches
(15 cm) from heat, turning once, until medium-rare, about 10 minutes.
Transfer to cutting board and tent with foil; let stand for 5 minutes.

4 Meanwhile, in small saucepan, bring reserved marinade to boil.
Remove from heat; whisk in vinegar and sugar. Gradually whisk in
olive oil. Let cool slightly.

5 Slice meat diagonally across the grain into thin slices; add to bowl.
Pour dressing over top; toss gently to coat.

Makes 4 servings. PER SERVING: about 305 cal, 24 g pro, 15 g total fat (4 g sat. fat),
18 g carb, 4 g fibre, 35 mg chol, 903 mg sodium. % RDI: 11% calcium, 31% iron, 40% vit A,
168% vit C, 49% folate.

12 oz	flank marinating steak	375 g
2 tbsp	each fish sauce, lime juice and hoisin sauce	25 mL
4 tsp	minced gingerroot	20 mL
1 tbsp	dry sherry	15 mL
1	clove garlic, minced	1
½ tsp	Asian chili paste	2 mL
½ tsp	sesame oil	2 mL
8 cups	torn red leaf lettuce	2 L
2 cups	snow peas (6 oz/175 g)	500 mL
1	sweet red pepper, thinly sliced	1
Half	small English cucumber	Half
1 cup	bean sprouts	250 mL
1 tbsp	balsamic vinegar	15 mL
½ tsp	granulated sugar	2 mL
2 tbsp	extra-virgin olive oil	25 mL

Grilled T-Bone Steak with Zesty Barbecue Sauce

You can also serve your steak with a coin of herbed butter: softened butter
mixed with minced garlic and chopped fresh chives and parsley. – Emily

4	T-bone grilling steaks (each about 6 oz/175 g)	4
2 tbsp	extra-virgin olive oil	25 mL
¼ tsp	each salt and pepper	1 mL
ZESTY BARBECUE SAUCE:		
1 cup	beef stock	250 mL
1 cup	chili sauce	250 mL
½ cup	fancy molasses	125 mL
2 tbsp	wine vinegar	25 mL
4 tsp	Dijon mustard	20 mL
2 tsp	chili powder	10 mL
2 tsp	Worcestershire sauce	10 mL
1 tsp	celery seeds, crushed	5 mL
1 tsp	ground cumin	5 mL
½ tsp	each salt and pepper	2 mL

1 Brush steaks with oil; sprinkle with salt and pepper. Place on greased grill over high heat; close lid and grill until medium-rare, about 5 minutes per side, or until desired doneness.

2 Brush Zesty Barbecue Sauce over steaks just before removing from grill or serve alongside steak.

Makes 4 servings. PER SERVING: about 290 cal, 26 g pro, 15 g total fat (4 g sat. fat), 12 g carb, 1 g fibre, 46 mg chol, 588 mg sodium. % RDI: 3% calcium, 28% iron, 2% vit A, 5% vit C, 6% folate.

Zesty Barbecue Sauce

1 In saucepan, combine stock, chili sauce, molasses, vinegar, mustard, chili powder, Worcestershire sauce, celery seeds, cumin, salt and pepper. Stir in ⅔ cup (150 mL) water; bring to boil. Reduce heat and simmer until reduced to 2 cups (500 mL), about 20 minutes. (MAKE-AHEAD: **Transfer to airtight container and refrigerate for up to 2 weeks.**)

Makes 2 cups (500 mL). PER 2 TBSP (25 mL): about 50 cal, 1 g pro, trace total fat (0 g sat. fat), 12 g carb, 1 g fibre, 0 mg chol, 379 mg sodium. % RDI: 3% calcium, 6% iron, 2% vit A, 5% vit C, 3% folate.

Devilled Beef Ribs

The devil is in the mustard and horseradish. You may need to specially order beef ribs from the butcher. – Daphna

1 DEVIL SAUCE: In saucepan, heat oil and butter over medium-high heat; sauté onion, stirring occasionally, until softened, 3 to 5 minutes. Add garlic, sugar, lemon juice, thyme and cayenne; cook, stirring, for 4 minutes. Let cool slightly.

2 Whisk together Dijon and grainy mustards, horseradish, salt, pepper and hot pepper sauce; whisk into onion mixture. Add more hot pepper sauce, if desired; stir in parsley. Let cool.

3 In large shallow dish, arrange ribs in single layer. Set aside ½ cup (125 mL) of the Devil Sauce for dipping. Brush both sides of ribs with remaining Devil Sauce. Cover and marinate in refrigerator for 3 hours.

4 Reserving marinade, place ribs, curved side down, on greased grill over medium heat. Brush with some of the marinade; close lid and grill for 5 minutes. Turn, brush with some of the remaining marinade and grill for 5 minutes. Repeat twice. Sprinkle with salt. Grill until glazed and crusty, about 10 minutes longer. Transfer to platter and tent with foil; let stand for 5 minutes. Cut into serving-size pieces and serve with reserved Devil Sauce.

Makes 6 to 8 servings. PER EACH OF 8 SERVINGS: about 296 cal, 20 g pro, 21 g total fat (7 g sat. fat), 8 g carb, 1 g fibre, 54 mg chol, 667 mg sodium. % RDI: 6% calcium, 19% iron, 4% vit A, 7% vit C, 6% folate.

4 lb	meaty beef ribs	2 kg
¼ tsp	salt	1 mL
DEVIL SAUCE:		
¼ cup	vegetable oil	50 mL
2 tbsp	butter	25 mL
1	large onion, minced	1
3	cloves garlic, minced	3
2 tbsp	packed brown sugar	25 mL
2 tbsp	lemon juice	25 mL
2 tsp	dried thyme	10 mL
¼ tsp	cayenne pepper	1 mL
⅓ cup	each Dijon and grainy mustard	75 mL
¼ cup	horseradish	50 mL
¾ tsp	each salt and pepper	4 mL
¼ tsp	hot pepper sauce (approx)	1 mL
¼ cup	minced fresh parsley	50 mL

Indian Spiced Beef Koftas

I like to serve these spicy barbecued meatballs with a fresh mix of chopped tomatoes, onions, cucumbers and coriander. – Elizabeth

2 tbsp	minced gingerroot	25 mL
2	cloves garlic, minced	2
1	jalapeño or hot green chili pepper, seeded and minced	1
2 tbsp	vegetable oil	25 mL
1	egg yolk	1
1 tbsp	cornstarch	15 mL
½ tsp	each salt and turmeric	2 mL
¼ tsp	ground coriander	1 mL
1 lb	lean ground beef	500 g

1 In large bowl, stir together ginger, garlic, jalapeño, oil, egg yolk, cornstarch, salt, turmeric and coriander; mix in beef. Divide into 8 portions; shape each into ball.

2 Thread 2 balls onto each of 4 metal or soaked wooden skewers; squeeze each ball into 3-inch (8 cm) sausage shape.

3 Place koftas on greased grill over medium-high heat; close lid and grill, turning once, until koftas are lightly browned and no longer pink inside, about 15 minutes.

Makes 4 servings. PER SERVING: about 272 cal, 22 g pro, 19 g total fat (5 g sat. fat), 4 g carb, trace fibre, 111 mg chol, 350 mg sodium. % RDI: 2% calcium, 17% iron, 5% vit A, 10% vit C, 4% folate.

" Living in England in the '60s introduced me to the seductive blend of Indian spices. I am still totally hooked! – *Elizabeth* **"**

Slow and Easy Java Ribs

Ground coffee and ribs? You'll just have to trust me here. A whisper of coffee mingles with the spices and adds a little crunch. – Emily

1 Trim any visible fat from ribs; remove membrane from underside if attached. Place ribs in large shallow dish.

2 In small bowl, combine coffee, sugar, chili powder, paprika, salt, cumin, cinnamon and ginger; rub all over ribs. Cover and marinate in refrigerator for 4 hours. (MAKE-AHEAD: **Refrigerate for up to 24 hours.**)

3 Place ribs on greased grill over medium-low heat; close lid and grill, turning 4 times and brushing with some of the oil, until tender and bones are visible at ends, 1½ to 2 hours. Cut into 2- or 3-rib pieces.

Makes 6 to 8 servings. PER EACH OF 8 SERVINGS: about 494 cal, 29 g pro, 39 g total fat (13 g sat. fat), 7 g carb, 1 g fibre, 137 mg chol, 1,005 mg sodium. % RDI: 7% calcium, 20% iron, 17% vit A, 5% vit C, 1% folate.

3	racks pork back ribs (about 5 lb/2.2 kg total)	3
¼ cup	ground coffee beans (not instant)	50 mL
3 tbsp	packed brown sugar	50 mL
2 tbsp	each chili powder and paprika	25 mL
1 tbsp	salt	15 mL
2 tsp	ground cumin	10 mL
½ tsp	each cinnamon and ground ginger	2 mL
2 tbsp	vegetable oil	25 mL

Italian Sausage and Tomato Kabobs

I love the versatility of sausages and keep them in the freezer to use in pasta sauces or to grill up for a panini. – Daphna

4	mild Italian sausages (about 1 lb/500 g)	4
32	cubes (1 inch/2.5 cm) Italian bread	32
24	cherry tomatoes	24
¼ cup	extra-virgin olive oil	50 mL
3 tbsp	balsamic vinegar	50 mL
2 tbsp	chopped fresh oregano	25 mL
¼ tsp	each salt and pepper	1 mL
1 tbsp	grated Parmesan cheese	15 mL

fridge NOTES

- **If you don't have a microwave oven, simmer the sausages in a saucepan of water for five minutes.**

- **For more zing, look for fresh hot Italian sausages or use spiced sausage, such as garlic or chorizo.**

1 Prick sausages all over; place in microwaveable dish. Cover with plastic wrap; microwave at High until firm, about 5 minutes. Let cool slightly; cut into quarters.

2 Onto each of 8 metal or soaked wooden skewers, alternately thread 4 bread cubes, 3 tomatoes and 2 sausage pieces. In small bowl, whisk together oil, vinegar, oregano, salt and pepper; brush about one-quarter over kabobs.

3 Place kabobs on greased grill over medium-high heat; brush with about 2 tbsp (25 mL) of the remaining oil mixture. Close lid and grill, turning and basting twice with remaining oil mixture, until sausage is browned and bread is crisp, about 8 minutes. Serve sprinkled with cheese.

Makes 4 servings. PER SERVING: about 440 cal, 20 g pro, 30 g total fat (8 g sat. fat), 23 g carb, 2 g fibre, 49 mg chol, 1,046 mg sodium. % RDI: 5% calcium, 19% iron, 10% vit A, 22% vit C, 12% folate.

Grilled Vegetable Panini

You can make these sandwiches ahead and heat them in a sandwich press or on a barbecue. – Emily

1 Seed, core and cut red and yellow peppers into quarters; place in large bowl. Trim stems off mushrooms; add caps to bowl. Slice zucchini lengthwise; add to bowl.

2 Whisk together oil, vinegar, garlic, mustard, salt and pepper; pour all but 2 tbsp (25 mL) over vegetables and toss to coat.

3 Place vegetables on greased grill over medium-high heat; close lid and grill, turning once, until tender-crisp, 10 to 15 minutes. Thickly slice mushrooms.

4 Whisk mayonnaise, mint and tahini into reserved oil mixture; spread on cut sides of buns. Sandwich vegetables in buns. (MAKE-AHEAD: **Wrap in plastic wrap and refrigerate for up to 4 hours.**) Cut in half to serve.

Makes 8 servings. PER SERVING: about 253 cal, 6 g pro, 15 g total fat (2 g sat. fat), 26 g carb, 3 g fibre, 5 mg chol, 432 mg sodium. % RDI: 5% calcium, 15% iron, 13% vit A, 158% vit C, 25% folate.

2	each sweet red and yellow or green peppers	2
2	portobello mushrooms	2
2	zucchini	2
¼ cup	extra-virgin olive oil	50 mL
¼ cup	wine vinegar	50 mL
1	clove garlic, minced	1
½ tsp	Dijon mustard	2 mL
½ tsp	each salt and pepper	2 mL
½ cup	light mayonnaise	125 mL
2 tbsp	chopped fresh mint	25 mL
2 tbsp	tahini	25 mL
4	large crusty buns, halved	4

By the Sea

*A*ll three of us are big fans of fish for both weeknight meals and entertaining, and we are determined to reel in more devotees through our show. That was easy to do the day we prepared salmon papillote. When we slit the puffed parchment to reveal the pink fillets, the glorious aroma filled the studio, and no one could resist diving in. We're so lucky that we don't have to live right by the sea to enjoy its bounty. Discover what's at your own local seafood department or fishmonger and get set to fry, grill, poach or roast a tasty meal. – Emily

- Beer-Battered Fish and Onion Rings
- Porcini-Dusted Cod with Roasted Garlic Mashed Potatoes
- Monkfish Stew
- Fresh Tuna Salade Niçoise
- Tea-Smoked Salmon
- Tarragon Monkfish Kabobs
- Salmon en Papillote with Fennel and Roasted Peppers
- Herb-Roasted Trout
- Escovitched Fish
- Poached Salmon with Beurre Blanc

Beer-Battered Fish and Onion Rings

Here's how to bring this takeout favourite home. Beer's the secret to the crunchy coating. – Elizabeth

1¾ cups	all-purpose flour	425 mL
1½ tsp	salt (approx)	7 mL
¼ tsp	cayenne pepper	1 mL
1	bottle (341 mL) beer	1
1	small Spanish onion	1
	Vegetable oil for deep-frying	
1 lb	haddock or cod fillets	500 g
	Lemon wedges	
	Tartar sauce	

1 In bowl, whisk together 1½ cups (375 mL) of the flour, 1½ tsp (7 mL) salt and cayenne. Whisk in beer until smooth. Let stand for 15 minutes.

2 Meanwhile, cut onion into ½-inch (1 cm) thick slices. Separate into rings.

3 Pour enough oil into deep-fryer or deep heavy-bottomed pot to come at least 2 inches (5 cm) up side. Heat to 375°F (190°C) or until 1-inch (2.5 cm) cube of bread turns golden in 30 seconds. Using fork, dip 4 onion rings into batter, letting excess drip off; transfer to deep-fryer and cook, turning once, until golden brown, about 1 minute. Using slotted spoon, transfer to paper towel–lined rimmed baking sheet. Keep warm in 250°F (120°C) oven for up to 1 hour. Repeat with remaining onion rings.

4 Meanwhile, cut fillets into serving-size pieces. Dredge fish in remaining flour, shaking off excess. Dip fish into batter, letting excess drip off; fry in oil, turning once, until golden brown, about 7 minutes. Using slotted spoon, transfer to paper towel–lined rimmed baking sheet to drain.

5 Sprinkle with salt to taste. Serve with lemon wedges and tartar sauce.

Makes 4 servings. PER SERVING: about 447 cal, 27 g pro, 17 g total fat (1 g sat. fat), 43 g carb, 2 g fibre, 65 mg chol, 772 mg sodium. % RDI: 6% calcium, 24% iron, 2% vit A, 10% vit C, 32% folate.

Porcini-Dusted Cod with Roasted Garlic Mashed Potatoes

This dish is all about flavour: the woodsy essence of porcini mushrooms and the mellow depth of roasted garlic. – Daphna

1 Cut fish into 6 equal pieces; sprinkle with salt and pepper. Set aside.

2 In clean coffee grinder, grind mushrooms into fine powder; spread in shallow dish. Dip fish into mushroom powder, turning to coat. Place on plate; cover loosely with plastic wrap and refrigerate for 4 hours. (MAKE-AHEAD: **Refrigerate for up to 24 hours.**)

3 ROASTED GARLIC MASHED POTATOES: Meanwhile, cut tips off top of each garlic head; remove any loose papery skin, leaving head unpeeled. Wrap in foil. Roast in 425°F (220°C) oven until very soft when squeezed, about 40 minutes.

4 Meanwhile, in large saucepan of lightly salted boiling water, cover and cook potatoes until just tender, 15 to 20 minutes. Drain well and return to saucepan; heat over low heat, shaking pan occasionally, until completely dry, about 2 minutes. Turn off heat. Squeeze garlic from skins; mash into potatoes along with butter. Add cream, chives, salt and pepper; mash or stir until fluffy.

5 In cast-iron skillet or grill pan, melt butter over medium-high heat until starting to brown; cook fish, skin side down (if applicable), for 3 minutes. Transfer to 425°F (220°C) oven and roast until fish is opaque and flakes easily when tested, about 10 minutes.

6 Mound potatoes on each plate; top with fish. Drizzle browned butter over top.

Makes 6 servings. PER SERVING: about 483 cal, 32 g pro, 20 g total fat (12 g sat. fat), 44 g carb, 3 g fibre, 125 mg chol, 1,025 mg sodium. % RDI: 9% calcium, 12% iron, 19% vit A, 32% vit C, 16% folate.

2 lb	cod, halibut or snapper fillets	1 kg
1 oz	dried porcini mushrooms	30 g
¼ tsp	each salt and pepper	1 mL
3 tbsp	butter	50 mL
ROASTED GARLIC MASHED POTATOES:		
2	heads garlic	2
7	potatoes (about 3 lb/1.5 kg), peeled and cut into chunks	7
¼ cup	butter	50 mL
¾ cup	18% cream	175 mL
3 tbsp	chopped fresh chives	50 mL
¾ tsp	salt	4 mL
½ tsp	pepper	2 mL

Monkfish Stew

Perfect for a cold winter night, this colourful one-pot meal is best served in a wide soup bowl with lots of bread to sop up the juices. – Emily

2	potatoes	2
4	carrots	4
1 lb	monkfish or halibut fillets (skin removed)	500 g
½ tsp	salt	2 mL
¼ tsp	pepper	1 mL
2 tsp	extra-virgin olive oil	10 mL
2	onions, chopped	2
3	cloves garlic, minced	3
1½ tsp	dried thyme	7 mL
1	bay leaf	1
1½ cups	fish or vegetable stock	375 mL
¾ cup	dry white wine	175 mL
¼ tsp	saffron threads	1 mL
1	can (19 oz/540 mL) tomatoes, drained and chopped	1
2 tbsp	finely chopped fresh parsley	25 mL

1 Peel potatoes if desired; cut potatoes and carrots into finger-size sticks. Set aside.

2 Remove any membranes from fish; cut into 1-inch (2.5 cm) cubes. Sprinkle with half each of the salt and pepper. In large nonstick skillet, heat oil over medium-high heat; cook fish until opaque and barely flakes when tested, about 4 minutes. Transfer to plate.

3 Add potatoes, carrots, onions, garlic, thyme, bay leaf and remaining salt and pepper to pan; cook over medium heat, stirring often, for 4 minutes.

4 Stir in stock, wine and saffron; bring to boil. Reduce heat, cover and simmer, stirring occasionally, until vegetables are almost tender, about 20 minutes. Stir in tomatoes; simmer, uncovered, just until vegetables are tender, about 15 minutes.

5 Return fish to pan; simmer until steaming, about 2 minutes. Discard bay leaf. Serve sprinkled with parsley.

Makes 4 servings. PER SERVING: about 265 cal, 22 g pro, 5 g total fat (1 g sat. fat), 31 g carb, 5 g fibre, 29 mg chol, 634 mg sodium. % RDI: 9% calcium, 17% iron, 189% vit A, 42% vit C, 26% folate.

Fresh Tuna Salade Niçoise

In this composed salad, the tuna is grilled rare. It gives a fresh, sophisticated update to a classic bistro salad from the south of France. – Daphna

1 In saucepan of boiling salted water, cover and cook potatoes just until tender, 20 to 25 minutes. Remove with slotted spoon; let cool slightly. Cut into quarters.

2 In same pan, cover and cook green beans until tender-crisp, 5 to 7 minutes. Drain and chill in cold water; drain again.

3 Cut each tomato into 6 wedges. Slice red onion. Cut eggs into quarters. Set aside.

4 Brush both sides of tuna with oil; sprinkle with salt and pepper. Place on greased grill over medium-high heat; close lid and grill, turning once, until firm and pink outside yet still rare inside, 6 to 8 minutes. Cut into ¼-inch (5 mm) thick slices.

5 DRESSING: In bowl, whisk together vinegar, mustard, garlic, anchovy paste, salt and pepper; gradually whisk in oil until blended. Set aside.

6 On large serving platter, attractively arrange potatoes, green beans, tomatoes, onion, eggs, tuna and olives; drizzle with dressing.

Makes 6 servings. PER SERVING: about 570 cal, 36 g pro, 35 g total fat (6 g sat. fat), 30 g carb, 5 g fibre, 189 mg chol, 947 mg sodium. % RDI: 8% calcium, 29% iron, 81% vit A, 50% vit C, 26% folate.

5	new red potatoes (unpeeled), 1½ lb (750 g)	5
1 lb	green beans, trimmed	500 g
5	plum tomatoes	5
Half	small red onion	Half
4	hard-cooked eggs	4
1½ lb	fresh tuna fillet	750 g
2 tbsp	extra-virgin olive oil	25 mL
Pinch	each salt and pepper	Pinch
⅓ cup	Niçoise or other black olives	75 mL
DRESSING:		
¼ cup	red wine vinegar	50 mL
1 tbsp	Dijon mustard	15 mL
1	clove garlic, minced	1
2 tsp	anchovy paste	10 mL
¼ tsp	each salt and pepper	1 mL
½ cup	extra-virgin olive oil	125 mL

Tea-Smoked Salmon

You can rig up your wok to hot-smoke salmon Chinese-style. Be sure to do your smoking on a day when you can open the window! – Elizabeth

1 lb	salmon fillet (skin on)	500 g
2½ tsp	salt	12 mL
1½ tsp	finely grated gingerroot	7 mL
½ tsp	granulated sugar	2 mL
1 tbsp	packed brown sugar	15 mL
2 tsp	soy sauce	10 mL
1½ tsp	five-spice powder	7 mL
½ cup	radish sprouts	125 mL
SMOKING:		
¼ cup	tea leaves	50 mL
¼ cup	white rice	50 mL
2 tbsp	packed brown sugar	25 mL
SALMON ROE GARNISH:		
2 oz	salmon roe	60 g
3 tbsp	sake (Japanese wine)	50 mL
1 tsp	finely grated gingerroot	5 mL
1 tsp	lemon juice	5 mL

1 Rub salmon fillet with salt, ginger and granulated sugar. Place on plate, cover with plastic wrap and refrigerate for 12 hours. (MAKE-AHEAD: **Refrigerate for up to 24 hours.**)

2 Lightly rub excess salt and ginger off fillet; discard any accumulated juices on plate. In small bowl, mix together brown sugar, soy sauce and five-spice powder; spread on top of salmon. Cut piece of foil about same size as salmon; place on round wire rack that fits inside wok. Poke several holes in foil; place salmon on foil.

3 SMOKING: Line wok with foil. Place tea leaves, rice, brown sugar and 1 tbsp (15 mL) water on foil. Cover and heat over high heat until smoking. Add salmon; cover with lid. Wrap wet tea towel around edge of wok to prevent smoke from escaping. Smoke until fish just begins to flake when tested, about 15 minutes. Remove and let cool. (MAKE-AHEAD: **Place on rack on plate, uncovered, in refrigerator for up to 24 hours. This will make fish easier to slice thinly.**)

4 SALMON ROE GARNISH: Meanwhile, in small bowl, mix salmon roe with sake; let stand for 2 minutes. Drain. Stir ginger with lemon juice. Break salmon into chunks or slice salmon; place over bed of radish sprouts. Top with garnish.

Makes 4 to 6 servings. PER EACH OF 6 SERVINGS: about 208 cal, 14 g pro, 7 g total fat (1 g sat. fat), 20 g carb, trace fibre, 68 mg chol, 1,113 mg sodium. % RDI: 2% calcium, 4% iron, 2% vit A, 8% vit C, 13% folate.

Tarragon Monkfish Kabobs

Monkfish – also known as poor man's lobster – is a mild-tasting firm-fleshed fish great for grilling, and it won't overpower the marinade. – Emily

1 In large bowl, whisk together wine, oil, olives, tarragon, garlic, salt and pepper. Remove any membrane from fish; cut fillets into 1½-inch (4 cm) chunks. Add to bowl and toss gently to coat. Leaving about ¼ inch (5 mm) between chunks, thread onto 6 metal or soaked wooden skewers.

2 Place on greased grill over medium-high heat; close lid and grill, turning once, until fish is opaque and flakes easily when tested, about 5 minutes.

Makes 6 servings. PER SERVING: about 133 cal, 17 g pro, 7 g total fat (1 g sat. fat), trace carb, trace fibre, 28 mg chol, 139 mg sodium. % RDI: 1% calcium, 4% iron, 1% vit A, 2% vit C, 4% folate.

3 tbsp	each dry white wine and extra-virgin olive oil	50 mL
2 tbsp	minced oil-cured black olives	25 mL
1 tbsp	chopped fresh tarragon or basil (or ½ tsp/2 mL dried)	15 mL
2	cloves garlic, minced	2
¼ tsp	each salt and pepper	1 mL
1½ lb	monkfish fillets	750 g

" When we think kabobs, we tend to think chicken and meat. But this is also a wonderful way to prepare fish. – *Emily* **"**

fridge NOTE

- For added flavour and a more colourful presentation, you can thread fresh bay leaves onto skewers between fish chunks. Just remember not to eat the bay leaves.

Salmon en Papillote with Fennel and Roasted Peppers

For dinner parties, bring the salmon packages to the table hot from the oven.
When you slit the parchment, the aroma is so inviting. – Emily

1	small bulb fennel	1
4	roasted red peppers, drained and sliced	4
4	salmon fillets (about 1½ lb/750 g total)	4
2 tbsp	chopped fresh Italian parsley	25 mL
2 tbsp	extra-virgin olive oil	25 mL
2 tbsp	licorice liqueur, such as Pernod (optional)	25 mL
4	cloves garlic, minced	4
1 tsp	grated lemon rind	5 mL
½ tsp	each salt and pepper	2 mL
	Lemon wedges	

1 Cut stalks off fennel. Halve fennel from top to root end; cut out core. Cut into thin slices. Place one-quarter of the slices on 1 side of each of four 18-inch (45 cm) long pieces of parchment paper or foil. Sprinkle with red peppers. Top with salmon.

2 In bowl, combine parsley, oil, liqueur (if using), garlic, lemon rind, salt and pepper; spoon over salmon. Fold paper over top; fold open edges over in small pleats to seal and form semicircular package.

3 Bake on rimmed baking sheet in 425°F (220°C) oven until fennel is tender and fish flakes easily when tested, 15 to 20 minutes. Serve with lemon wedges.

Makes 4 servings. PER SERVING: about 422 cal, 36 g pro, 26 g total fat (5 g sat. fat), 12 g carb, 3 g fibre, 100 mg chol, 414 mg sodium. % RDI: 4% calcium, 10% iron, 44% vit A, 345% vit C, 31% folate.

fridge **NOTE**

- Fatty fish, such as salmon, is rich in omega-3 fatty acids, which are associated with lowering the risk of heart disease.

Herb-Roasted Trout

The subtlety of fresh herbs goes beautifully with mild trout, and the vibrant greens are a striking visual contrast. – Daphna

1 In small bowl, stir together parsley, oregano, sage, lemon rind, oil, salt and pepper. Place fish, skin side down, on parchment paper–lined rimmed baking sheet. Press parsley mixture onto fish.

2 Roast in top third of 450°F (230°C) oven until fish is opaque and flakes easily when tested, about 10 minutes. Serve with lemon wedges.

Makes 4 servings. PER SERVING: about 290 cal, 32 g pro, 16 g total fat (1 g sat. fat), 2 g carb, 1 g fibre, 90 mg chol, 344 mg sodium. % RDI: 12% calcium, 6% iron, 13% vit A, 22% vit C, 16% folate.

2 tbsp	each minced fresh parsley, oregano and sage	25 mL
2 tbsp	finely grated lemon rind	25 mL
2 tbsp	extra-virgin olive oil	25 mL
½ tsp	each salt and pepper	2 mL
4	trout fillets (each about 6 oz/175 g)	4
	Lemon wedges	

Escovitched Fish

Hot pickled escovitched fish is eaten all day long in Jamaica – for breakfast, as an appetizer or for dinner. Good, man! – Elizabeth

2 lb	tilapia or red snapper fillets	1 kg
½ cup	all-purpose flour	125 mL
½ tsp	each salt and pepper	2 mL
2 tbsp	vegetable oil (approx)	25 mL
PICKLING LIQUID:		
1	Scotch bonnet pepper, seeded	1
1	chayote	1
1	carrot	1
1	large red onion, sliced	1
1 cup	apple cider vinegar	250 mL
12	whole allspice	12
6	peppercorns	6
1 tsp	granulated sugar	5 mL
Pinch	salt	Pinch

1 Pat fish dry. In shallow dish, whisk flour with salt and pepper; dredge fish in flour mixture to coat all over, shaking off excess. Place on waxed paper–lined rimmed baking sheet.

2 Heat large nonstick skillet over medium heat; brush generously with oil. Fry fish, in batches and adding more oil as necessary, until golden brown and crisp, about 3 minutes per side. Drain on paper towel–lined tray. Arrange in single layer in 13- x 9-inch (3 L) glass baking dish.

3 PICKLING LIQUID: Slice pepper thinly and place in saucepan. Cut chayote and carrot into ¼-inch (5 mm) matchstick strips and add to pan along with onion, vinegar, 1 cup (250 mL) water, allspice, peppercorns, sugar and salt; bring to boil, stirring. Pour over fish. Let cool for 30 minutes. Cover and refrigerate for 2 hours. (MAKE-AHEAD: **Refrigerate for up to 24 hours.**) Serve cold.

Makes 6 to 8 servings. PER EACH OF 8 SERVINGS: about 196 cal, 25 g pro, 5 g total fat (1 g sat. fat), 12 g carb, 2 g fibre, 42 mg chol, 188 mg sodium. % RDI: 5% calcium, 6% iron, 26% vit A, 13% vit C, 10% folate.

fridge **NOTE**

- **Look for chayote, a.k.a. chocho, in Caribbean grocery stores. It has a lovely apple-pear taste.**

Poached Salmon with Beurre Blanc

Poaching is an easy technique well suited to fish. The poaching liquid (court bouillon) cooks it gently and infuses it with flavour. – Emily

1 In shallow Dutch oven or skillet large enough to hold fish in single layer, combine 6 cups (1.5 L) water, wine, onion, celery, parsley, bay leaves, lemon, tarragon, peppercorns, thyme and salt; bring to boil. Reduce heat to medium and simmer for 20 minutes. (**MAKE-AHEAD: Cover and set aside for up to 6 hours; return to simmer.**)

2 Add salmon to pan; cover and cook at bare simmer until fish flakes easily when tested, 7 to 9 minutes. Using slotted spatula, transfer fish to plate and keep warm. Strain, reserving liquid.

3 In saucepan over high heat, bring 1 cup (250 mL) of the reserved liquid, vinegar, shallots and pepper to boil; boil until reduced to ¼ cup (50 mL), 5 to 6 minutes.

4 Reduce heat to low. Whisk in butter, 1 cube at a time; whisk in cream. Serve over salmon. Garnish with chives.

Makes 6 servings. PER SERVING: about 465 cal, 34 g pro, 35 g total fat (14 g sat. fat), 1 g carb, trace fibre, 141 mg chol, 280 mg sodium. % RDI: 3% calcium, 5% iron, 18% vit A, 10% vit C, 25% folate.

1 cup	dry white wine	250 mL
1	onion, sliced	1
2	stalks celery, sliced	2
6	sprigs parsley	6
2	bay leaves	2
Half	lemon, sliced	Half
1½ tsp	dried tarragon	7 mL
1 tsp	black peppercorns	5 mL
½ tsp	each dried thyme and salt	2 mL
6	salmon fillets (each about 6 oz/175 g)	6
⅓ cup	white wine vinegar	75 mL
2 tbsp	finely chopped shallots	25 mL
Pinch	white or black pepper	Pinch
½ cup	cold butter, cut in small cubes	125 mL
1 tbsp	whipping cream	15 mL
1 tbsp	chopped fresh chives and/or parsley	15 mL

" I serve this a lot for family brunches. Its delicate texture and flavour are lovely for a late-morning meal. – *Emily* "

Let's Celebrate!

There are so many reasons to celebrate – holidays, birthdays, weddings and anniversaries, graduations, promotions, babies. We've had fun theming many shows around special occasions. Christmas, Hanukkah, New Year's and Ramadan come to mind, as do the shows when we've indulged our love of decorating birthday cakes. And here's another reason I have to celebrate: I've noticed that when friends and family gather nowadays, it's inspired more by "I'd love to do this" than by "I have to do this." Entertaining itself has become fun and food more playful, without compromising tradition. Hosts set their own stage according to their notions of elegance, passionately presenting memorable food and inspiring warm memories. – Daphna

- Shrimp Newburg
- Pesce Frillo
- Lobster Cocktail with Ginger Vinaigrette
- Chicken Phyllo Bundles
- Charmoula Roast Turkey Breast
- Peppery Prime Rib
- Grainy Mustard–Glazed Ham
- Salad of Greens and Candied Walnuts
- Traditional Challah
- Chocolate Fig Honey Cake
- Pumpkin Cake
- Pool Party Cake
- Ma'amoul

Shrimp Newburg

Here's an elegant entrée for a special occasion. Boiling the shrimp shells in wine gives the silky sauce an intense shrimp flavour. – Emily

4 lb	large raw shrimp	2 kg
1 tbsp	butter	15 mL
4	shallots, finely chopped	4
2 tbsp	tomato paste	25 mL
½ tsp	paprika	2 mL
1 cup	dry white wine	250 mL
2 cups	whipping cream	500 mL
Pinch	pepper	Pinch
2 tbsp	chopped fresh parsley	25 mL
1 tbsp	chopped fresh chives	15 mL
RICE:		
1 tbsp	butter	15 mL
1	shallot, finely chopped	1
1	carrot, diced	1
2 cups	long-grain rice	500 mL
1 tsp	salt	5 mL

1 Peel and devein shrimp, reserving shells. Cover and refrigerate shrimp. (MAKE-AHEAD: **Refrigerate for up to 8 hours.**)

2 In large shallow saucepan, melt butter over medium heat; cook shallots, stirring often, until softened, about 3 minutes. Add tomato paste and paprika; cook, stirring, for 1 minute. Add reserved shrimp shells; cook, stirring, until pink, about 2 minutes.

3 Add wine and 2 cups (500 mL) water; bring to boil, scraping up any brown bits from bottom of pan. Reduce heat and simmer gently for 20 minutes. Strain through fine-mesh sieve into clean saucepan, pressing shells to extract liquid. Discard shells. (MAKE-AHEAD: **Let cool for 30 minutes; refrigerate until cold. Cover and refrigerate in airtight container for up to 8 hours. Reheat before continuing.**)

4 Add cream and pepper; bring to boil. Boil, stirring, until reduced by half, about 10 minutes. Add reserved shrimp; cook until pink, about 5 minutes. Stir in parsley.

5 RICE: Meanwhile, in saucepan, melt butter over medium heat; cook shallot and carrot until softened, about 5 minutes. Stir in rice. Add 4 cups (1 L) water and salt; bring to boil. Reduce heat to medium-low; cover and cook until water is absorbed and rice is tender, about 20 minutes. Fluff with fork. Serve shrimp mixture over rice. Garnish with chives.

Makes 8 to 10 servings. PER EACH OF 10 SERVINGS: about 470 cal, 32 g pro, 22 g total fat (12 g sat. fat), 34 g carb, 1 g fibre, 274 mg chol, 484 mg sodium. % RDI: 8% calcium, 22% iron, 44% vit A, 7% vit C, 8% folate.

Pesce Fritto

*Be sure to pat the fish dry so that the batter coats it well. And keep in mind
that this batter is also great for calamari, shrimp and vegetables.* – Emily

1 BATTER: In bowl, whisk together flour, baking powder, lemon rind, salt and pepper; whisk in 1 cup (250 mL) water until smooth. Set aside.

2 Cut cod into 3-inch (8 cm) chunks. Pat dry with paper towel.

3 In deep-fryer or deep heavy-bottomed pot, heat oil to 375°F (190°C) or until 1-inch (2.5 cm) cube of white bread turns golden in 30 seconds. Using fork, dip cod, 1 piece at a time, into batter, letting excess drip back into bowl. Deep-fry, in batches and turning halfway through, until golden, about 3 minutes. Using slotted spoon, transfer to paper towel–lined rimmed baking sheet. Keep warm in 250°F (120°C) oven for up to 30 minutes.

Makes 8 to 10 servings. PER EACH OF 10 SERVINGS: about 157 cal, 17 g pro, 5 g total fat (1 g sat. fat), 9 g carb, trace fibre, 39 mg chol, 194 mg sodium. % RDI: 3% calcium, 6% iron, 1% vit A, 2% vit C, 9% folate.

2 lb	cod or halibut fillets	1 kg
	Vegetable oil for deep-frying	
BATTER:		
1 cup	all-purpose flour	250 mL
2 tsp	baking powder	10 mL
½ tsp	grated lemon rind	2 mL
½ tsp	salt	2 mL
Pinch	pepper	Pinch

" In my family, a fish meal on Christmas Eve is traditional, and this is the dish my mom and grandmother always make. Like them, I'm a big fan of deep-frying. – *Emily* "

Lobster Cocktail with Ginger Vinaigrette

Celebrate New Year's Eve and other grand occasions with an elegant starter course from Boba restaurant in Toronto. – Daphna

12 oz	fresh cooked lobster meat (about 2 lobsters)	375 g
½ cup	diced avocado	125 mL
½ cup	diced mango	125 mL
Quarter	sweet red pepper	Quarter
1 cup	baby greens or mesclun	250 mL
2 tbsp	julienned daikon	25 mL
DRESSING:		
2 tbsp	lime juice	25 mL
1 tbsp	soy sauce	15 mL
1 tbsp	chopped fresh basil	15 mL
1	small green onion, minced	1
1 tsp	liquid honey	5 mL
½ tsp	grated gingerroot	2 mL
½ tsp	Asian chili paste or hot pepper sauce	2 mL
¼ tsp	each salt and pepper	1 mL
½ cup	vegetable oil	125 mL

1 DRESSING: Whisk together lime juice, soy sauce, basil, onion, honey, ginger, chili paste, salt and pepper. Gradually whisk in oil.

2 Break lobster meat into chunks, saving any claws for garnish. In bowl, combine lobster, avocado and mango; pour in half of the dressing and toss to combine. Cover and refrigerate for 30 minutes. (MAKE-AHEAD: **Refrigerate lobster mixture and remaining dressing separately for up to 2 hours.**)

3 Cut red pepper in half crosswise; slice into thin matchstick-size strips. Arrange greens in bottom of each of 8 cocktail glasses. Top each with ¼ cup (50 mL) of the lobster mixture. Garnish with red pepper strips, daikon and reserved lobster claws; drizzle with remaining dressing.

Makes 8 servings. PER SERVING: about 192 cal, 9 g pro, 15 g total fat (1 g sat. fat), 5 g carb, 1 g fibre, 31 mg chol, 369 mg sodium. % RDI: 3% calcium, 4% iron, 9% vit A, 22% vit C, 9% folate.

Chicken Phyllo Bundles

I love the combination of chicken and feta, and here they make little bundles of bliss. Phyllo always adds a fancy touch. – Emily

1 Starting at right side with knife parallel to board, slice each chicken breast in half almost but not all the way through to create pocket; place in glass dish. Whisk together wine, oil, garlic, bay leaves, oregano, pepper and salt; pour over chicken. Cover and marinate in refrigerator for 12 hours. (MAKE-AHEAD: **Refrigerate for up to 24 hours.**) Drain chicken, reserving 2 tbsp (25 mL) of the marinade and omitting bay leaves.

2 Stir together feta cheese, egg, Parmesan cheese, parsley and reserved marinade. Place each chicken breast on work surface. Insert generous 2 tbsp (25 mL) of the cheese mixture into pocket of each.

3 Place 1 sheet of phyllo on work surface, keeping remainder covered with damp tea towel to prevent drying out. Brush lightly with some of the butter; top with second sheet. Centre stuffed chicken breast on phyllo about 2 inches (5 cm) from bottom. Fold bottom over chicken; fold sides over and roll up. Place, seam side down, on greased rimmed baking sheet. Repeat with remaining phyllo and chicken. Brush tops with remaining butter.

4 Bake in 350°F (180°C) oven until tops are browned and chicken is no longer pink inside, about 45 minutes.

Makes 8 servings. PER SERVING: about 615 cal, 41 g pro, 37 g total fat (19 g sat. fat), 28 g carb, 1 g fibre, 189 mg chol, 994 mg sodium. % RDI: 21% calcium, 19% iron, 23% vit A, 5% vit C, 26% folate.

8	boneless skinless chicken breasts (2 lb/1 kg total)	8
½ cup	white wine	125 mL
¼ cup	extra-virgin olive oil	50 mL
3	cloves garlic, minced	3
2	bay leaves	2
2 tsp	dried oregano	10 mL
½ tsp	pepper	2 mL
¼ tsp	salt	1 mL
10 oz	feta cheese, crumbled	300 g
1	egg	1
2 tbsp	grated Parmesan cheese	25 mL
2 tbsp	chopped fresh parsley	25 mL
16	sheets phyllo pastry	16
¾ cup	butter, melted	175 mL

fridge NOTE

- Feta cheese varies in saltiness. Taste it before adding to dishes, so you can decide whether to: adjust the salt level in the recipe; or soak the feta briefly in cold water to reduce saltiness (drain and pat dry).

Charmoula Roast Turkey Breast

This is an impressive dish for Hanukkah and other celebrations. Charmoula is a herb and spice mixture of Moroccan origin. – Daphna

½ cup	finely chopped fresh coriander	125 mL
⅓ cup	finely chopped fresh parsley	75 mL
2	cloves garlic, minced	2
¼ cup	extra-virgin olive oil	50 mL
2 tbsp	lemon juice	25 mL
1 tsp	each paprika and salt	5 mL
½ tsp	ground cumin	2 mL
¼ tsp	cayenne pepper	1 mL
¼ tsp	pepper	1 mL
Pinch	cinnamon	Pinch
1	boneless turkey breast (3 lb/1.5 kg)	1

1 In bowl, stir together coriander, parsley, garlic, oil, lemon juice, paprika, salt, cumin, cayenne pepper, pepper and cinnamon.

2 Pat turkey breast dry. Starting at right side with knife parallel to board, slice turkey breast in half lengthwise just to within 1 inch (2.5 cm) of edge; open flat like book. Spread half of the seasoning mixture over cut surface. Starting at 1 long edge, roll up. Tie kitchen string around each end and at centre to secure. Rub remaining seasoning mixture over roll. Place on greased rack in roasting pan.

3 Roast in 325°F (160°C) oven until juices run clear when turkey is pierced and meat thermometer registers 185°F (85°C), about 2 hours. Transfer to cutting board and tent with foil; let stand for 15 minutes before slicing thinly.

Makes 8 servings. PER SERVING: about 244 cal, 40 g pro, 8 g total fat (1 g sat. fat), 1 g carb, trace fibre, 111 mg chol, 359 mg sodium. % RDI: 2% calcium, 17% iron, 3% vit A, 7% vit C, 5% folate.

fridge NOTE

- **For other occasions, brush this fragrant charmoula coating over salmon fillets, chicken breasts or lamb chops. Grill and enjoy.**

Peppery Prime Rib

With a premium oven roast such as a juicy prime rib, you don't need to do any gussying up; stay classic with peppercorns and mustard. – Daphna

1 Place roast, bone side down, on rack in roasting pan; set aside. Using mallet, coarsely crush peppercorns between waxed paper; transfer to small bowl. Stir in mustard, thyme and oil; spread all over roast. Roast in 325°F (160°C) oven until meat thermometer registers 140°F (60°C) for rare, about 2½ hours, or until desired doneness.

2 Transfer to cutting board and tent with foil; let stand for 15 minutes. Cut off string. Stand roast so bones are vertical; cut meat away from bones. Place meat, cut side down, on board and carve thinly.

Makes 12 servings. PER SERVING: about 275 cal, 34 g pro, 14 g total fat (5 g sat. fat), 1 g carb, trace fibre, 78 mg chol, 218 mg sodium. % RDI: 3% calcium, 23% iron, 5% folate.

1	prime rib premium oven roast (about 6½ lb/3 kg)	1
1 tbsp	black peppercorns	15 mL
½ cup	grainy or Dijon mustard	125 mL
2 tsp	dried thyme	10 mL
2 tsp	extra-virgin olive oil	10 mL

Grainy Mustard–Glazed Ham

A ham is never complete without a glaze. This one features ginger and chutney and makes a gorgeous platter for Easter dinner. – Elizabeth

1	fully cooked bone-in smoked ham, 12 to 15 lb (5.5 to 6.75 kg)	1
1	bottle (341 mL) beer	1
⅔ cup	strained mango chutney	150 mL
⅓ cup	packed brown sugar	75 mL
¼ cup	grainy Dijon mustard	50 mL
1 tbsp	dry mustard	15 mL
1 tbsp	cider vinegar	15 mL
1½ tsp	ground ginger	7 mL

1 Place ham, meaty side up, in roasting pan. Pour beer over ham. Cover with foil, tucking around pan to keep in beer aromas. Roast in 325°F (160°C) oven for 2 hours, basting occasionally with beer.

2 Meanwhile, in bowl, stir together chutney, sugar, Dijon and dry mustards, vinegar and ginger; set aside.

3 Remove ham from oven. Slide sharp knife under skin and lift off gently. Trim fat layer to ¼ inch (5 mm). Diagonally score fat side of ham in diamond pattern.

4 Brush about one-third of the mustard mixture over ham. Roast, brushing twice more with mustard mixture, until outside is crusty and rich caramel brown and meat thermometer inserted in centre registers 140°F (60°C), about 1 hour.

5 Transfer to cutting board and tent with foil; let stand for 20 to 30 minutes before carving.

Makes 16 to 20 servings. PER 4-OZ (125 G) SERVING: about 209 cal, 29 g pro, 6 g total fat (2 g sat. fat), 9 g carb, 0 g fibre, 62 mg chol, 1,694 mg sodium. % RDI: 1% calcium, 9% iron, 1% vit A, 2% folate.

Salad of Greens and Candied Walnuts

This salad has become the Baird family Christmas Day starter course, but you can make it to rave reviews any time of the year. – Elizabeth

1 CANDIED WALNUTS: In small bowl, combine walnuts, corn syrup, sugar, salt and cayenne; toss to coat (nuts may clump together). Spread on parchment paper–lined rimmed baking sheet. Bake in 325°F (160°C) oven, stirring occasionally to break up clumps, until golden and sugar is bubbling, about 15 minutes. Let cool completely on pan. Break apart if necessary. (MAKE-AHEAD: **Store in airtight container for up to 5 days.**)

2 WALNUT OIL DRESSING: In jar with tight-fitting lid, shake together shallots, walnut oil, sherry vinegar, vegetable oil, salt and pepper. (MAKE-AHEAD: **Refrigerate for up to 24 hours.**)

3 Remove coarse stems from watercress; place leaves in large bowl. Break romaine into bite size pieces and add to bowl. Shred radicchio; add to bowl. Add dressing; toss lightly to coat. Sprinkle with candied walnuts, and Stilton cheese (if using).

Makes 12 servings. PER SERVING: about 139 cal, 3 g pro, 12 g total fat (1 g sat. fat), 8 g carb, 2 g fibre, 0 mg chol, 115 mg sodium. % RDI: 5% calcium, 8% iron, 24% vit A, 38% vit C, 44% folate.

2	bunches watercress or arugula	2
2	hearts romaine lettuce (1½ lb/750 g total)	2
1	small head radicchio	1
½ cup	crumbled Stilton cheese (optional)	125 mL
CANDIED WALNUTS:		
1 cup	walnut halves	250 mL
2 tbsp	corn syrup	25 mL
1 tbsp	granulated sugar	15 mL
¼ tsp	each salt and cayenne pepper	1 mL
WALNUT OIL DRESSING:		
¼ cup	minced shallots, chives or green onions	50 mL
¼ cup	walnut oil	50 mL
2 tbsp	sherry vinegar	25 mL
1 tbsp	vegetable oil	15 mL
¼ tsp	salt	1 mL
Pinch	pepper	Pinch

Traditional Challah

Braided egg bread is traditional at the Jewish Sabbath meal. Shaped into a crown, it resonates with deeper meaning at Rosh Hashanah. – Daphna

2 tsp	granulated sugar	10 mL
½ cup	warm water	125 mL
1	pkg active dry yeast (or 1 tbsp/15 mL)	1
3½ cups	all-purpose flour (approx)	875 mL
1 tsp	salt	5 mL
¼ cup	liquid honey	50 mL
¼ cup	butter, melted (or vegetable oil)	50 mL
2	eggs, lightly beaten	2
2	egg yolks	2
¾ cup	golden raisins	175 mL
TOPPING:		
1	egg yolk, lightly beaten	1
1 tbsp	sesame seeds	15 mL

1 In large bowl, dissolve sugar in warm water. Sprinkle in yeast; let stand until frothy, about 10 minutes. Using wooden spoon, stir in 3 cups (750 mL) of the flour and salt. Add honey, butter, eggs and egg yolks; stir until dough forms.

2 Turn out dough onto lightly floured surface; knead until smooth and elastic, about 10 minutes, adding enough of the remaining flour as necessary to prevent sticking. Place in greased bowl, turning to grease all over. Cover with plastic wrap; let rise in warm draft-free place until doubled in bulk and indentation remains when dough is poked with 2 fingers, about 1 hour. Punch down dough; knead in raisins. Let rest for 5 minutes.

3 To make crown: Roll out dough into 30-inch (75 cm) long rope. Holding 1 end in place, wind remaining rope around end to form fairly tight spiral that is slightly higher in centre. Transfer to greased rimmed baking sheet.

4 To make braid: Divide dough into quarters; roll each into 18-inch (46 cm) long rope. Place side by side on greased rimmed baking sheet; pinch together at 1 end. Starting at pinched end, move second rope from left over rope on its right. Move far right rope over 2 ropes on left. Move far left rope over 2 ropes on right. Repeat until braid is complete; tuck ends under braid.

5 Cover crown loaf or braid loaf with plastic wrap; let rise in warm draft-free place until doubled in bulk, about 1 hour.

> " One of my biggest pleasures is sharing my love of baking with my son, Jacob. Making challah has been a weekly tradition since he was a preschooler, and now he knows all the steps. – *Daphna* "

6 TOPPING: Stir egg yolk with 1 tsp (5 mL) water; brush over loaf. Sprinkle with sesame seeds.

7 Bake in centre of 350°F (180°C) oven until golden brown and loaf sounds hollow when tapped on bottom, 35 to 45 minutes. Let cool on rack.

Makes 1 loaf, 16 slices. PER SLICE: about 190 cal, 5 g pro, 5 g total fat (2 g sat. fat), 32 g carb, 1 g fibre, 70 mg chol, 184 mg sodium. % RDI: 2% calcium, 12% iron, 5% vit A, 25% folate.

VARIATION

Bread Machine Challah (for dough only): Replace active dry yeast with 2½ tsp (12 mL) quick-rising (instant) dry yeast. Into pan of machine, add (in order) water, honey, sugar, butter, eggs, egg yolks, salt, flour and yeast. (Do not let yeast touch liquids.) Choose dough setting. When complete, remove from pan. Knead in raisins. Let rest for 5 minutes. Shape, brush with topping and bake as directed.

fridge NOTE

- Follow this technique when kneading: With floured hands, fold dough in half toward you. Beginning at side opposite fold, lean into dough with heels of palms, pressing down and pushing dough away. Turn dough a quarter turn to the right. Repeat folding, pressing and turning dough, sprinkling work surface lightly with more flour as needed, until smooth and elastic, about 10 minutes.

Chocolate Fig Honey Cake

Honey is a natural preservative that lengthens this Rosh Hashanah cake's storage time for up to one week and boosts it moistness. – Elizabeth

1⅓ cups	liquid honey	325 mL
1 cup	strong brewed tea	250 mL
1 tbsp	grated lemon or orange rind	15 mL
2¾ cups	all-purpose flour	675 mL
2 tsp	each baking powder and cinnamon	10 mL
½ tsp	each baking soda, ground ginger and allspice	2 mL
¼ tsp	salt	1 mL
1 cup	diced dried figs	250 mL
4	eggs	4
¼ cup	vegetable oil	50 mL
1 tbsp	vanilla	15 mL
1 cup	granulated sugar	250 mL
3 oz	bittersweet or semisweet chocolate, chopped	90 g

1 Grease 10-inch (4 L) tube or 10-inch (3 L) Bundt pan; set aside.

2 In small saucepan, bring honey just to boil; remove from heat. Stir in tea and grated lemon rind. Set aside to let cool slightly.

3 In bowl, whisk together flour, baking powder, cinnamon, baking soda, ginger, allspice and salt; stir in figs. Set aside.

4 In large bowl, beat eggs until pale and frothy, about 5 minutes. Beat in oil and vanilla. Beat in sugar, 2 tbsp (25 mL) at a time, until slightly thickened and bubbling, about 5 minutes. Alternately fold in flour and honey mixtures, making 3 additions of flour mixture and 2 of honey mixture, to make thin batter. Pour into prepared pan.

5 Bake in centre of 325°F (160°C) oven until cake tester inserted into centre comes out clean, 60 to 70 minutes. Let cool in pan on rack for 30 minutes. Using knife, loosen edges of cake; turn out onto rack and let cool completely.

6 In heatproof bowl over hot (not boiling) water, melt chocolate. Dip tines of fork into chocolate; drizzle over cake.

Makes 12 to 16 servings. PER EACH OF 16 SERVINGS: about 317 cal, 5 g pro, 8 g total fat (2 g sat. fat), 61 g carb, 3 g fibre, 47 mg chol, 124 mg sodium. % RDI: 4% calcium, 14% iron, 3% vit A, 3% vit C, 16% folate.

Pumpkin Cake

This cake features all the traditional spices of pumpkin pie and is a stunning alternative for your Thanksgiving feast. – Emily

1 Grease bottom and side of 10-inch (4 L) tube pan with removable bottom and tube; line bottom with parchment paper. Set aside.

2 In bowl, beat butter with sugar until fluffy. Beat in eggs, 1 at a time, beating well after each addition. Beat in vanilla.

3 In separate bowl, whisk together flour, baking powder, salt, nutmeg, cinnamon, ginger, cardamom, cloves and baking soda. Stir in walnuts.

4 Alternately stir flour mixture and pumpkin purée into butter mixture, making 3 additions of flour mixture and 2 of pumpkin purée. Scrape batter into prepared pan.

5 STREUSEL: In small bowl, whisk together flour, sugar and cinnamon. Using pastry blender or 2 knives, cut in butter until mixture clumps together. Stir in walnuts. Sprinkle over batter in pan.

6 Bake in centre of 325°F (160°C) oven until streusel is golden brown and cake tester inserted in centre comes out clean, about 1¾ hours.

7 Let cool in pan on rack for 15 minutes. Loosen side of cake with knife; holding onto centre tube, lift cake from pan. Let cool completely on rack. Run knife around tube. Using wide spatulas, gently lift out cake; peel off paper. (MAKE-AHEAD: **Wrap in plastic wrap and store at room temperature for up to 3 days. Or overwrap with heavy-duty foil and freeze for up to 2 weeks.**)

Makes 16 servings. PER SERVING: about 468 cal, 6 g pro, 21 g total fat (10 g sat. fat), 67 g carb, 2 g fibre, 85 mg chol, 372 mg sodium. % RDI: 8% calcium, 20% iron, 66% vit A, 2% vit C, 19% folate.

1 cup	butter, softened	250 mL
3 cups	packed brown sugar	750 mL
4	eggs	4
1 tbsp	vanilla	15 mL
3 cups	all-purpose flour	750 mL
2 tsp	baking powder	10 mL
1 tsp	each salt, nutmeg and cinnamon	5 mL
½ tsp	each ground ginger and cardamom	2 mL
¼ tsp	ground cloves	1 mL
¼ tsp	baking soda	1 mL
½ cup	chopped walnuts, toasted	125 mL
1	can (14 oz/398 mL) pumpkin purée	1

STREUSEL:

⅓ cup	all-purpose flour	75 mL
¼ cup	packed brown sugar	50 mL
¼ tsp	cinnamon	1 mL
¼ cup	cold butter, cubed	50 mL
½ cup	chopped walnuts, toasted	125 mL

Pool Party Cake

You can make the cake, blue water jelly and icing ahead, leaving the fun part – creating the pool – to do with the kids. – Elizabeth

1	pkg (85 g) blue jelly powder	1
1	White Butter Cake (recipe, page 215)	1
2 cups	Basic Butter Icing (recipe, page 215)	500 mL
44	multicoloured cream-filled wafers	44
1	each piece red and green shoestring licorice, each 7 inches (18 cm)	1
	Pink chocolate rounds, multicoloured sprinkles and chocolate finger cookies	
	Doughnut-shaped jelly candies	
	Gumballs	

1 Line bottom and sides of 13- x 9-inch (3.5) metal cake pan with plastic wrap; set aside.

2 Make jelly powder according to manufacturer's instructions but using only ¾ cup (175 mL) cold water; pour into prepared pan. Refrigerate, uncovered, until completely set, about 1 hour.

3 Meanwhile, cut cake into kidney shape; place on cake board. Using spoon, hollow out ½ inch (1 cm) from top of cake, leaving ¾-inch (2 cm) thick walls as border. Freeze cake scraps for another use.

4 Using palette knife, spread icing over sides and border of cake. Trim multicoloured wafers to 2-inch (5 cm) lengths or to match height of cake. Alternating colours, press wafers onto side of cake for fence, leaving 2-inch (5 cm) space uncovered for ladder.

5 Using spatula, scoop up long slabs of blue jelly; arrange in hollowed-out centre of cake, rippling to resemble waves.

6 Cut red licorice piece in half; arrange both halves on space on side of cake for ladder railings, pressing ends into cake to secure. Cut green licorice into small pieces for ladder steps; secure in place with icing.

7 At end opposite from ladder, press wafer in place for diving board; decorate with pink chocolate rounds and multicoloured sprinkles for landscape. Arrange chocolate finger cookies for wooden planking. Just before serving, place toy people in doughnut-shaped candy for swimmers in rafts. Add gumballs for beach balls.

Makes 16 to 20 servings. PER EACH OF 20 SERVINGS: about 330 cal, 3 g pro, 15 g total fat (8 g sat. fat), 48 g carb, trace fibre, 65 mg chol, 267 mg sodium. % RDI: 4% calcium, 9% iron, 13% vit A, 10% folate.

fridge NOTE

- If you don't have a cake board, make one by covering a strong piece of cardboard or a cutting board with foil.

This irresistible cake has tickled the funny bones of many birthday boys and girls of all ages. – *Elizabeth*

White Butter Cake

1 Grease 13- x 9-inch (3.5 L) cake pan. Line bottom with parchment or waxed paper. Set aside. In bowl, whisk together eggs, ⅓ cup (75 mL) of the milk and vanilla; set aside.

2 In separate large bowl, whisk together flour, sugar, baking powder, orange rind and salt. Beat in butter and remaining milk until fluffy, about 2 minutes. Beat in egg mixture in 3 additions, beating well and scraping down side of bowl between additions.

3 Scrape batter into prepared pan, smoothing top. Bake in centre of 350°F (180°C) oven until cake springs back when lightly touched and tester inserted in centre comes out clean, 40 to 45 minutes. Let cool in pan on rack for 20 minutes. Run knife around edge of cake; invert onto baking sheet and peel off parchment. Reinvert onto rack; let cool completely. (MAKE-AHEAD: **Wrap in plastic wrap and store at room temperature for up to 1 day or overwrap with heavy-duty foil and freeze for up to 2 weeks.**)

Basic Butter Icing

1 In bowl, beat butter until light. Gradually beat in sugar alternately with cream, making 3 additions of sugar and 2 of cream. (MAKE-AHEAD: **Cover and refrigerate for up to 3 days; beat again before using.**) **Makes about 2 cups (500 mL).**

WHITE BUTTER CAKE:		
4	eggs	4
1⅓ cups	milk	325 mL
1 tbsp	vanilla	15 mL
4 cups	sifted cake-and-pastry flour	1 L
2 cups	granulated sugar	500 mL
5 tsp	baking powder	25 mL
1 tbsp	grated orange rind	15 mL
1 tsp	salt	5 mL
1 cup	butter, softened	250 mL
BASIC BUTTER ICING:		
½ cup	butter, softened	125 mL
2½ cups	icing sugar	625 mL
⅓ cup	whipping cream	75 mL

Ma'amoul

These date-filled delights, inspired by Nadine Ghalayini of Maple, Ontario,
are also delectable with a pistachio or walnut filling. – Emily

¼ cup	orange blossom water	50 mL
2 cups	all-purpose flour	500 mL
1 cup	semolina	250 mL
1 tbsp	granulated sugar	15 mL
½ tsp	salt	2 mL
1 cup	butter, cubed	250 mL
1½ cups	pitted dates, chopped	375 mL
2 tbsp	icing sugar	25 mL

fridge NOTE

- **You can use a patterned wooden ma'amoul mould with a geometric pattern to shape the cookies. Dust lightly with flour before pressing in a filled unbaked cookie. Tap lightly on counter to remove cookie.**

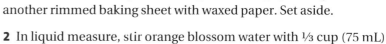

1 Line rimmed baking sheet with parchment paper, or grease; line another rimmed baking sheet with waxed paper. Set aside.

2 In liquid measure, stir orange blossom water with ⅓ cup (75 mL) water; refrigerate until cold.

3 In large bowl, whisk together all-purpose flour, semolina, granulated sugar and salt. Using pastry blender or 2 knives, cut in butter until mixture resembles fine bread crumbs. Drizzle orange blossom water over flour mixture, stirring briskly with fork until dough holds together. Press into ball; flatten into disc. Wrap in plastic wrap and refrigerate for 15 minutes. (MAKE-AHEAD: **Refrigerate for up to 3 days; let stand at room temperature for 15 minutes before rolling out.**)

4 Meanwhile, in saucepan, bring dates and 1 cup (250 mL) water to boil over medium-high heat; reduce heat and simmer until thickened and smooth, about 5 minutes. Let cool.

5 Drop dough by 2 tbsp (25 mL) onto waxed paper–lined baking sheet to make 26 mounds. Roll each into ball. Place 1 ball in palm of hand; press thumb halfway into centre of ball, forming cup shape to hold date filling. Spoon in 1 tsp (5 mL) filling; fold dough over filling and pinch edges to seal. Repeat with remaining balls and filling. Place, pinched side down and about 1 inch (2.5 cm) apart, on parchment paper–lined baking sheet. Refrigerate until firm, about 15 minutes.

(not used)

> **"** Eid-ul-Fitr is the celebration marking
> the end of Ramadan and a month of fasting.
> These cookies are a traditional treat. – *Emily* **"**

6 Bake in centre of 400°F (200°C) oven until bottoms are golden brown, 20 to 25 minutes. Transfer to rack. Dust with icing sugar. (MAKE-AHEAD: **Layer between waxed paper in airtight container and store at room temperature for up to 4 days. Or freeze for up to 2 weeks; after thawing, dust again with icing sugar.**)

Makes 26 cookies. PER COOKIE: about 153 cal, 2 g pro, 7 g total fat (4 g sat. fat), 21 g carb, 1 g fibre, 19 mg chol, 117 mg sodium. % RDI: 1% calcium, 4% iron, 7% vit A, 6% folate.

VARIATION

Nut-Filled Cookies: Omit dates. In bowl, combine 1 cup (250 mL) ground pistachios or walnuts, ⅓ cup (75 mL) granulated sugar and 2 tbsp (25 mL) orange or rose blossom water until stiff mixture forms. Fill and bake as above. Makes 26 cookies.

fridge NOTES

- **Look for semolina and orange blossom water in bulk, health food and Middle Eastern grocery stores. If you can't find orange blossom water, substitute grated orange rind.**

- **If making the variation, buy natural-colour pistachios (not dyed red) in bulk stores or the bulk section of your supermarket. Always try to buy nuts at a location with a high turnover for the freshest selection. If buying in bulk, transfer to resealable plastic bags and store in freezer to extend freshness.**

- **Stuffed dates are a Middle Eastern delicacy. Pit and slice halfway through, then fill with a small oval of marzipan and half a toasted almond. Roll in granulated sugar.**

Our Very Best Desserts

Last impressions last. A grand finale is what guests will remember, so give them something really spectacular to talk about. Nobody knows this better than we three enthusiastic dessert doyennes. There must be something that speaks to our soul as we measure out the flour, beat the butter until light and fluffy, witness the miracle of sugar and water turning into caramel and watch choux pastry rise from shiny blobs to airy puffs. It's hard to resist the temptation to do more desserts on the show, but as our mothers have told us, you have to eat your main course first. So, after a surfeit of appetizers, mains and salads, it's time to finish the feast with our very best desserts. – Elizabeth

- Profiteroles with Ice Cream and Chocolate Rum Sauce
- Raspberry Cream Tart
- Frozen Mango Mousse in Coconut Tuiles
- Peaches and Cream Pie
- Apple Tartlets with Caramel Sauce
- Best-Ever Apple Pie
- Grasshopper Pie
- Lemon Meringue Pie
- Mocha Cheesecake
- Apricot Cheesecake in Phyllo Pastry
- Glazed Lemon Cake
- Bananas Foster
- Baked Apples with Amaretti Crunch and Crème Anglaise
- Poached Pears in Six Spices
- Maple Pecan Fudge

◄ **Food stylist Wendy Trusler sets up the various stages of Elizabeth's recipe**

Profiteroles with Ice Cream and Chocolate Rum Sauce

Profiteroles are miniature choux pastry puffs. The pastry recipe (opposite) makes about 30 profiteroles; use half a batch to make this dessert. – Emily

16	profiteroles (half batch of Choux Pastry, recipe, page 221)	16
4 cups	coffee, vanilla or chocolate ice cream	1 L
CHOCOLATE RUM SAUCE:		
6 oz	semisweet chocolate, chopped	175 g
¼ cup	butter	50 mL
1 tsp	instant coffee granules	5 mL
1 tbsp	rum	15 mL

1 CHOCOLATE RUM SAUCE: In small saucepan, combine chocolate, ⅔ cup (150 mL) water, butter and coffee granules; warm over low heat, stirring frequently, until chocolate is melted. Remove from heat; stir in rum.

2 Slice top third off each profiterole, reserving tops. Pull out any moist dough inside. Soften ice cream in refrigerator for 15 minutes, if necessary. Fill each profiterole with scoop of ice cream; replace tops.

3 For each serving, arrange 2 profiteroles in chilled bowl. Drizzle with Chocolate Rum Sauce and serve immediately.

Makes 8 servings. PER SERVING: about 404 cal, 6 g pro, 26 g total fat (16 g sat. fat), 36 g carb, 2 g fibre, 116 mg chol, 229 mg sodium. % RDI: 9% calcium, 9% iron, 21% vit A, 12% folate.

fridge NOTE

- **Transform profiteroles into decadent chocolate éclairs. Shape them into tubes and bake; slice in half and fill with whipped cream. Drizzle with melted chocolate.**

Choux Pastry

1 In heavy saucepan, combine 1 cup (250 mL) water, butter and salt; bring to boil. Remove from heat; add flour all at once, stirring vigorously with wooden spoon until mixture forms smooth ball that leaves side of pan.

2 Return to medium-low heat; cook, stirring constantly, for 2 minutes. Let cool for 5 minutes.

3 Using electric mixer, beat in eggs, 1 at a time, beating well after each addition; continue beating until dough is smooth and shiny.

4 Using spoon or pastry bag fitted with star tip, drop 1 tbsp (15 mL) dough per profiterole, about 2 inches (5 cm) apart, onto parchment paper–lined or greased rimless baking sheets. Bake in centre of 400°F (200°C) oven until puffed, golden and crisp, about 25 minutes.

Makes about 30 profiteroles. PER PROFITEROLE: about 52 cal, 1 g pro, 4 g total fat (2 g sat. fat), 3 g carb, trace fibre, 34 mg chol, 59 mg sodium. % RDI: 2% iron, 4% vit A, 4% folate.

½ cup	butter, cubed	125 mL
¼ tsp	salt	1 mL
1 cup	all-purpose flour	250 mL
4	eggs	4

fridge NOTE

- Profiteroles are an impressive party dessert. You can fill them with ice cream up to a week ahead. We recommend wrapping each one individually and enclosing the lot in an airtight container.

Raspberry Cream Tart

*The irresistible combo of buttery pastry, vanilla-scented filling and fresh
fruit topping makes French fruit tarts a summer classic.* – Daphna

1¼ cups	all-purpose flour	300 mL
1½ tsp	granulated sugar	7 mL
¼ tsp	salt	1 mL
⅓ cup	cold unsalted butter, cubed	75 mL
¼ cup	whipping cream	50 mL
PASTRY CREAM:		
1 cup	milk	250 mL
1	egg	1
¼ cup	granulated sugar	50 mL
2 tbsp	all-purpose flour	25 mL
1 tsp	cornstarch	5 mL
2 tsp	butter	10 mL
1 tsp	vanilla	5 mL
TOPPING:		
2 cups	raspberries	500 mL
2 tbsp	apple jelly (optional)	25 mL

1 In large bowl, whisk together flour, sugar and salt. Using pastry blender or 2 knives, cut in butter until in fine crumbs with a few larger pieces. Drizzle with cream, tossing with fork until dough clumps together. Turn out onto lightly floured surface. Press into ball; flatten into disc. Wrap in plastic wrap and refrigerate for 30 minutes.

2 Let stand at room temperature until softened enough to roll out, about 20 minutes. On lightly floured surface, roll out into ⅛-inch (3 mm) thick circle; fit into 9-inch (23 cm) tart pan with removable bottom. Trim edge, leaving ½-inch (1 cm) overhang; fold under and press to adhere. Refrigerate for 30 minutes.

3 Prick pastry bottom with fork. Line with foil; fill evenly with pie weights or dried beans. Bake in centre of 400°F (200°C) oven just until edge starts to turn golden, 15 to 20 minutes. Remove weights and foil; bake until uniformly golden, about 10 minutes. Let cool on rack.

4 PASTRY CREAM: In small saucepan, heat milk until bubbles form around edge. Meanwhile, in bowl, whisk together egg, sugar, flour and cornstarch until pale and slightly thickened. Gradually whisk in milk. Return to saucepan.

5 Cook over medium heat, whisking, just until bubbling, about 5 minutes; simmer, whisking, until mixture is thick enough to mound on spoon, about 2 minutes. Remove from heat; whisk in butter and vanilla. Transfer to clean bowl. Place plastic wrap directly on surface; refrigerate until firm, about 3 hours. Spoon pastry cream into prepared crust; smooth top.

> **❝** Baking is a wonderful pleasure. I started my professional career as a pastry chef and I still adore creating – and eating – all kinds of desserts. – *Daphna* **❞**

6 TOPPING: Starting at edge, arrange raspberries in concentric circles on top. In small saucepan, heat apple jelly (if using) with 2 tsp (10 mL) water until melted; brush over berries. Refrigerate until set, about 1 hour.

Makes 8 servings. PER SERVING: about 247 cal, 5 g pro, 13 g total fat (8 g sat. fat), 29 g carb, 2 g fibre, 58 mg chol, 109 mg sodium. % RDI: 5% calcium, 8% iron, 13% vit A, 13% vit C, 16% folate.

VARIATION

Strawberry Cream Tart: Use 4 cups (1 L) thinly sliced strawberries instead of the raspberries. Arrange, tips up, in slightly overlapping rows.

fridge NOTES

- When rolling out pastry, lift your rolling pin slightly as you near the edge to make sure that it does not become thinner than the centre. Thin edges will bake and brown faster and turn brittle.

- After making the pastry and forming it into a disc, wrap and refrigerate it for 30 minutes to relax the flour, which ensures a tender pastry. Because the butter becomes very firm when chilled, let the pastry stand at room temperature for about 20 minutes before rolling out; it will crack if rolled when hard.

Frozen Mango Mousse in Coconut Tuiles

Elegantly thin cookie shells filled with homemade mousse make a show-stopping dessert. Garnish with mango slices or strawberries. – Elizabeth

3 tbsp	butter, softened	50 mL
⅓ cup	granulated sugar	75 mL
½ cup	all-purpose flour	125 mL
2	egg whites, lightly beaten	2
½ tsp	coconut extract	2 mL
FROZEN MANGO MOUSSE:		
2	ripe mangoes (1½ lb/750 g total)	2
½ cup	granulated sugar	125 mL
3 tbsp	rum or coconut liqueur	50 mL
2 tbsp	lime juice	25 mL
½ cup	whipping cream	125 mL

1 FROZEN MANGO MOUSSE: Peel, pit and coarsely chop mangoes; place in food processor. Add sugar, rum and lime juice; purée until smooth to make 3 cups (750 mL). Transfer to bowl. In separate bowl, whip cream; fold into purée. Freeze in shallow metal pan until almost firm, about 3 hours. Break mousse into chunks; purée in food processor. Freeze in airtight container until firm, about 1 hour. (Or pour into ice-cream maker; freeze according to directions.) (MAKE-AHEAD: **Freeze for up to 2 weeks.**) Using ice-cream scoop, scoop into 12 balls; place on waxed paper–lined baking sheet. Return to freezer. (MAKE-AHEAD: **Cover and freeze for up to 24 hours.**)

2 In bowl, beat butter with sugar until fluffy. Stir in flour, in 2 additions, until mixture is crumbly. Stir in egg whites, 1 tbsp (15 mL) at a time, until creamy. Stir in coconut extract.

3 On parchment paper–lined rimless baking sheet, draw two 5-inch (12 cm) circles 2 inches (5 cm) apart. Turn paper over. Drop 2 tbsp (25 mL) of the batter onto centre of each circle. With offset palette knife or spoon, spread to fill circle. Bake in centre of 400°F (200°C) oven just until golden brown at edges, 6 to 8 minutes.

4 Working quickly, slide palette knife under each tuile; place in 4½-inch (11 cm) diameter bowl and gently press into tulip shape. If tuile is too brittle, return to oven for 30 seconds. Let tuile stand until firm enough to hold shape; transfer to rack and let cool completely. Let baking sheet cool; repeat with remaining batter. (MAKE-AHEAD: **Store in airtight container for up to 3 days.**) To serve, fill each tuile with 2 scoops of Frozen Mango Mousse.

Makes 6 servings. PER SERVING: about 326 cal, 3 g pro, 13 g total fat (8 g sat. fat), 48 g carb, 2 g fibre, 44 mg chol, 86 mg sodium. % RDI: 2% calcium, 4% iron, 40% vit A, 33% vit C, 11% folate.

Peaches and Cream Pie

Here's The Canadian Living Test Kitchen's hands-down pick of peach pies. Enjoy in August when Canadian peaches are juicy. – Elizabeth

1 PASTRY: In large bowl, whisk together flour, salt and lemon rind. Using pastry blender or 2 knives, cut in shortening and butter until in fine crumbs with a few larger pieces.

2 In liquid measure, stir together egg yolk, lemon juice and enough ice water to make ¼ cup (50 mL). Drizzle over dry ingredients, tossing with fork until ragged dough clumps together. Turn out onto lightly floured surface. Press into ball; flatten into disc. Wrap in plastic wrap and refrigerate for 30 minutes.

3 On lightly floured surface, roll out pastry into 12-inch (30 cm) circle; fit into 9-inch (23 cm) glass pie plate. Trim edge, leaving ½-inch (1 cm) overhang; fold overhang under and flute edge. (MAKE-AHEAD: **Cover and refrigerate for up to 2 days.**)

4 In bowl, stir sugar with flour; whisk in sour cream and almond extract. Add peaches; stir to coat. Scrape into pie shell; set aside.

5 TOPPING: In bowl, stir flour with sugar; using pastry blender or 2 knives, cut in butter until crumbly. Mix in almonds; sprinkle evenly over filling.

6 Bake in bottom third of 425°F (220°C) oven for 15 minutes. Reduce heat to 350°F (180°C); bake until pastry and topping are golden and filling starts to bubble around edge, about 35 minutes. Let cool on rack.

Makes 8 servings. PER SERVING: about 487 cal, 6 g pro, 24 g total fat (11 g sat. fat), 64 g carb, 3 g fibre, 64 mg chol, 248 mg sodium. % RDI: 6% calcium, 19% iron, 18% vit A, 8% vit C, 20% folate.

½ cup	granulated sugar	125 mL
¼ cup	all-purpose flour	50 mL
¾ cup	sour cream or Balkan-style yogurt	175 mL
Dash	almond extract	Dash
5 cups	thickly sliced peeled peaches (about 5 large)	1.25 L
PASTRY:		
1¾ cups	sifted cake-and-pastry flour	425 mL
½ tsp	salt	2 mL
½ tsp	finely grated lemon rind	2 mL
⅓ cup	cold shortening, cubed	75 mL
¼ cup	cold butter, cubed	50 mL
1	egg yolk	1
1 tsp	lemon juice or cider vinegar	5 mL
	Ice water	
TOPPING:		
½ cup	all-purpose flour	125 mL
½ cup	packed brown sugar	125 mL
¼ cup	cold butter, cubed	50 mL
⅓ cup	slivered almonds	75 mL

Apple Tartlets with Caramel Sauce

These flat tartlets are worth every minute invested in making them. The recipe is from Toronto pastry queen Dufflet Rosenberg. – Emily

2 tbsp	granulated sugar	25 mL
PASTRY:		
2 cups	all-purpose flour	500 mL
¼ tsp	salt	1 mL
1 cup	cold butter, cubed	250 mL
½ cup	whipping cream	125 mL
ALMOND FILLING:		
1 cup	ground almonds (about 4 oz/125 g)	250 mL
¾ cup	icing sugar	175 mL
¼ cup	butter	50 mL
1 tsp	grated lemon rind	5 mL
¼ tsp	almond extract	1 mL
¼ tsp	vanilla	1 mL
CARAMELIZED APPLES AND SAUCE:		
2 lb	apples, peeled, cored and sliced	1 kg
¼ cup	lemon juice	50 mL
⅔ cup	granulated sugar	150 mL
1 cup	whipping cream	250 mL

1 Line rimmed baking sheet with parchment paper; set aside.

2 PASTRY: In food processor, blend flour with salt. Add butter; pulse until mixture resembles coarse crumbs. Add cream; pulse until mixture just comes together.

3 Turn out onto lightly floured surface. Roll out into 9- x 7-inch (23 x 18 cm) rectangle; fold in half to make 7- x 4-inch (18 x 10 cm) rectangle. Rotate pastry 90 degrees. Repeat rolling and folding once. Wrap in plastic wrap; refrigerate for 3 hours. (MAKE-AHEAD: **Refrigerate for up to 2 days or overwrap with heavy-duty foil and freeze for up to 2 weeks.**)

4 ALMOND FILLING: In food processor, pulse almonds with icing sugar until combined. Add butter, lemon rind, almond extract and vanilla; pulse to combine well. Refrigerate until chilled, about 2 hours.

5 CARAMELIZED APPLES AND SAUCE: In large bowl, toss apples with lemon juice; set aside. In large skillet, heat sugar over medium-high heat until melted and amber colour. Add apples; cook, stirring often, until barely tender and still holding shape, 5 to 10 minutes. Drain in colander set over bowl, reserving juice. Set apples aside in refrigerator.

6 In small saucepan, boil reserved juice from apples over medium-high heat until thickened and syrupy, about 4 minutes. Add cream; boil, stirring, until reduced by half, about 5 minutes. Set aside.

> **"** Tartlets take apple pie from homey to elegant. I think guests feel special when served an individual, restaurant-style dessert. – *Emily* **"**

7 On lightly floured surface, roll out pastry to ⅛-inch (3 mm) thickness. Cut out eight 5-inch (12 cm) rounds; place on prepared pan and freeze until firm, about 45 minutes.

8 Place 2 tbsp (25 mL) of the almond filling in centre of each round. Arrange overlapping apple slices in circle over filling, leaving ½-inch (1 cm) border uncovered. Cover with plastic wrap and freeze until firm, about 10 minutes. (MAKE-AHEAD: **Overwrap with heavy-duty foil and store in freezer for up to 1 day.**)

9 Sprinkle tartlets with granulated sugar. Bake in centre of 425°F (220°C) until pastry is golden and crisp, about 25 minutes. Serve with drizzle of caramel sauce.

Makes 8 servings. PER SERVING: about 712 cal, 7 g pro, 48 g total fat (26 g sat. fat), 68 g carb, 4 g fibre, 135 mg chol, 341 mg sodium. % RDI: 7% calcium, 14% iron, 38% vit A, 7% vit C, 19% folate.

fridge NOTE

- Fruit pastries are always delicious with cream – whipped, sour or iced, as in vanilla ice cream. For a touch of France, serve with crème fraîche, sometimes available in specialty dairy cases, or easy to make at home: Whisk together 1 cup (250 mL) each sour cream and whipping cream. Refrigerate until thickened, 24 to 48 hours. Makes 2 cups (500 mL).

Best-Ever Apple Pie

I recommend Northern Spy apples for pie. Their spicy, not-too-sweet flavour heightens the contrast between crisp pastry and juicy filling. – Elizabeth

¾ cup	shortening	175 mL
3 tbsp	butter, softened	50 mL
2¼ cups	all-purpose flour	550 mL
¾ tsp	salt	4 mL
½ cup	ice water	125 mL
FILLING:		
8 cups	thinly sliced peeled cored tart apples (about 2⅔ lb/1.35 kg)	2 L
2 tbsp	lemon juice	25 mL
½ cup	granulated sugar	125 mL
3 tbsp	all-purpose flour	50 mL
½ tsp	cinnamon	2 mL
GLAZE:		
1	egg yolk	1
2 tsp	granulated sugar	10 mL

1 In bowl, beat shortening with butter until smooth; stir in flour and salt until coarse and ragged looking. Pour in ice water all at once; stir until loose dough forms.

2 Press dough into 2 balls. On well-floured surface, gently press each into ¾-inch (2 cm) thick disc. Wrap in plastic wrap and refrigerate for 1 hour. (MAKE-AHEAD: **Refrigerate for up to 5 days or freeze in air-tight container for up to 2 weeks; let stand at room temperature for 15 minutes before rolling out.**)

3 On floured surface, roll out 1 of the discs into 13-inch (33 cm) circle. Fit into 9-inch (23 cm) pie plate; trim edge even with plate.

4 FILLING: In large bowl, toss apples with lemon juice. Stir together sugar, flour and cinnamon; sprinkle over apples and toss until coated. Scrape into pie shell. Brush pastry rim with water.

5 Roll out remaining pastry to same-size circle. Drape over filling; trim, leaving ¾-inch (2 cm) overhang. Fold overhang under bottom pastry rim; seal and flute edge. Cut 6 steam vents in centre.

6 GLAZE: Whisk egg yolk with 1 tbsp (15 mL) water; brush over top. Sprinkle with sugar.

7 Bake in bottom third of 425°F (220°C) oven for 15 minutes. Reduce heat to 350°F (180°C); bake until golden, filling is bubbling and apples are tender when pierced with knife through vent, about 40 minutes. Let cool on rack.

Makes 8 servings. PER SERVING: about 401 cal, 4 g pro, 20 g total fat (6 g sat. fat), 54 g carb, 4 g fibre, 36 mg chol, 213 mg sodium. % RDI: 1% calcium, 12% iron, 5% vit A, 7% vit C, 20% folate.

Grasshopper Pie

Head down memory lane and enjoy this diner dessert. Although this is a cream pie, it's light and airy – almost like a mousse. – Emily

1 In food processor, whirl chocolate wafer cookies until in fine crumbs. With motor running, pour in butter; whirl until crumbs are moistened. Press evenly over bottom and up side of 9-inch (23 cm) pie plate. Bake in centre of 350°F (180°C) oven until firm, about 10 minutes. Let cool on rack.

2 FILLING: Pour milk into large heatproof bowl. Sprinkle gelatin over milk; let stand for 5 minutes. Whisk in egg yolks, sugar and salt. Place over saucepan of simmering water and cook, stirring constantly, until gelatin and sugar are completely dissolved and mixture is smooth, about 8 minutes. Remove from heat; stir in crème de menthe and crème de cacao.

3 In bowl or roasting pan large enough to hold bowl of gelatin mixture, combine enough water and ice cubes to come halfway up side of pan. Nestle bowl of gelatin mixture into ice-cube mixture. Stir gelatin mixture often until cold and consistency of raw egg whites, about 10 minutes.

4 Whip cream. Gently stir one-third into gelatin mixture; fold in remainder. Return to ice-cube mixture and chill, without stirring, until filling is thick enough to mound on spoon, about 10 minutes. Scrape over prepared crust; smooth top. Refrigerate until firm, about 4 hours. (MAKE-AHEAD: **Cover and refrigerate for up to 24 hours.**)

5 GARNISH: Whip cream; pipe or dollop attractively over pie. Garnish with chocolate shavings, and sugared mint leaves (if using).

Makes 8 servings. PER SERVING: about 474 cal, 6 g pro, 31 g total fat (17 g sat. fat), 40 g carb, 1 g fibre, 185 mg chol, 242 mg sodium. % RDI: 7% calcium, 10% iron, 30% vit A, 13% folate.

30	chocolate wafer cookies (three-quarters 200 g pkg)	30
⅓ cup	butter, melted	75 mL
FILLING:		
¾ cup	milk	175 mL
1	pkg unflavoured gelatin	1
4	egg yolks	4
½ cup	granulated sugar	125 mL
Pinch	salt	Pinch
3 tbsp	crème de menthe	50 mL
3 tbsp	crème de cacao	50 mL
1 cup	whipping cream	250 mL
GARNISH:		
½ cup	whipping cream	125 mL
⅓ cup	semisweet or bittersweet chocolate shavings	75 mL
	Sugared mint leaves (optional)	

Lemon Meringue Pie

I find pastry making very relaxing. This oft-requested pie features "blind baking," the technique of baking the crust before filling it. – Daphna

1½ cups	all-purpose flour	375 mL
¼ tsp	salt	1 mL
¼ cup	each cold butter and shortening, cubed	50 mL
1	egg yolk	1
1 tsp	lemon juice	5 mL
	Ice water	

FILLING:

1¼ cups	granulated sugar	300 mL
6 tbsp	cornstarch	100 mL
½ tsp	salt	2 mL
4	egg yolks, beaten	4
1 tbsp	grated lemon rind	15 mL
½ cup	lemon juice	125 mL
3 tbsp	butter	50 mL

MERINGUE:

5	egg whites, at room temperature	5
¼ tsp	cream of tartar	1 mL
⅓ cup	instant dissolving (fruit/berry) sugar	75 mL

1 In bowl, whisk flour with salt. Using pastry blender or 2 knives, cut in butter and shortening until in fine crumbs with a few larger pieces.

2 In liquid measure, whisk egg yolk with lemon juice; whisk in enough ice water to make ⅓ cup (75 mL). Drizzle over dry ingredients, stirring briskly with fork until ragged dough forms. Press into ball; flatten into disc. Wrap in plastic wrap and refrigerate for 30 minutes. (MAKE-AHEAD: **Refrigerate for up to 3 days; let stand at room temperature for 15 minutes before rolling out.**)

3 On lightly floured surface, roll out pastry to ⅛-inch (3 mm) thickness. Fit into 9-inch (23 cm) pie plate. Trim edge, leaving 1-inch (2.5 cm) overhang; fold overhang under and flute edge. Line with foil; fill evenly with pie weights or dried beans. Bake in bottom third of 400°F (200°C) oven for 15 minutes. Remove weights and foil. Prick shell all over; bake until golden, about 10 minutes. Let cool on rack.

4 FILLING: In heavy saucepan, stir together sugar, cornstarch and salt; stir in 2 cups (500 mL) water and bring to boil over medium-high heat, stirring constantly. Reduce heat to medium-low and simmer for 3 minutes, stirring constantly. Remove from heat; whisk one-quarter into egg yolks. Whisk back into pan. Increase heat to medium; cook, stirring, for 2 minutes. Remove from heat; stir in lemon rind and juice and butter. Set aside.

5 MERINGUE: In bowl, beat egg whites with cream of tartar until soft peaks form. Beat in sugar, 1 tbsp (15 mL) at a time, until stiff peaks form.

6 Pour filling over prepared crust; smooth top. Starting at edge and using spatula, spread meringue around outside of hot filling to seal to crust. Spread remaining meringue over centre of filling, swirling with back of spoon to make peaks. Bake in centre of 400°F (200°C) oven until golden, 5 to 6 minutes. Let cool on rack until set, about 5 hours.

Makes 8 servings. PER SERVING: about 428 cal, 6 g pro, 18 g total fat (8 g sat. fat), 62 g carb, 1 g fibre, 139 mg chol, 335 mg sodium. % RDI: 2% calcium, 9% iron, 15% vit A, 10% vit C, 8% folate.

fridge NOTES

- Grate lemon rind finely to release as much of the flavour as possible. We like to use a microplane, or rasp.

- Overstirring or too high heat can break a cornstarch-thickened filling; use a gentle touch with the whisk.

- Be sure to spread the meringue on the filling while still warm. This helps the meringue cling to the filling and prevents it from weeping.

" From pride of place in the rotating pastry case of the '50s diner to the menus of today's chi-chi bistros, luscious lemon meringue pie never goes out of style. – *Daphna* **"**

Mocha Cheesecake

Coffee and chocolate are a match made in heaven. Thank goodness we can enjoy them here on earth! – Elizabeth

1½ cups	chocolate cookie crumbs	375 mL
3 tbsp	butter, melted	50 mL
1 tsp	instant coffee granules or instant espresso powder	5 mL
FILLING:		
8 oz	milk chocolate, chopped	250 g
4 oz	bittersweet chocolate, chopped	125 g
3	pkg (each 8 oz/250 g) cream cheese, softened	3
¾ cup	granulated sugar	175 mL
3	eggs	3
1 cup	whipping cream	250 mL
3 tbsp	coffee liqueur	50 mL

fridge NOTE

- **You can also freeze the cheesecake in a rigid airtight container for up to two weeks. If you don't have a container large enough to freeze cheesecakes or pies, wrap them in heavy-duty foil.**

1 Grease 9½-inch (2.75 L) springform pan. Centre pan on large square of foil; press foil to side of pan. Set aside.

2 In small bowl, stir together cookie crumbs, butter and coffee granules until evenly moistened. Press into bottom and ½ inch (1 cm) up side of prepared pan. Bake in centre of 325°F (160°C) oven until firm, about 10 minutes. Let cool.

3 FILLING: Meanwhile, in bowl over saucepan of hot (not boiling) water, melt milk chocolate, stirring occasionally; let cool to room temperature. Repeat with bittersweet chocolate in separate bowl.

4 In large bowl, beat cream cheese until smooth; beat in sugar, scraping down side of bowl often. Beat in eggs, 1 at a time, beating well after each and scraping down side of bowl. Beat in cream, liqueur and milk chocolate until blended. Transfer one-third of the batter to separate bowl; whisk in bittersweet chocolate. Pour bittersweet chocolate batter over prepared crust; using offset spatula, smooth top. Pour remaining batter over top; smooth top.

5 Set springform pan in larger pan; pour in enough hot water to come 1 inch (2.5 cm) up side of springform pan. Bake in centre of 325°F (160°C) oven until set around edge but centre is still jiggly, about 1 hour. Turn off oven; let stand in oven for 1 hour.

6 Transfer springform pan to rack and remove foil; let cool completely. Cover with plastic wrap and refrigerate until chilled, about 4 hours. (MAKE-AHEAD: **Refrigerate for up to 3 days.**)

Makes 12 servings. PER SERVING: about 592 cal, 10 g pro, 46 g total fat (27 g sat. fat), 41 g carb, 2 g fibre, 160 mg chol, 336 mg sodium. % RDI: 11% calcium, 17% iron, 40% vit A, 8% folate.

Apricot Cheesecake in Phyllo Pastry

Light cream cheese, cottage cheese and sour cream make this cheesecake a lower-fat choice. – Daphna

9	sheets phyllo pastry	9
1/3 cup	butter, melted	75 mL
1	egg white, lightly beaten	1
APRICOT PURÉE:		
1/2 cup	dried apricots (about 4 oz/125 g)	125 mL
1/4 cup	granulated sugar	50 mL
CHEESECAKE:		
2	pkg (each 8 oz/250 g) light cream cheese	2
1¾ cups	1% cottage cheese	425 mL
2/3 cup	granulated sugar	150 mL
2	eggs	2
1/2 cup	light sour cream	125 mL
1 tbsp	cornstarch	15 mL
2 tsp	grated lemon rind	10 mL
1 tsp	vanilla	5 mL

1 APRICOT PURÉE: In small saucepan, bring apricots and ⅔ cup (150 mL) water to boil; reduce heat and simmer until very soft, about 5 minutes. Reserving liquid, drain apricots and transfer to food processor. Add sugar and 3 tbsp (50 mL) of the reserved liquid; purée until smooth, adding up to 1 tbsp (15 mL) more liquid if necessary. (MAKE-AHEAD: **Refrigerate in airtight container for up to 5 days.**)

2 CHEESECAKE: In food processor, blend together cream cheese, cottage cheese and sugar. Blend in eggs, 1 at a time. Blend in sour cream, cornstarch, lemon rind and vanilla; set aside.

3 Place 1 sheet of phyllo on work surface, keeping remainder covered with damp tea towel to prevent drying out. Brush with some of the butter. Place in greased 9-inch (2.5 L) springform pan, flattening against bottom and into corner and scrunching top to align with rim. Repeat with second sheet of phyllo, rotating to cover side of pan completely. Brush third sheet with some of the egg white; repeat arranging in pan. Repeat layering with remaining phyllo, brushing every third sheet with egg white.

4 Pour in one-third of the batter. Dollop one-third of the purée over top; swirl with tip of knife to create marbled effect. Repeat layers twice. Bake in centre of 325°F (160°C) oven until edge is set but centre is still jiggly, about 1 hour. Turn off oven; let stand in oven for 1 hour. Transfer to rack; let cool completely. Cover and refrigerate until chilled, about 6 hours. (MAKE-AHEAD: **Refrigerate for up to 2 days.**) Remove side of pan. Scrve at room temperature.

Makes 12 servings. PER SERVING: about 324 cal, 12 g pro, 15 g total fat (8 g sat. fat), 36 g carb, 1 g fibre, 78 mg chol, 472 mg sodium. % RDI: 9% calcium, 9% iron, 18% vit A, 2% vit C, 11% folate.

Glazed Lemon Cake

*This recipe is a tradition at the Harris family reunion in Mitchell, Ontario,
but you don't have to get relatives together to enjoy it. –Elizabeth*

1 cup	butter, softened	250 mL
2 cups	granulated sugar	500 mL
4	eggs	4
2 tbsp	grated lemon rind	25 mL
1 tsp	vanilla	5 mL
3 cups	all-purpose flour	750 mL
1 tbsp	baking powder	15 mL
½ tsp	salt	2 mL
1¼ cups	milk	300 mL
TOPPING:		
½ cup	icing sugar	125 mL
2 tsp	grated lemon rind	10 mL
1 tbsp	lemon juice	15 mL

1 Grease and flour 10-inch (3 L) Bundt pan; set aside.

2 In large bowl, beat butter with sugar until light and fluffy; beat in eggs, 1 at a time, beating well after each addition. Beat in lemon rind and vanilla. In separate bowl, whisk together flour, baking powder and salt. Using wooden spoon, stir into butter mixture alternately with milk, making 3 additions of flour mixture and 2 of milk. Pour into prepared pan.

3 Bake in centre of 350°F (180°C) oven until cake tester inserted in centre comes out clean, about 50 minutes. Let cool in pan on rack for 10 minutes. Turn out onto rack and let cool.

4 TOPPING: In bowl, whisk together icing sugar and lemon rind and juice; drizzle over cake.

Makes 12 to 16 servings. PER EACH OF 16 SERVINGS: about 325 cal, 5 g pro, 13 g total fat (8 g sat. fat), 48 g carb, 1 g fibre, 84 mg chol, 263 mg sodium. % RDI: 5% calcium, 9% iron, 14% vit A, 3% vit C, 16% folate.

Bananas Foster

When you need a stylish dessert, this one is simple, sinfully rich and so quick to make. – Elizabeth

1 Using ice-cream scoop, place 8 balls ice cream on waxed paper–lined rimmed baking sheet; set aside in freezer.

2 In skillet or chafing dish, melt butter over medium heat; stir in sugar until dissolved. Add bananas, cut side down; cook, turning once, until just barely tender, about 5 minutes. Sprinkle with cinnamon and nutmeg.

3 Pour rum, and banana liqueur (if using), over bananas, shaking pan to distribute liquid. Averting face, ignite with long wooden match. Using long-handled spoon, baste bananas until flames subside.

4 Place 2 of the reserved scoops of ice cream in each of 4 chilled bowls. Top with bananas and serve immediately.

2 cups	vanilla ice cream	500 mL
3 tbsp	unsalted butter	50 mL
3 tbsp	packed brown sugar	50 mL
2	ripe bananas, peeled and halved lengthwise	2
¼ tsp	cinnamon	1 mL
Pinch	nutmeg	Pinch
⅓ cup	light or dark rum	75 mL
2 tbsp	banana liqueur or brandy (optional)	25 mL

Makes 4 servings. PER SERVING: about 333 cal, 3 g pro, 16 g total fat (10 g sat. fat), 39 g carb, 1 g fibre, 52 mg chol, 59 mg sodium. % RDI: 9% calcium, 4% iron, 16% vit A, 7% vit C, 4% folate.

Baked Apples with Amaretti Crunch and Crème Anglaise

I get kidded about baked apples. I can't resist them, especially tarted up with maple syrup and stuffed with almond cookies. – Elizabeth

½ cup	apple cider	125 mL
⅓ cup	maple syrup	75 mL
2 tbsp	butter	25 mL
¼ tsp	each cinnamon and nutmeg	1 mL
6	large apples	6
1 cup	coarsely crushed amaretti cookies	250 mL
½ cup	dried cherries or dried cranberries	125 mL
3 tbsp	toasted slivered almonds	50 mL
CRÈME ANGLAISE:		
1½ cups	milk	375 mL
3	eggs	3
¼ cup	granulated sugar	50 mL
Pinch	salt	Pinch
½ tsp	vanilla	2 mL

1 CRÈME ANGLAISE: In heavy saucepan, heat milk just until bubbles form around edge. In bowl, whisk together eggs, sugar and salt; gradually whisk in milk. Return to pan; cook over medium-low heat, stirring constantly with wooden spoon, until thick enough to coat back of spoon, 3 to 5 minutes. Do not boil.

2 Immediately strain milk mixture through fine sieve into bowl. Stir in vanilla. Let cool at room temperature for 30 minutes. Place plastic wrap directly on surface and refrigerate until chilled, about 2 hours. (MAKE-AHEAD: **Refrigerate for up to 24 hours.**)

3 In saucepan, bring cider, maple syrup, butter, cinnamon and nutmeg to boil, stirring frequently; reduce heat and simmer until reduced to 1 cup (250 mL), about 10 minutes.

4 Using melon baller or corer, core each apple, making 1-inch (2.5 cm) diameter cavity and leaving bottom intact. Peel apples one-quarter of the way down from tops; place upright in greased 11- x 7-inch (2 L) glass baking dish. Pour syrup over top; cover loosely with foil. Bake in centre of 375°F (190°C) oven, basting occasionally, until very tender, 50 to 60 minutes.

5 In small bowl, combine amaretti crumbs, cherries and almonds; pack into apple cavities, mounding any excess on top and around sides. Baste with syrup. Bake, uncovered, until filling is crisp on top, about 10 minutes. Serve warm with chilled crème anglaise.

Makes 6 servings. PER SERVING: about 439 cal, 8 g pro, 13 g total fat (6 g sat. fat), 80 g carb, 6 g fibre, 110 mg chol, 145 mg sodium. % RDI: 14% calcium, 11% iron, 14% vit A, 15% vit C, 9% folate.

Poached Pears in Six Spices

Pears are one of my favourite fruits. Their unique shape, flavour and texture are so appealing for desserts. – Daphna

1 In large heavy saucepan, stir together wine, 2½ cups (625 mL) water, sugar and lemon juice until sugar is dissolved. Add lemon rind, ginger, cinnamon, star anise, cloves, cardamom pods and peppercorns; bring to boil.

2 Meanwhile, peel pears. Using melon baller or small spoon, core through bottoms, leaving stems intact. Add to pan; reduce heat and simmer, turning pears occasionally, until tender, 20 to 30 minutes. Using slotted spoon, transfer pears to bowl.

3 Bring syrup to boil; boil until reduced to 1 cup (250 mL), 15 to 20 minutes. Strain. Place each pear on dessert plate; spoon syrup over top.

Makes 6 servings. PER SERVING: about 243 cal, 1 g pro, 1 g total fat (0 g sat. fat), 57 g carb, 3 g fibre, 0 mg chol, 5 mg sodium. % RDI: 2% calcium, 6% iron, 12% vit C, 4% folate.

2½ cups	dry red wine	625 mL
1 cup	granulated sugar	250 mL
2 tbsp	lemon juice	25 mL
2	strips (2 x 1 inch/5 x 2.5 cm) lemon rind	2
4	slices gingerroot	4
2	sticks cinnamon, halved	2
4	whole star anise	4
½ tsp	whole cloves	2 mL
½ tsp	whole cardamom pods	2 mL
¼ tsp	peppercorns	1 mL
6	Bosc pears	6

fridge NOTE

- **For a presentation that will wow your guests, slice poached pears several times on an angle without cutting all the way through to the top. Twist each pear and let it fan out atop a pool of the scrumptious spiced sauce.**

Maple Pecan Fudge

For the creamiest texture, let the fudge stand for at least 12 hours before packing it into gift boxes – or devouring it, square by square. – Emily

¾ cup	chopped pecans	175 mL
2 cups	packed brown sugar	500 mL
1 cup	whipping cream	250 mL
½ cup	pure maple syrup	125 mL
2 tbsp	butter, cubed	25 mL
Pinch	baking soda	Pinch
1 tsp	vanilla	5 mL

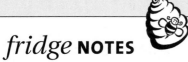

fridge NOTES

- **If the mixture does not foam up high when it comes to a boil, stir in another pinch of baking soda.**

- **Making candy can be hot stuff. Always use a candy thermometer; it's heatproof, accurately indicates the various candy stages and clips right to your pan.**

1 Line 8-inch (2 L) square glass baking dish with foil, leaving 1-inch (2.5 cm) overhang; grease foil. Set aside.

2 Spread pecans on rimmed baking sheet; toast in 350°F (180°C) oven until fragrant, about 8 minutes. Set aside.

3 Grease side of heavy saucepan. Add sugar, cream, maple syrup, butter and baking soda; cook over medium heat, stirring constantly with wooden spoon, until sugar is dissolved and mixture is boiling. Boil, without stirring, until candy thermometer registers soft-ball stage of 238°F (114°C) or ½ tsp (2 mL) of the syrup dropped into very cold water forms soft ball that flattens when removed from water, about 8 minutes. Immediately pour into clean wide-bottom bowl, without scraping pan clean. Let cool on rack until candy thermometer registers 100°F (38°C) or until mixture feels just slightly warm to the touch, 1 to 2 hours.

4 Using wooden spoon, beat in vanilla. Beat until very thick and most of the gloss disappears, about 7 minutes. (Or pour mixture into heavy-duty stand mixer with paddle attachment; beat at medium-low speed for 15 minutes.)

5 Quickly stir in pecans. Immediately scrape into prepared pan; smooth top. Let cool in pan on rack. Using foil overhang as handles, remove from pan; cut into pieces. (MAKE-AHEAD: **Wrap in foil and store in cool dry place, not refrigerator, for up to 2 weeks.**)

Makes about 1 lb (500 g), 32 pieces. PER PIECE: about 113 cal, trace pro, 5 g total fat (2 g sat. fat), 17 g carb, trace fibre, 12 mg chol, 51 mg sodium. % RDI: 2% calcium, 3% iron, 3% vit A.

Index

CONTRIBUTORS

All recipes were created by the cohosts and The Canadian Living Test Kitchen with the exception of the ones by these contributors: Riki Dixon (p. 4), Shannon Ferrier (p. 8), Tarrah Laidman-Lodboa (p. 13), Unni Simenson (p. 16), Yvan Lebrun (p. 17), Jean Soulard (p. 18), The Rebel House (p. 21), M. Lee Leuschner (p. 23), Gail Hall (p. 26), Roger Holmes (p. 27), Karen Barnaby (p. 28), Café au Livre (p. 31), Ida Pusateri (pp. 62, 142), Heather Howe (pp. 91, 147), Dufflet Rosenberg (pp. 106, 226), Rose Murray (p. 116), Barbara Gordon and Bob Bermann (p. 204), Lesleigh Landry (p. 225) and Edythe Diebel (p. 234). We gratefully acknowledge their contributions.

ABOUT OUR NUTRITION INFORMATION

- To meet nutrient needs each day, moderately active women 25 to 49 need about 1,900 calories, 51 g protein, 261 g carbohydrate, 25 to 35 g fibre and not more than 63 g total fat (21 g saturated fat). Men and teenagers usually need more. Canadian sodium intake of approximately 3,500 to 4,500 mg daily should be reduced. Percentage of recommended daily intake (% RDI) is based on the highest recommended intakes (excluding those for pregnant and lactating women) for calcium, iron, vitamins A and C, and folate.

- Figures are rounded off. They are based on the first ingredient listed when there is a choice and do not include optional ingredients.

- Abbreviations: cal = calories, pro = protein, carb = carbohydrate, sat. fat = saturated fat, chol = cholesterol